THE COUNTRY
HOUSE MURDERS

THE COUNTRY HOUSE MURDERS

Edited by
Jonathan Goodman

GUILD PUBLISHING
LONDON

This edition published 1988 by
Book Club Associates
by arrangement with
W.H. Allen & Co Plc

Printed and bound in Great Britain by
Adlard & Son Ltd, The Garden City Press

Contents

For Philip and Diane Chadwick

A Doom With a View

It is my belief, Watson, founded upon my experience, that the lowest and vilest alleys in London do not present a more dreadful record of sin than does the smiling and beautiful countryside. . . . Look at these lonely houses, each in its own fields. . . . Think of the deeds of hellish cruelty, the hidden wickedness which may go on, year in, year out, in such places, and none the wiser.

So said Sherlock Holmes in the course of the adventure that became known by the name of its eventual setting, which (I cannot resist a further quotation) was extolled by its tenant to the prospective governess of his cockroach-smacking son as a "Charming rural place. The Copper Beeches, five miles on the far side of Winchester. It is the most lovely country, my dear young lady, and the dearest old country house." Perhaps as a side-effect of Holmes's unexcepting dependence upon generalizations, he tended to exaggerate, and he may have done so when relishing the extent of rustic wrongdoing; but though the published crime statistics of his day were less artfully contrived, and so are more easily swallowed, than are those latest ones that we are straightfacedly assured are about right, they are still not imprecise enough to be worth consulting in aid of confirming or contradicting Holmes's belief. At the risk of sparking an epidemic of apoplexy among The Baker Street Irregulars and other, less august bands of The Detective's Disciples, I shall voice my suspicion that Holmes had been taken in by an optical illusion.

Particularly when the crime is murder, the newsworthiness of a crime, as well as the likelihood of its being written about, read about, long after the event, often depends as much upon the charm of the scene of the crime as upon what made the scene criminous. The ecclesiastic surroundings of William Durrant's stranglings, etc., ensured for him a vicarious immortality; had James Camb discarded Gay Gibson's body via a window of a

I

riparian dwelling rather than through a port-hole of an ocean-going liner, his name would not have become the differentiating part of a title in the "Notable British Trials", and he might not have felt impelled to amend it after his early release from a so-called life sentence and before his commission of crimes that bore similarities to the one that he was lucky not to have been hanged for; the Lovers' Lane locus of the murder of the Reverend Edward Hall and his favourite female chorister, Mrs Eleanor Mills — and the shading of their mutual remains by a crab-apple tree — helped to raise the case above the humdrum; if Charles and Florence Bravo had chosen to reside somewhere less quaint of design and emphatic of name than The Priory, Charles's demise would have engendered less controversy soon afterwards and ever since. And, generally speaking, crimes in the smiling and beautiful countryside are apt to receive more coverage than are similar crimes in an urban setting. Supposing that Holmes was aloof from that fact, his observation was and is questionable.

Holmes's chronicler, by giving literary preference to out-of-town adventures, implied a sort of substance to the optical illusion, and thereby made its perception commonplace. Prior to Holmes's outings in *The Strand*, comparatively few authors of mystery fiction had told rural tales; in 1912, five years before the account appeared of what turned out to be Holmes's *actual* final bow, E. C. Bentley published the country-housed *Trent's Last Case*, harbinger of what is rightly termed the "golden age" of long detective tales, so many of which occupied country houses that those that did not now seem deliberately, just for the sake of a change, set elsewhere. And so the optical illusion was lent a further sort of substance; and the number of its perceivers grew. The fictive encouragement of the notion that country houses — ranging from bijou to stately, and with an extravagant Mousetrap in between — are popular as scenes of crime may have been aided and abetted by certain novelists' twistings of trial testimony on behalf of tales; at least five of the cases recounted in *this* volume have been made a basis of novels.

Even if, when compiling *The Pleasures of Murder*, I had foreseen sequels, this volume among them, I doubt if I would have sensibly left out Richard D. Altick's essay on Samuel Dougal's doings at the latterly late Miss Camille Holland's moated farm, which surely made the still-sturdy place the one that looms largest in the country-housed species of murder.

A Doom with a View

Though the absence of that case from this collection is conspicuous, the omission of Professor Altick's eminently pleasurable essay from the earlier volume would have seemed, to me, more conspicuous still.

Fearing that an entirety of indoor cases might make for claustrophobia, I have included some alfresco affairs; but none of those was more than a short stroll from habitation, and all have associations with country houses, both before and after the fact of murder, that are sufficiently material, I think, to warrant their presence here.

JONATHAN GOODMAN

The Killing at Road Hill House

F. Tennyson Jesse

THE CASE of Constance Kent is one of the most curious examples of the murder from revenge, for it is free from that admixture of sex-interest which causes most murders of this nature to be dubbed *crime passionel*. This case has been loosely and incorrectly classed as a murder of jealousy, but, as a matter of fact, if we look thoroughly into the matter it is obvious that, although jealousy was to a great extent present in Constance Kent's mind, the actual motive of the murder was purely one of revenge. She herself declared in a letter to Dr Bucknill that she had "no ill-will against the little boy except as one of the children of her stepmother," and explained that if any remark was made at any time which, in her opinion, was disparaging to any member of the first family, she treasured it up and "determined to avenge it". Also, in a letter to her solicitor, Mr Rodway, she referred to "my feelings of revenge". She deliberately chose the much-loved little boy of the second family as the most powerful weapon with which she could hit back at her stepmother for certain ill-judged remarks which that unfortunate lady had made. Indeed, although Constance allowed the matter to swell to much too great proportions in her mind, it is true that any sensitive young girl would have felt bitterly one taunt which Mrs Kent, doubtless in a moment of exasperation, flung at her. Knowing perfectly well, as she did, that Constance's mother had died insane, yet the second Mrs Kent actually spoke to the girl words conveying her own conviction that Constance was getting as mad as her mother had been. It was not the slur on herself, but that on her dead mother, that Constance felt so bitterly, and those words were going eventually to cost the second Mrs Kent the life of her little boy.

The case is interesting, not only because of the revelation it gives of the heart of a strange girl, but also as an example of the gulf that divides present-day thought from that of 1860.

4

None of the problems of adolescence, with which a modern counsel for the defence would have made such powerful play, were invoked by Constance Kent's advocate. It is quite certain that the doctrines of Freud and his followers could not have been left out of a similar trial taking place nowadays, but in Constance Kent's day it was considered that justice had been sufficiently tempered with mercy when the woman of twenty-one was sentenced to penal servitude for life for the crime committed when an ill-balanced girl of sixteen.

The drama of Constance Kent's mind, though the stage was a narrow one, was impressive. It has been said that in religion there are all experiences, and, if so, this girl, in the terrific onslaught which conscience made upon her unwilling soul, must have known the whole gamut of spiritual warfare and submission.

On the morning of Saturday, 30 June 1860, the household of Mr Kent, an Inspector of Factories, living at the little village of Road, on the Wiltshire-Somerset border, awoke tranquilly as usual.

The character of Mr Kent is worth a careful survey. He suffered extremely during the years between that fatal Saturday and the date in 1865 when the truth was made plain. He may stand as a symbol of the different morality obtaining in the middle of the last century. His first wife had shown signs of insanity after the birth of her third child, and yet he made her the mother of four more children who died in infancy, and of the unfortunate Constance and a boy called William. After which, not unreasonably as it may seem to us, her mania became so acute and violent that she had to be kept under restraint.

From 1845 until 1852 Mr Kent's household was looked after by Miss Pratt, his daughters' governess, and in the year following Mrs Kent's death Miss Pratt became Mrs Kent the Second. The eldest boy, who seems to have resented the fact of the erstwhile governess taking the place of his mother, went to sea and died abroad, leaving three girls and William in the first family. Mr Kent's habits having been in no way changed by his sad experience, he promptly became the father of three more children by his second wife, and she was expecting a fourth when the calamity from which they were never to recover fell upon the unfortunate inmates of Road Hill House. Under the weight of this misfortune, which attacked no one with the virulence with which it did the unlucky father, who for years went under the

Road Hill House

imputation of being a murderer, his character shone out with
that resignation to Fate which he would probably have called
"submission to the inscrutable decrees of Providence". It is
impossible that he could not have known, or, if he did not
actually know, at least suspect with an awful sense of certainty,
the true culprit, but never at any time did he do other than try to
shield her from suspicion by his own unfailing kindness and
considerateness towards her. How he prevailed on Mrs Kent to
keep her tongue still will never be known. Perhaps it was
because of the ghastly suspicion that must always have filled his
wife's eyes when she looked at his daughter, that Constance was
allowed to take a step so much rarer in those days than it would
be now — that of living away from home.

At first she went to live in a convent in France; after that she
became a paying guest in St Mary's Home, Brighton — an
Anglican Sisterhood — and it was the influence of this latter
place, led up to, perhaps, who knows how much, by the spiritual
influences in the French convent, which led her to the ultimate
bourne of her pilgrimage.

There must have been four broken hearts connected with the
affair at Road Hill House: Constance's own — that queer,
vindictive, yet tender organ which was at once the root and
solution of all her troubles; that of her father, who was ruined

Constance Kent, circa *1856*

socially and professionally by the suspicions which rested upon him; that of his wife, the former Miss Pratt, to whom the shock of her little child's murder must have been unforgettable; and, lastly, that of Inspector Whicher, the officer who all along had believed in the guilt of the young girl, and had even engineered her arrest, and who had been so covered with obloquy and adverse criticism that his career was spoiled. There can have been few, if any, cases in which one man was so convinced of the guilt of the true criminal as the Inspector, and yet in which the lack of evidence necessary to convict was such that, had not the guilty party ultimately confessed, several innocent people would have remained under an unmerited shadow to the end of their lives.

Mr Kent little knew when, according to his mid-Victorian concepts of belief in Providence, he was continuing to subject a mentally unsound woman to the trial of annual childbirth, what misery he was laying up in store for himself and for others. It is true that Constance had been a difficult problem ever since his marriage with her former governess. Children, like servants and dogs, are instinctive snobs, and Constance added to her jealousy of her father's new family an arrogant suspicion of the woman she had been accustomed to know in a very different position to that now held by her.

Constance and William, the two nearest in age of Mr Kent's first family, had always clung to each other, partly in affection and partly in that sense of being banded together against the world to which imaginative children become the prey. This alliance between the two children was brought painfully into publicity some four years previous to the tragedy by the fact of the sudden disappearance of the two of them. The following day they were discovered at Bath. Constance had cut off her hair, dressed in some of William's clothes and, with him, run away, probably with the usual romantic idea of childhood — that of going to sea. William had been the first to give in under cross-examination at Bath. Constance had remained impassive, spent the night in the police station, and been taken home next day, always in the same state of sullen calm, and this although she was only a child of twelve. It is idle now to think of what gifts of strength and steadfastness this child must have possessed — gifts which could have been turned, with a more individual upbringing than fell to the lot of the young in those days, to such excellent uses. Instead, her brooding sullenness, her way of thinking herself ill-used, and her deadly habit of nursing an injury were allowed to accumulate within her like poison so long as she preserved outward decorum.

The family of Road Hill House was apparently a happy as well as a prosperous one, until the fatal awakening of 30 June 1860.

Elizabeth Gough, nursemaid to the three young children who

8

constituted the family of the second Mrs Kent, awoke that morning at about five o'clock and, leaning out of her bed to pull the bedclothes more closely over the youngest little girl — a baby of about twelve months, who slept beside her — she noticed the cot of the four-year-old boy, Francis Savile, was empty. One of the points raised against Elizabeth Gough in the days that followed was that she felt no alarm on discovering that one of her charges was missing. This was explained by stating that Mrs Kent, being often anxious about her children, was apt to take them into her own room if they cried. Gough, who was exceedingly tired from a very hard day's work the day before — the sort of day's work that no servant now would undertake — turned over and slept again until a quarter past six. She then arose, dressed, made her bed, tidied her room, and read her usual chapter from the Bible with the utmost calm, and not until about an hour passed in these various exercises did she go to disturb her mistress, who was in a delicate state of health. To her placid inquiry as to whether Mrs Kent had Master Savile came a startling answer in the negative, and on hearing the child had vanished from the nursery Mrs Kent came running from her bed. The news that the child was missing ran through the house. The two elder girls, who slept in a room above Mrs Kent's, said they had seen nothing of the child, and Constance came out to the door of her little room over Mr Kent's dressing-room to hear what all the fuss was about.

The first discovery of importance was made by the house-maid, and consisted of the fact that the window in the drawing-room, which had been fastened and shuttered by Mrs Kent the night before, was open. There were no traces of footsteps in the mould outside the window and no marks of violence on the fastenings. Mr Kent, convinced — as who would not have been convinced in similar circumstances, set about only by his own family and trusted dependants? — that the kidnapper (for so far they had thought of nothing worse) had come from without, set off at once in his trap for the nearest police station, which was at Trowbridge. The news of the child's disappearance ran through the village as it had run through the house, and soon volunteers turned out to help in the search. Two men, called Benger and Nutt, searched the grounds, for Road Hill House stood back from the road in its own garden. Away from the house, in the shrubbery at the back, there stood a disused closet, and in this, wrapped in a blanket, crammed down in the vault, the body of the little boy was discovered. His head had been nearly severed from his body and, in addition, there was a deep wound above the heart, apparently inflicted after death, as it had not bled.

The men carried the body into the house, and the news was broken to Mrs Kent and the girls. Mr Kent himself arrived soon after, closely followed by the police, of whom the head was a certain Superintendent Foley — one of the most egregious idiots who ever made a mess of an inquiry, a true descendant of Dogberry.

So far no suspicion rested upon anybody in the household, and Foley stationed two of his men in the kitchen that night, with what object does not appear to be quite clear. It was hardly likely that the murderer would make a second appearance and come creeping about the house reconstructing the crime, which, apparently, was what Mr Foley expected.

The inquest was held on the Monday, and, short as the space of time was between the discovery of the murder and this second event, there had already arisen, in that irrational and inexplicable manner in which such feelings do spring into life, a strong suspicion against the household of Mr Kent among the populace. There are always people who can be wise after the event, and villages where everyone knows everything there is to be known about everyone else — and even a great deal more! — are crowded with these sapient beings.

It was considered extraordinary and suspicious that the nursemaid allowed such a long time to elapse between her discovery that the little boy's cot was empty and her visit to her mistress, but this criticism — which was to swell to much more serious proportions a little later — was not, by the Monday, so plainly expressed as the suspicion against certain members of the Kent family.

It is difficult at this lapse of time to obtain a true estimate of the various characteristics that went to make that complicated little world at Road Hill House, but it does seem as though the Kents could not have been very popular, for people to turn so readily to such dark thoughts about them.

Crowds are notoriously brutal things; for a crowd, to express the mob spirit at all, has to do so by working on its common factor. Before a crowd of men can be strung to simultaneous expression, some one chord of interest in which they all share has to be struck; their common factor has to be found, and the common factor is never by any chance a refined or specially

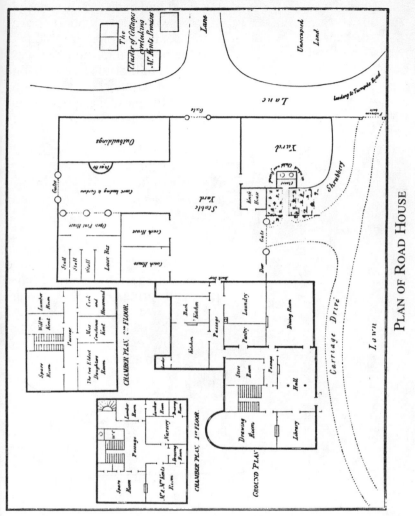

PLAN OF ROAD HOUSE

beautiful quality. If so, it would not be a common factor. The hunting instinct is possibly the most certain common factor that there is. If skilfully worked upon, it can become a dangerous blood-lust of the mob, and though there may be righteous indignation and genuine horror intermingled with the groans and epithets bestowed by a crowd upon a criminal, it is perfectly certain that the hunting instinct has the larger share. Probably every criticism that had ever been levelled carelessly against Mr

Kent now came up again in the minds of those who had uttered them. There are some people to whom a marriage such as Mr Kent's second marriage had been is always suspect; and there are sure to have been those who considered that his relationship with his children's former governess had not been what it should have been in their pre-marital days, though this was an imputation for which there was not a shadow of excuse or reason. A stepmother also is inseparably connected in the minds of the vulgar with indifference, if not with something worse. As a matter of fact, though Mrs Kent may not have known — indeed, obviously had not known — how to deal with such a difficult nature as that of the young girl Constance, her other stepdaughters had seemed to be very fond of her, and, undoubtedly, she must have exercised much self-restraint in the difficult and anguished days and months that followed her loss.

Feeling was running high, not only against Mr and Mrs Kent, but against the stepchildren. The youthful escapade of William and Constance came uppermost again in people's minds and on their tongues, and such was the obvious manifestation of ill-feeling from those who crowded the Temperance Hall — where the inquest was held — that the Coroner refused to allow the children to be examined in that place, but adjourned the inquest to Road Hill House. There Constance and William were examined, as had been the nurse and housemaid responsible for the inspection of the fastenings of the drawing-room window on the night of the crime. The two men who found the body had also been examined, but they had nothing to say beyond their description of the condition in which they had found it, and nothing was elicited from the family or the servants except the statement that not anything had been seen or heard by anyone in the house. The whole affair seemed shrouded in complete mystery.

There was no one who could have had any apparent motive for the murder. It was to no burglar's interest to steal and kill one child. Mr Kent was obviously not a man to object to the proportions that his family had assumed, the nurse had apparently been fond of her little charge, and Mrs Kent was obviously heartbroken.

A verdict of "Wilful Murder" was returned against "a person or persons unknown".

Where there is no motive, the busy-minded at once begin to seek one out, and it is, perhaps, not surprising that the first suspicions of the authorities should have been directed against the nurse, Elizabeth Gough. She was taken into custody, but no charge was made against her by the local police, and she was allowed to go free again.

The public voice now began to grumble loudly against the way in which the affair was being conducted. The Coroner, Mr Sylvester, had refused to examine Mrs Kent at the inquest, and this action of his brought much censure upon him.

In *The Times* of Wednesday, 11 July, the following passage occurs:

We must speak and do our part in enquiring who is guilty of this foul deed. Every effort, say the local papers, has been made to detect the murderer, but hitherto without effect. Perhaps so; but we are of opinion that many efforts yet untried may be made, and that in due time the murderer will be brought to justice. Without intending any disrespect to the Coroner or his jury, we take the liberty of saying that the circumstances demand a much more searching investigation than they have received at the hands of those functionaries. The Secretary of State must take it up, and the case must be sifted by a Commission under his authority. As far as we can understand the story, it seems that the house was thoroughly closed up on the night preceding the murder. In the morning the house was partly open; but it does not appear to have been opened by violence from without. Therefore the inference is plain that the secret lies with someone who was within. This seems so plain that we do not hesitate for an instant to say that, however painful such a proceeding may be, and however for a while the innocent may seem to suffer with the guilty, yet it must be held that the persons who composed the household must collectively be responsible for this murderous and dreadful event. Not one of them ought to be at large till the whole mystery is cleared up. Let a *cordon judiciaire* be drawn round the house, and let parents and nurse, master and servants, be confined within it until the truth is found. We cannot divest ourselves of the belief that the child suffered death at the hands of someone belonging to the house. We beg to ask you, what was the antecedent state of the family circle? It has been stated that two of the children once ran away because of some family disagreement. Have there been any recent repetitions of these disagreements? On what terms were the children of the first wife with those of the second? Had there been any previous strife in which the murdered child was involved? Was the father a good father? It is very painful to have such questions suggested, and we feel for all parties while we write them, but no fear of hurting anyone's feelings must be allowed to stifle enquiry. Of the servants we should like to learn more. What were their antecedents, habits and characters? On what terms were they with one another, with the children and with their master and mistress? Had anything occurred to provoke spite towards children or employers? Were any of them, or was anybody in the house, subject to mental delusions or violent impulses? . . .

We should like to know why the father went to Trowbridge immediately the child was missed; why he thought that it had been stolen, and how he accounted to himself for the *modus operandi* of the thief; why he didn't first search the premises, raise the neighbourhood and call in all conceivable help. We are willing to make allowances for a father's agitation, indecision, mistakes and confusion under such desperate circumstances, but at the same time we should like to know how what he did that day weaves in with the context of his temperament and habits.

It will be seen from the above that feeling was already running very high against the unfortunate Mr Kent, and the theory that already began to weave itself in people's minds was that he had been concerned in the crime.

It was on the Tuesday, 10 July, that Superintendent Foley apprehended Elizabeth Gough on suspicion, and on the following Monday, 16 July, she was brought before the Bench and liberated. Already, so swift was the revulsion of opinion in the public mind, people began to say that Elizabeth Gough was undoubtedly innocent.

Meanwhile, Detective Inspector Whicher had been sent down from Scotland Yard to take charge of the case. Almost at once he came to the conclusion — from which he was never afterwards to be turned — that the guilty party was the sixteen-year-old Constance Kent. On Friday, 20 July, a meeting of magistrates was held behind closed doors, and to it Inspector Whicher brought Constance in custody. She sat mute throughout the inquiry, with her eyes cast down, but Whicher described how, when he read the warrant to her, she burst into tears and kept on saying: "I am innocent! I am innocent!"

She was remanded and taken to Devizes Gaol, while maintaining a dogged silence.

People now began to say that Detective Inspector Whicher had certainly found out the truth, and all the suspicious circumstances connected with Constance began to be remembered. One of the chief of these circumstances was the fact that a night-dress of Constance Kent had disappeared — "at the laundress's," said the Kent family, who had previously complained of missing articles, but the laundress herself stoutly denied that she ever had the night-dress in question. Laundresses are notoriously careless, and the fact that there had been garments missing before made the Kents very sure of their ground. Also, the housemaid was certain that she had put Constance's night-dress into the linen-basket as usual; but it was certainly an unfortunate coincidence for Constance that it should be the night-dress she was wearing the week of the murder that had disappeared.

When Whicher asked Constance on 16 July how it was that she could only produce two night-dresses, whereas the linen-list showed three, she replied that she only had two, as the laundry had lost the third for her. This answer did not seem entirely satisfactory to Whicher, as he had discovered from the housemaid that while she was writing the list and sorting out the linen-basket, Constance sent her on an unnecessary errand, and so was left alone for a few minutes in the same room with all the dirty linen.

Elizabeth Gough was cross-examined before a magistrate on 27 July, when Constance was again brought up before them. In spite of the suspicion that had rested upon herself, the nursemaid showed no tendency to try to divert it upon Constance. Indeed, she stated in evidence: "I have never heard Miss Constance say anything unkind towards the little boy that is dead." And when she was asked: "Did you ever see her conduct herself unkindly towards the little boy?" she replied definitely in the negative.

Two of Constance's schoolfellows were then examined, but nothing more was elicited from them than a slight recountal of a few vague complaints of her home such as any imaginative child might have given. Emma Moody, the first girl to be examined, deposed that:

> I said upon one occasion, when we were talking about the holidays — we were going for a walk towards Road — I said: "Won't it be nice to go home shortly?" She said: "Yes, perhaps it may be to your home, but mine is different." She also led me to infer that she didn't dislike these children. She said that the second family were much better treated than herself and her brother William. She said this on several occasions. We were talking of dress at one time, and she said: "Mamma will not let me have what I like. If I said I would have a brown dress she would let me have black, or just the contrary."

What girl is there who might not have said the like, even about her own mother, let alone a stepmother? What girl of sixteen has ever seen quite eye to eye with her mother in the matter of dress?

Evidence was also given to the effect that the night-dress found on Constance's bed on the morning of the murder was quite free from blood stains; in fact, it was extraordinarily clean, considering that the day was a Saturday, and that the garment had been in wear for a week — with the starch still stiff in the frills in the collar and waistbands.

The story of the missing night-gown was gone into, but seemed to have no bearing on the case, and Mr Edlin, who was representing the prisoner, asked the Bench to liberate the prisoner and restore her to her friends, and declared with some truth that:

There was not one tittle of evidence against her, not one word on which the finger of infamy could be pointed against her. Although a most atrocious murder had been committed, it had been followed by a judicial murder not less atrocious. If the murderer were never discovered it would never be forgotten that this young lady had been dragged like a common felon to Devizes Gaol. The fact alone was quite sufficient to ensure the sympathy of every man in the county and the kingdom. The steps which had been taken must blast her hopes and prospects for life, and those steps had been taken solely on the suspicion of an inspector of police, acting under the influence of the reward which had been offered. The fact respecting the missing bedgown had been cleared up to the satisfaction of every one who had heard the evidence that day, and no doubt could remain that this little peg, upon which this fearful charge had been grounded, had fallen to the ground. He asked the magistrates, therefore, to pause and say whether for one moment longer this young lady should be kept in custody. Without reproaching Inspector Whicher for what he had done, he must say that the hunting up of the schoolfellows of Miss Constance Kent reflected ineffable disgrace upon those who had been the means of bringing them there. Nothing that had been elicited from those young ladies showed anything like *animus* on the part of the prisoner towards the deceased child, nor had any motive been established which would induce the prisoner to imbrue her hands in the blood of the poor little child. He appealed to the Bench, therefore, the case for the prosecution being exhausted — and a weaker one he had never heard — to perform their duty to the country and to the prisoner by at once saying that the evidence adduced satisfied them that the charge was groundless, and that Miss Constance Kent should at once be discharged.

Mr Edlin's speech was followed by applause, and Constance Kent was forthwith discharged. She returned home and, according to a contemporary description from *The Times*, a most affecting scene followed:

> Her sisters and parents clasped her in the most passionate and excited manner, embracing her most tenderly, and the sobbing and weeping and embraces were continued for a considerable time. At length, however, it subsided, and since then the young lady has presented a very subdued and contemplative demeanour.

By now a violent reaction had set in in the public mind in favour of Constance, and Inspector Whicher was overwhelmed with abuse for ever having made the arrest.

Public opinion veered round once more, and the next person to be blasted by its breath was Mr Kent. It had already determined that Elizabeth Gough, or her imaginary paramour, was guilty. It had then absolved her and fastened upon Constance. It now acquitted Constance and fastened firmly upon Mr Kent, with Elizabeth Gough as an accessory, on the theory that he had had an illicit affair with Elizabeth Gough, that little Savile had awakened and seen more than he should — more than he could be trusted to keep his childish tongue still about — and that Mr Kent had deliberately murdered his child to preserve his own fair name.

The fact that up till now he had been accused of favouring his second family too much did not in the least check those who were trying to make out that he had wantonly sacrificed his most dearly loved child of that family.

One indignant gentleman wrote to *The Times* as follows:

> Suppose — and every step of this case, except the actual murder, is based on supposition — suppose that something, call it an intrigue, a burglary, or what you will, was taking place beneath the roof that night, suppose the child awaking from sleep 'saw a man where a man should na' be', would not that supply a motive for the crime?
>
> To my mind, two things that occurred the next morning are fraught with suspicion — the ostentatious reading of the Bible for an hour by the nurse, who knew that the child was missing, and who ought immediately to have made enquiry in Mrs Kent's room; and the decision which was at once arrived at by certain parties that the child had been murdered.
>
> If the police would follow out these two points, they would, perhaps, be more successful than they were in their "fussy activity" about the night-dress of a schoolgirl.

There certainly seemed grounds, to a casual observer, for suspecting Elizabeth Gough, but there was really no point against her that was not easily disproved. Her enemies declared that it was extraordinary that she had slept through the entrance of the abductor, and the removal of the child; yet what is odd about that in a young woman of twenty-three, who had been up until about eleven the night before, and who had, in company with the only other two servants kept by this family of nine people, been busy all the previous day in extra cleaning?

In spite of the accumulation of ill-feeling against the unfortunate nursemaid and still more unfortunate Mr Kent, Elizabeth Gough was liberated and the chairman of the inquiry spoke very favourably of her behaviour in her time of trial. The only thing which had become clear through all the inquiries and the maze of suggestions was that the murder must undoubtedly have been committed by a member of the household. One of the three servants, or Mr or Mrs Kent, or one of the three older children must beyond question have been guilty of that innocent blood. There had been no marks of violence on the opened window of the shutters; no stranger to the house had opened all those doors and found his way unerringly to the little cot, and thence to the outside closet. Guilty one of the members of that household undoubtedly was, and the stigma of guilt clung to them all.

On Saturday, 11 August, a statement was made which temporarily diverted suspicion from Elizabeth Gough. A working man gave himself up and confessed to the murder. He stated that Mr Kent had himself handed the child to him out of the drawing-room window; he said that he was promised by Mr Kent a sum of money, but that he had not been paid and, as he was sure the curse of God was upon him, he had confessed.

This man was found to be insane and to have no connection with the crime, but the feeling against Mr Kent was running so high by this time that a great many people believed the story.

As to Inspector Whicher, his action was even commented on in the House of Commons, it being held that the Inspector in question had acted in a most objectionable manner; after all his boastings of the evidence he could produce, the young lady was discharged by the magistrates, and they believed there was not the slightest doubt that she was innocent of the charge.

The result of all this was that the nursemaid was apprehended in September, and in October was again brought before the magistrates, and again released.

In November an extraordinary incident came to light. Apparently on the fatal Saturday, when the police were searching the kitchen at Road Hill House, they discovered in the boiler of the furnace a chemise covered with blood. The egregious Foley had dismissed the incident as of no importance and had never mentioned it, although he had probably placed his two policemen in the kitchen that night to see whether anyone got up to try to destroy what was perhaps an incriminating garment. The fact that nobody did so apparently settled the matter for Mr Foley, and he troubled no more about it.

As a matter of fact, it transpired that the stains on the chemise had nothing to do with the crime, and were simply the result of an ordinary incident of nature to which Constance had at that time become subject, and which in these days would be taken into account as affecting her unbalanced condition. Nevertheless, the fact remains that the ineffable Foley had found a bloodstained garment concealed about the house on the day of the crime and had not thought it worth mentioning. It is no wonder that Inspector Whicher wrote very bitterly to say that he had been kept in ignorance of this discovery.

The Kent family was ruined; they had to leave Road, and took up their abode in Wales, trying to live as quietly and inconspicuously as possible. Only Mr Whicher still clung to his opinion, in spite of all the disgrace that had befallen him.

The American Civil War must have come as a blessing to the Kent family, for the Road Mystery passed out of the newspapers, and in their obscure Welsh home let us hope that their wounds began to heal as well as was possible, considering the misery of the accusations that they must always have felt dogged their footsteps.

Meanwhile Constance lived in her French convent and grew to womanhood. There is a photograph extant of her, taken when still a schoolgirl, in which she looks, to our modern eyes, to be a grown-up woman, and for this the fashions of the day are to blame — the hair bundled into a net at the back; prim collar and tie; the dark velvet jacket spreading out pyramid-wise over a swelling crinoline; the boat-shaped hat with the drooping plume — such as would have been worn at that same period by women twenty years older than herself. All these things combine to make a schoolgirl of that period look very much more of a sedate and settled woman than she can possibly have been.

Also, Constance Kent's features were of the regular and strongly marked variety — good-looking enough, bright, and perhaps too determined for the period in which she lived.

It is difficult — in fact, it is impossible — with any certainty to reconstruct the character of those who lived in a day before our own consciousness, and the utmost it is permissible to do is to draw deductions, not only from the circumstances of their lives but from the contemporary accounts of any reactions to such circumstances. Psychology was not then a science, as it is now, and, though doubtless much that would be clear to our modern eyes in the flame of our greater illumination remained dark — even unguessed at by those of that generation — yet without doubt we wander, nowadays, down many false and devious paths, missing the plain truth left for us to see upon the high road, in a manner which they were spared. The many complicated streams which went to make up that complex creature — for complex and abnormal she must have been — Constance Kent, were taken into small account by the doctors and lawyers of her day.

Contemporary writers dwell on the cold-bloodedness of the crime as its most monstrous feature, without seeing that it was

Constance Kent
From a photograph taken circa 1862

the very abnormality of that cold-bloodedness which should have marked her out for special treatment.

Constance Kent's salvation, like her damnation, came from within herself, and the really interesting thing about her, as far as it is possible to judge at this distance of time, is the fact that apparently she was not — as the congenital female criminal invariably is — a *poseuse*. She did not commit the crime for the sake of notoriety. She was normal enough to wish to remain unsuspected; and therefore we can rule her out at once from the great class of congenital youthful criminal into which she might, to superficial observation, seem to fall.

Neither, when she took the tremendous step of confessing, do we find her, to put it vulgarly, "out to make a splash". She went through with the thing as plainly as might be. There seems to me to be no valid reason for doubt that it was genuinely the working of her conscience that drove Constance Kent to the confession that electrified England in the year 1865.

I lay stress on these points because they are extremely rare in any criminal, and so rare as to be practically unique in a female criminal; and it is upon the inner evidence afforded to the mind by these points that Constance Kent, at least in the opinion of the writer, deserves to be placed in the class of occasional criminals and not in that of the congenital criminal, in spite of all the morbid stigmata which her crime displays, and which would seem to place her in the latter category.

Therefore, arguing along these lines, it is permissible to say that with a more understanding upbringing, such as she might have obtained nowadays, Constance Kent, with her determin-ation, her force of feeling, and her rare power of secrecy, might have made a very fine thing of her life, instead of turning it into a sordid tragedy.

What imaginative child is there who has not seen himself in some violent and picturesque role? — saving his whole family from a burning house, or suffering, misunderstood, in silence, for another's fault and eventually being cleared with honour in the eyes of his accusers?

Doubtless Constance Kent had begun by voicing to her schoolfellows her discontent with her father's new marriage and the state of things at home; and had found that the recital of such picturesque woe as is involved by having a stepmother gained her sympathy from her schoolfellows. This, in its turn, would make the whole situation more real to herself, so that she would see slights where none were meant, and would hug to herself the idea that she was a misunderstood and unappreciated, unwanted daughter of the first family, whom her father had ceased to love. It is all the more remarkable with this inflation of the imagination from which she evidently suffered — as does every intelligent child, given the necessary circumstances — that she so successfully should have pulled out of that quagmire of theatricality which besets the feet of adolescence, and have met at last face to face in the stern conflict, for which there was no issue save a hard and fast decision, the spectre which inhabited her soul.

In 1863 Constance was sent to live at Brighton, at St Mary's Home, which was under the spiritual direction of the Rev. A. D. Wagner, who was Perpetual Curate of St Paul's Church. Fully to understand the tremendous effect which these surroundings had upon Constance Kent, it is necessary that one should recapture in some degree the peculiar religious atmosphere of that time, so alien from us now. Every daily paper was full of the doings of the so-called Puseyites. Questions of ritual, ranging from the wearing of surplices to the use of the private confessional, convulsed England daily.

The world has grown past this particular view of life in almost every religion professed by its inhabitants. Tolerance, mutual respect, candid acknowledgement of ignorance as to the actual attributes both of the Deity and the human soul, have taken the place of the passionate and heartfelt arguments not only upon questions of ritual, but also upon questions of dogma. Being prepared for Confirmation by such an honest, fiery-souled, thoroughly convinced man as Mr Wagner so worked upon the mind of Constance Kent that she came to believe the world well lost if she could yet by any means save her soul.

In those days, no such simple creed as sustains most of us blundering humans nowadays was held, except by a very few, who concealed the fact; and there is this to be said for the black-and-whiteness, the hard-and-fastness of the creed which Constance Kent found closing about her every day — it had a definite practical value.

Constance Kent's confession lifted the cloud that for five years past had rested upon her father, upon an innocent nurse-maid, upon the whole family — in fact, upon the entire household that had once lived at Road Hill.

For let there be no mistake about it — there was no necessity, save that of spiritual compulsion, for the confession of Constance Kent. The affair would never have been raked up again, and she had not that dire necessity which even most hardened criminals would feel — of confession to save the neck of some innocent person. She could only have had two motives — one purely spiritual and the other theatrical; and as I have pointed out, I see no evidence of the latter dread quality surviving into her adult years. Undoubtedly it swayed her childhood and adolescence, but then so it does that of every imaginative young creature.

Religion then, extremely clear-cut religion which there was no evading, tracked Constance down. It has often been said, and with great truth, that the religion of the Victorians was a very hypocritical affair of Sundays only, of best clothes, of outward conformity, and that it held no real part in the lives of those who professed it.

From this charge the Ritualistic Movement, with all its tiresomeness, its absurd fussing over unimportant points, was at least free. It presented to the people the forms and privileges of Catholicism, and, unlike the Continentals, accustomed to those forms and privileges from their youth and able to come to some sort of terms with them, the English people had to conform their practice to their new belief if they were not to be written down utter triflers and hypocrites.

Constance's mind cannot, it is needless to say, have been at rest during the time that had elapsed since the murder. She must have known that she was even more than suspect by her family in that she was allowed to live away from them, and was moved from Home to Home, always under supervision. The thing she had done must have assumed more and more dreadful proportions in her preoccupied mind. Only the stubbornness of her strong nature can have enabled her to carry through with her attitude of pretended innocence for so long. When one realizes that for the whole of that time letters must have passed between her and her family — for the Victorians were rigid about these conventions — and, further, realizes that a deadly suspicion must have weighted the pen of her father whenever he wrote to her, and a deadlier knowledge dragged at hers, it is possible to begin to understand what an unreal and nightmare quality those years must have held.

There must, of course — for so resilient is human nature — have been times when she thought and hoped to forget it, when she cheated herself into an almost forgetfulness. The novelty of the scenes abroad, the strange language, the different life, must all have helped her towards the illusion that it was not only possible to forget, but possible perhaps that the whole thing had been a mistake.

But the Hound of Heaven was on her track, if ever He were on that of mortal being, and it was in cheerful, banal, prosperous Brighton that Constance was finally tracked down.

She admitted her guilt to Mr Wagner, though under the seal of confession, and, therefore, of course, his tongue was tied; but in Holy Week in the year 1865, worked on doubtless by the solemn and dreadful pageant of successive services, she came to her great decision and informed Miss Gream, the Superior of the Order, and Mr Wagner that she had made up her mind to make public confession.

Mr Wagner gave her the advice that any priest of the Catholic Church would have given her — that is to say, he told her that what she contemplated was right; that without so doing she could not hope to obtain peace for her soul, but that he himself could reveal nothing that she told in confession.

Constance Kent went up to town and delivered herself up at Bow Street before the Chief Magistrate, Sir Thomas Henry; Mr Wagner and the Mother Superior went with her. She was taken to Sir Thomas Henry's private room; she was dressed in mourning, with a heavy lace veil which entirely hid her face. She told her story formally, though quietly. Superintendent Durkin and Mr Williamson — Chief Inspector of the Detective Force — were in charge of her.

It is curious to notice how local and public feeling were inimical at first to Mr Wagner and Miss Gream. The good Protestant people were suspicious of undue influence of Romanizing tendencies — of the sinister coercion they had heard existed in convents.

Sir Thomas Henry asked Constance: "Am I to understand, Miss Kent, that you have given yourself up of your own free act and will on this charge?" She replied: "Yes."

He then went on to warn her, as in duty bound, that anything she said would be written down and might be used in evidence. To which she replied that she quite understood. With the scrupulous fairness generally observed towards prisoners in England, Sir Thomas then asked: "Is this paper now produced before me in your own handwriting and written of your own free will?" She replied that it was.

The charge was then entered as follows: "Constance Emilie Kent of 2 Queen Square, Brighton, charged upon her own confession with having alone and unaided on the night of the 29th of June 1860 murdered at Road Hill House, Wiltshire, one Francis Savile Kent."

Sir Thomas then asked her: "Have you any objection to signing the statement you have here made? I must again remind you that it is the most serious crime that can be committed, and that your statement will be used against you at your trial. I have had the words written copied upon this charge-sheet, but I do not wish you to sign it unless you desire to do so."

Constance in answer said that she would do so, and he replied:

"There is no occasion for you to sign the charge unless you wish it. I will have your statement attached to the depositions, and I will again ask you if you have made it by your own desire, and without any inducement from any quarter whatever to give yourself up."

When he was reassured upon this point, Mr Wagner was then sworn, and deposed to having known Constance Kent for about twenty-one months, as an inmate of St Mary's Home.

Sir Thomas asked him whether he had made any inducement to Constance Kent to cause her to make the confession, and Mr Wagner replied in the negative. He explained that it had been entirely Constance Kent's own idea to come up to a London magistrate, and that apart from the confession, which she had made to him under the seal of the confessional, she had since made a statement similar to that upon the charge-sheet.

Sir Thomas was obviously one to whom the word "confessional" acted as an irritant, and he replied: "I will not go into that point here — it may be gone into at the trial — perhaps very fully.'"

Then, turning to Constance Kent, he added: "I hope you understand that whatever you say must be entirely your own free and voluntary statement and that no inducement that may have been held out to you is to have any effect upon your mind?"

CONSTANCE KENT: No inducement ever has, sir.

SIR THOMAS: I am anxious that you should most seriously consider that.

MR WAGNER: I wish to mention that many are in the habit of coming to confess to me as a religious exercise, but I never held out any inducement to her to make a public confession.

SIR THOMAS: Yes, I think you ought to mention that. Did you, in the first instance, induce her to make a confession to you?

MR WAGNER: No, sir, I did not seek her out or in any way ask her to come to confession. She herself wished to do so.

SIR THOMAS: If you think that the confession she now makes has been induced in consequence of anything which she has said to you or which you have said to her, you ought to say so.

MR WAGNER: I never even recommended it. I have been simply passive. I thought she was doing right, and so I did not dissuade her.

SIR THOMAS: But do you say that you did not persuade her?

MR WAGNER: I do say so.

Sir Thomas then once again warned Constance Kent that she was not bound to make any statement unless she desired to do so, and her deposition was then read over and she was asked if she wished to add anything to it, a question to which she replied in the negative.

Sir Thomas then explained that as the offence had been committed in Wiltshire, the trial would have to be there also, and he must send her to be examined before the Magistrate in that district.

The warrant was then made out and handed, with the other documents in the case, to Inspector Williamson, who took the prisoner in a cab to the railway station, still accompanied by Mr Wagner and Miss Gream, the conventual dress of the latter exciting much attention among the little group gathered outside Bow Street.

The thing worth comment, I suggest, about this interview is that Constance Kent did not make a scene. She was quite undramatic.

Her ordeal took place at Trowbridge, where she was brought up before the Magistrates sitting in Petty Sessions. Again she was dressed in deep mourning, with her thick veil, but even through that covering it was to be seen that her face was deeply flushed. The evidence was purely formal, and merely a recapitulation of what had taken place before Sir Thomas Henry, and the prisoner was committed for trial at the ensuing Wiltshire Assizes.

As a dramatic spectacle, the trial was, of course, a complete failure, for not only was there no doubt of the prisoner's guilt, but she refused to enter the conventional plea of "Not Guilty," and her defender, Mr Coleridge, QC, was therefore limited to a purely formal little speech before the sentence was passed.

It must, indeed, have been the strangest trial on record. It cannot have occupied more than a few minutes. The court was crowded. In the middle of a deep silence the Clerk of Assize spoke to the prisoner in the usual formula:

"Constance Emilie Kent, you stand charged with having wilfully murdered Francis Savile Kent at Road Hill House on 30 June 1860. How say you — are you guilty or not guilty?"

THE PRISONER — in a low tone of voice: Guilty.

MR JUSTICE WILLES: Are you aware that you are charged with having wilfully, intentionally, and with malice killed your brother?

THE PRISONER — with head bent low: Yes.

MR JUSTICE WILLES: And you plead guilty of that?

The prisoner hesitated. Mr Justice Willes waited for some minutes in breathless silence and then said: What is your answer?

The prisoner still remained silent.

MR JUSTICE WILLES: I must repeat to you that you are charged with having wilfully and intentionally and with malice killed and murdered your brother. Are you guilty or not guilty?

THE PRISONER — in a rather more firm voice: Guilty.

MR JUSTICE WILLES — to the Clerk of Assize: Let the plea be recorded.

A dead silence ensued for some minutes, which was broken by Mr Coleridge QC, afterwards Lord Chief Justice, who said:

My Lord, as counsel for the defence, acting on the prisoner's behalf, before your Lordship passes sentence, I desire to say two things — first, solemnly in the presence of Almighty God, as a person who values her own soul, she wishes me to say that the guilt is hers alone, and that her father and others who have so long suffered most unjust and cruel suspicion are wholly and absolutely innocent; and, secondly, she was not driven to this act, as has been asserted, by unkind treatment at home, as she met with nothing there but tender and forbearing love; and I hope I may add, my Lord, not improperly, that it gives me a melancholy pleasure to be the organ of these statements for her, because on my honour I believe them to be true.

THE CLERK OF ASSIZE — addressing the prisoner: Constance Emilie Kent, you have confessed yourself guilty of the murder of Francis Savile Kent; have you anything to say why sentence of death should not be passed upon you?

THE PRISONER: No.

Mr Justice Willes then assumed the black cap and addressed the prisoner in the following terms:

Constance Emilie Kent, you have pleaded guilty to an indictment charging you with the wilful murder of your brother Francis Savile

Kent on 30 June 1860. It is my duty to receive that plea which you have deliberately put forward, and it is a satisfaction to me to know that it was not done until after having had the advice of counsel, who would have freed you from this dreadful charge if you could have been freed thereof. I can entertain no doubt, after having read the evidence in the depositions, and considering this is your third confession of the crime, that your plea is the plea of a really guilty person. The murder was one committed under circumstances of great deliberation and cruelty. You appear to have allowed your feelings of jealousy and anger to have worked in your breast until at last they assumed over you the influence and the power of the Evil One.

Mr Justice Willes here became deeply affected and burst into tears, which prevented him from proceeding with his remarks for some minutes.

The prisoner at the bar, who up to this time had maintained the greatest composure, could no longer witness the proceedings with apparent indifference. Turning her head from the judge, she burst into a passion of tears, which was audible to every part of the court, and produced a profound impression upon all who were witnesses of the scene.

Mr Justice Willes continued as follows:

Whether Her Majesty, with whom alone the prerogative of mercy rests, may be advised to consider the fact of your youth at the time when the murder was committed, and the fact that you were convicted chiefly upon your own confession, which removes suspicion from others, is a question which it would be presumption for me to answer here. It well behoves you to live what is left of your life as one who is about to die, and to seek a more enduring mercy, by sincere and deep contrition, and by a reliance upon the only redemption and satisfaction for all the sins of the world. It only remains for me to discharge the duty which the law imposes upon the Court without alternative, and that is to pass upon you the sentence which the law adjudges for wilful murder: that you be taken from the place where you now stand to the place whence you came, from thence to the place of execution, and that you be hanged by the neck until your body be dead; that when your body be dead it be buried within the precincts of the gaol in which you were last confined: and may God have mercy on your soul.

The capital sentence was commuted to that of penal servitude for life.

A detailed account of the manner in which the crime was committed was afterwards furnished to the public by Dr Bucknill, the physician who had examined the prisoner by the desire of the government, in order to form an opinion as to the condition of her mind.

The following letter appeared in the public papers:

Sir,

I am requested by Miss Constance Kent to communicate to you the following details of her crime; which she has confessed to Mr Rodway, her solicitor, and to myself, and which she now desires to be made public.

Constance Kent first gave an account of the circumstances of her crime to Mr Rodway, and she afterwards acknowledged to me the correctness of that account when I recapitulated it to her. The explanation of her motive she gave to me when, with the permission of the Lord Chancellor, I examined her for the purpose of ascertaining whether there were any grounds for supposing that she was labouring under mental disease. Both Mr Rodway and I are convinced of the truthfulness and good faith of what she said to us.

Constance Kent says that the manner in which she committed her crime was as follows: A few days before the murder she obtained possession of a razor from a green case in her father's wardrobe, and secreted it. This was the sole instrument which she used. She also secreted a candle with matches, by placing them in the corner of the closet in the garden, where the murder was committed. On the night of the murder she undressed herself and went to bed, because she expected that her sisters would visit her room. She lay awake watching, until she thought that the household were all asleep, and soon after midnight she left her bedroom and went downstairs and opened the drawing-room door and window shutters. She then went up into the nursery, withdrew the blanket from between the sheet and the counterpane, and placed it on the side of the cot. She then took the child from his bed and carried him downstairs through the drawing-room. She had on her night-dress, and in the drawing-room she put on her goloshes. Having the child in one arm, she raised the drawing-room window with the other hand, went round the house and into the closet, lighted the candle and placed it on the seat of the closet, the child being wrapped in the blanket and still sleeping, and while the child was in this position she inflicted the wound in the throat. She says that she thought the blood would never come, and that the child was not killed, so she thrust the razor into its left side, and put the body, with the blanket round it, into the vault. The light burnt out. The piece of flannel which she had with her was torn from the old flannel garment placed in the waste bag, and which she had taken some time before and sewn it to use in washing herself. She went back to her bedroom, examined her dress, and found only two spots of blood on it. These she washed out in the basin, and threw the water, which was but little discoloured, into the foot-pan in which she had washed her feet overnight. She took another of her night-dresses and got into bed. In the morning her night-dress had become dry where it had been washed. She folded it up and put it into the drawer. Her three night-dresses were examined by Mr Foley, and she believes also by Mr Parsons, the medical attendant of the family. She thought the blood-stains had been effectually washed out, but on holding the dress up to the light a day or two afterwards, she found the stains were still visible. She secreted the dress, moving it from place to place, and she eventually burnt it in her own bedroom, and put the ashes or tinder into the kitchen grate. It was about five or six days after the child's death that she burnt the night-dress. On the Saturday morning, having cleaned the razor, she took an opportunity of replacing it unobserved in the case in the wardrobe. She abstracted her night-dress from the clothes basket when the housemaid went to fetch a glass of water. The stained garment found in the boiler hole had no connection whatever with the deed. As regards the motive of her crime, it seems that, although she entertained at one time a great regard for the present Mrs Kent, yet if any remark was at any time made which in her opinion was disparaging to any member of the first family, she treasured it up, and determined to revenge it. She had no ill-will against the little boy, except as one of the children of her stepmother. She declared that both her father and her stepmother had always been kind to her personally, and the following is a copy of a letter which she addressed to Mr Rodway on this point while in prison before her trial:

DEVIZES, *May 15th*

Sir,
It has been stated that my feelings of revenge were excited in consequence of cruel treatment. This is entirely false. I have received the greatest kindness from both the persons accused of subjecting me to it. I have never had any ill-will towards either of them on account of their behaviour to me, which has been very kind.

I shall feel obliged if you will make use of this statement in order that the public may be undeceived on this point.
I remain, sir,
Yours truly,
CONSTANCE E. KENT

To Mr R. Rodway
She told me that when the nursemaid was accused she had fully made up her mind to confess if the nursemaid had been convicted; and that she had also made up her mind to commit suicide if she herself was convicted. She said that she had felt herself under the influence of the devil before she committed the murder, but that she did not believe, and had not believed, that the devil had more to do with her crime than he had with any other wicked action. She had not said her prayers for a

year before the murder, and not afterwards until she came to reside at Brighton. She said that the circumstance which revived religious feelings in her mind was thinking about the Sacrament when confirmed.

An opinion has been expressed that the peculiarities evinced by Constance Kent between the ages of twelve and seventeen may be attributed to the then transition period of her life. Moreover, the fact of her cutting off her hair, dressing herself in her brother's clothes, and then leaving her home with the intention of going abroad, which occurred when she was only thirteen years of age, indicated a peculiarity of disposition, and great determination of character, which foreboded that, for good or evil, her future life would be remarkable.

This peculiar disposition, which led her to such singular and violent resolves of action, seemed also to colour and intensify her thoughts and feelings, and magnify into wrongs that were to be revenged any little family incidents or occurrences which provoked her displeasure.

Although it became my duty to advise her counsel that she evinced no symptom of insanity at the time of my examination, and that, so far as it was possible to ascertain the state of her mind at so remote a period, there was no evidence of it at the time of the murder, I am yet of opinion that, owing to the peculiarities of her constitution, it is probable that under prolonged solitary confinement she would become insane.

The validity of this opinion is of importance now that the sentence of death has been commuted to penal servitude for life; for no one could desire that the punishment of the criminal should be so carried out as to cause danger of a further and greater punishment not contemplated by the law.

I have the honour to remain your very obedient servant,

JOHN CHARLES BUCKNILL, MD

HILMERTON HALL, NEAR RUGBY
August 24th

It will be seen from this detailed confession that Inspector Whicher had been uncannily correct in what he had maintained at the time of the first inquiries about the murder — namely, that the night-dress which was sent to the wash that Saturday, and which the household had imagined was the night-dress she had been wearing the whole of the week, was a clean garment which she had put on after the murder, and the actual gown in which she had done the deed she had succeeded in destroying without it having been found.

Thus this unfortunate girl passed into a retreat more complete than that of any of the institutions in which she had lived since her commission of the crime. She served twenty years of her sentence and came out a middle-aged woman. For part of her sentence she was detained at Portland Prison, where she made many of the mosaics for St Peter's Church.

Certain it is that, in spite of the extremely brutal and callous crime which she committed, modern psychology would have found many excuses for her, but it is perhaps better that she should have been treated in the simpler and harder manner of those days.

For it would have been all but impossible, under present methods, for Constance Kent not to have acquired an inflated sense of her own importance, and the stark spiritual solitude in which she wrestled with her soul must have — surely it is permissible to think so? — gained her more peace in the long run than she could have acquired under different methods.

Hers was a harsh, strong, violent and revengeful nature, and for such, bare and rigid truth is the only comforter.

Editor's Note

In his book on the case, *Cruelly Murdered* (Souvenir Press, London 1979), Bernard Taylor reveals that in 1886, a year after Constance Kent's release from prison on "ticket of leave", she assumed the name of Ruth Emilie Kaye and emigrated to Australia, where her brother William, who was gaining fame as a naturalist, had settled with his second wife, his first wife having died young. From 1890 — when she volunteered to help victims of a typhoid epidemic — until 1932, she ministered to the sick; latterly at a nurses' home that she herself had set up. She was busy, too, as a founder-member of an organization dedicated to social reform. She died on Easter Monday, 1944, two months after her hundredth birthday, when she had received, among many tributes and messages of love and gratitude, a congratulatory telegram from the King and Queen.

Death on the Via Devana

Jonathan Goodman

I MAY not be quoting Alfred Hitchcock exactly, but he once
remarked that the murder tales he found most appealing made
him think of blood on a daisy. What he meant, I think, was that
he liked contrast between a crime and its setting: a dramatic
contradiction in terms. Murder behind lace curtains, perhaps.
Or murder marring a beauty spot, as in the case that came to be
known as the Mystery of the Green Bicycle.

It was a bike of another colour that twenty-one-year-old Bella
Wright pedalled towards the village of Stoughton (locally pronounced "Stoat'n"), where she lived with her parents, at about
eleven o'clock on the morning of Saturday, 5 July 1919, her last
day on earth. She was returning home after working the early-
morning shift at St Mary's Rubber Mills in Leicester, a couple of
miles to the west of the village.

Bella had been born in Leicester, which was where her family
had resided until a year or so before, when her father, after
being unemployed for a while, had found a job as a farm
labourer at Stoughton. After leaving school, Bella had spent
five years as a domestic servant until she was taken on at the
rubber mills in May 1917.

She was a chunkily built girl, darkly pretty. Though some
people complained that she was a "dreadful chatterbox", she
had many friends. Since round about Christmas, her main topic
of chatter had been Archibald Ward, a young man she had met
at the rubber mills. She and Archibald — Archie for short —
were engaged to be married. She did not wear an engagement
ring, but that was only because Archie had proposed by post,
after joining the navy for war service as a stoker — presently on
HMS *Diadem*.

Bella was counting the days till the middle of August, when,
all being well, Archie would be demobbed. She told friends and
relatives — *insisted* on telling them — of the latest additions to

33

her bottom drawer; of her uncertainty as to whether she should
buy a wedding gown, an awful extravagance, or please her
parents by wearing her mother's gown, recently unfolded from
within reams of tissue paper and found to be only slightly
discoloured but pungently smelling of mothballs; of how many
children she wanted and what their names would be.

The day of her death was hot and sunny. When she reached her
parents' cottage on the hillside at Stoughton, her cream-coloured
dress clung moistly to her body; her face, shadowed by a wide-
brimmed hat of white velour, sparkled with sweat. As she leaned
her cycle against the water butt beside the kitchen door, she
waved to her father, who was toiling in a nearby field. As soon as
she entered the kitchen, she sniffed the air – not to discern what
her mother was cooking on the range but in the hope that the
wedding gown that she had hung by the window the night before
smelt less of naphthalene. Perhaps it was her imagination, but the
stench seemed worse than ever. She told her mother so.

"Don't talk nonsense," Mrs Wright said. "My goodness, girl,
the wedding's not until the autumn, and there'll be no smell by
then. If there is, the guests will think it's incense."

That comment didn't please Bella. Refusing the mug of tea
offered by her mother, she went to her room, undressed, and
got into bed.

It was four o'clock when she awoke. She ate a cucumber
sandwich and a slice of seed-cake, then wrote some letters,
including the daily one to Archie. When her mother asked what
she was giggling about, she explained that she had made a joke
to Archie: something to do with the saying that sailors had girls
in every port. Mrs Wright told her to be careful — she might put
ideas in her fiancé's head.

She cycled to the village of Evington, a mile to the north,
bought some penny and halfpenny stamps at the post office, and
put her letters in the box. She returned home, but stayed there
for no more than an hour or so. Shortly after half-past six, she
rode off again, this time travelling east, past the church where
she expected to be wed — past the diminutive cemetery where
in a few days' time, her body would be buried.

It was half-past seven when she turned up at the cottage of her
uncle, George Measures, a road-worker, in the hamlet of
Gaulby, three miles east of Stoughton. As it happened,
Measures's son-in-law, James Evans, had come over for the day
from Ashby-de-la-Zouche, where he worked as a coal miner.

Bella was not alone when she arrived outside the cottage.

She was accompanied by a youngish man riding a pea-green bicycle. He remained in the road, his legs straddling the cycle, when Bella entered the cottage.

He was still there when, a few minutes later, James Evans looked out of the window. When Evans asked Bella who the man was, she said that she hadn't the faintest idea: "He's a perfect stranger," she added, explaining that he had overtaken her and tried to strike up a conversation. "Perhaps if I wait a while, he will be gone," she said.

But shortly before half-past eight, when Measures and Evans walked with Bella to the garden gate, the man was waiting for her. According to Measures and Evans, he said: "Bella, you *have* been a long time. I thought you had gone the other way." He spoke in a low but "squeaking" voice.

As Bella wheeled her cycle into the road, Evans, who was himself a keen cyclist, had a few words with the stranger, asking about his machine, which had a three-speed gear and a back-pedalling brake.

Bella and the stranger rode away together — towards Stoughton, as Measures and Evans believed.

George Measures's cottage
A recent photograph

35

At twenty minutes past nine, Joseph Cowell, the owner o
Elms Farm at Stretton Parva, a village two miles north-west o
Gaulby and the same distance north-east of Stoughton, took
stroll along a road known as the Via Devana, leading to Leicester

The dead body of a young woman was lying on the road. He
head was covered with blood. A few feet away, a bicycle la
askew, its front wheel pointing towards Leicester.

As Cowell dragged the body on to the grass verge, he notice
that the skin was still warm. The tall hedges made the roa
almost pitch black, and so he was unable to see something tha
added a sinister touch to the death of Bella Wright: the blood
claw-marks of a large bird were scribbled a dozen times over
backwards and forwards between the place where the body ha
originally lain and the gate of an adjoining meadow.

Cowell went in search of the local constable, George Hall. The
time was then about half-past nine. Either Cowell had difficulty
in tracking down PC Hall or the policeman was in no hurry to
start the investigation, for it wasn't until an hour later that he
located the body.

Constable Hall had had the foresight to phone a doctor
Ernest Williams, and the latter drove to the scene. Subsequen
tly, when he was asked what time he arrived, he said that it wa
quarter to eleven . . . or perhaps quarter *past* eleven — one o
the other, he wasn't sure which. His uncertainty on this poin
was symptomatic of a bumbling inefficiency that suggests tha
locals who were taken ill would have been well advised to stee
clear of his surgery and seek treatment from the nearest vet.

Whatever the time was when the doctor parked on the Vi
Devana, Constable Hall had by then commandeered a milk floa
and lifted the body on to it; and he had wheeled the dead girl'
cycle off the road. Also, perhaps — one cannot be sure of this —
he had looked in the slit-pockets of the girl's black skirt, hopin
to find some form of identification. All one can glean from Hall'
notes is that, at some time during the early stages of the investi
gation, he itemized the contents of the pockets: an empty purse
a box of matches, and a handkerchief. Nothing that gave th
corpse a name. Not until the small hours of the morning, whe
Bella Wright's father reported that she had not returned hom
after visiting her uncle, did Constable Hall have any idea of th
dead girl's identity.

By then, the body was lying in an empty cottage owned by Joseph Cowell. And, apart from Mr and Mrs Wright, no one was greatly concerned. Dr Williams, you see, had "examined" the body on the milk float and concluded that death was due to an accident: it was more than likely, he thought, that the front wheel of the girl's cycle had struck a stone and she had been catapulted head-first on to the road.

But at about seven o'clock on the Sunday morning, Constable Hall, a tidy-minded sort of chap, went back to the Via Devana to make sure that nothing had been left lying around. He noticed two things that seemed to him rather odd.

First, there was a bullet embedded in the road, five yards or so from where the body had been found; it looked to the constable as if it had been trodden on, perhaps by a horse. Having prised the misshapen bullet from the ground, Hall squinted at it and concluded that it had been fired from a hand-gun.

The constable also noticed the bloody claw-marks between the centre of the road and the gate to the meadow; there were some dozen tracks, and the top bar of the gate showed similar claw-marks. Hall walked into the meadow, and there discovered a dead bird — a raven, he thought. The bird was gorged with blood.

A recent photograph of the Via Devana, looking east. Bella Wright's body was found on the left, just past the road junction.

37

Hall went to the empty cottage that was being used as a mortuary. The night before, Dr Williams had not bothered to wipe any of the blood from the dead girl's face. Now Hall remedied that omission — and at once saw what looked like a bullet-hole, large enough to admit a pencil, an inch below the left eye.

He telephoned Dr Williams and suggested that perhaps a second examination was called for. When Williams heard the reasons for the suggestion, he hurried along to the cottage.

He nodded sagely when Hall indicated the hole in Bella Wright's cheek. Taking a pair of scissors from the bag he had remembered to bring with him, he snipped at the hair above the nape of the neck, and gradually cut towards the scalp. Now the scissors encountered resistance from coagulated blood. A few further snips revealed a much larger hole than that in the cheek: it was one and a half inches long and half an inch wide. There was little doubt — not even in Dr Williams's mind — that the hole was the exit-wound of a bullet. Putting two and two together, the doctor informed Constable Hall that Bella Wright had been shot in the face; the bullet had burrowed through her head, travelling diagonally upwards.

Focusing his attention —and later a microscope — on the area around the hole in the cheek, Williams observed that the skin was discoloured. At first, he thought this might be due to burning, indicating that the firearm had been held close to the face; but closer examination revealed downy hair around the wound. The discoloration was bruising, probably caused by the impact of the bullet.

Next day, Williams carried out a post-mortem examination with another doctor. There was no sign of bruising on the trunk or arms, but two small contusions were found near the right of the mouth. The doctors agreed that a number of scratches on the left hand and left cheek had almost certainly been caused by the gravel on the road. The girl was a virgin.

Belatedly, a murder investigation got under way. Members of the Leicester CID interviewed Bella Wright's uncle, George Measures, and his son-in-law, James Evans, and put together a description of the man on the green bicycle who had accompanied Bella to Measures's cottage on the Saturday evening, waited outside while she chatted with her relatives, and then ridden away with her.

The Chief Constable of Leicester offered a reward of five pounds for information leading to the man's apprehension — not an extravagant amount, perhaps because it was thought that many people would come forward. After all, the announcement included not only an extremely detailed word-picture of the man — with such details as his age (in his thirties), the fact that he had a "squeaking" voice, and full information about his clothing ("light rainproof coat with green plaid lining, grey-mixture jacket suit, grey cap," etc.) — but also a most precise description of his cycle: "gent's BSA, green enamelled frame, black mudguards" and so on, finishing up with the particularizing fact that "the three-speed control had recently been repaired with a length of new cable".

It was only a matter of time, surely — hours rather than days — before the squeaky-voiced man would be identified.

But no: though newspapers were now offering far more enticing rewards, weeks passed . . . months. Still the police had no worthwhile information.

Then, on Monday, 23 February 1920, over seven months after the murder, the green bicycle was brought to light by one of the most extraordinary flukes in the annals of crime.

On the morning of that Monday, a bargeman named Enoch Whitehouse was transporting a load of coal to the St Mary's Rubber Mills in Leicester — the very place where Bella Wright had worked. As he neared the New Lock in the centre of the town, he saw the tow-rope slacken, then dip below the surface of the canal. The rope tightened again, bringing with it part of a bicycle, which hung suspended for a few seconds before lurching back into the dark water.

Enoch Whitehouse delivered the coal at the St Mary's wharf, but his mind wasn't on his work. He kept thinking about the curious fish he had hooked. Later that day, he made careful enquiries, and learned that newspapers, both local and national, were still in the market for information helping towards the solution to the Mystery of the Green Bicycle.

Enoch rose earlier than usual the next day. Having fashioned a grappling-iron and attached it to a length of rope, he went on a fishing expedition to the spot near the New Lock. After casting about for half an hour or so, he felt the grappling-iron tugging against something. He pulled on the line, hand over hand, and the incomplete bicycle, just the frame and the front wheel, re-emerged from the canal. The frame was *green*.

Protecting his interests, Enoch informed the press of his find before carrying it to the Leicester police headquarters.

While a detective examined the incomplete bicycle, checking its features against the description given by Bella's uncle and his son-in-law, arrangements were made for the Leicester Corporation's dredger to be used in a search of the part of the canal near the New Lock. The dredging, which went on for several weeks, resulted in the reclamation of most of the missing parts: the rear wheel, gears, cranks, pedals.

And there was a bonus for the police. On 19 March, a revolver holster was fished up. As it was being lifted towards the embankment, some cartridges fell into the water, but twelve live cartridges and seven blanks were left in the soggy case; later, ten live cartridges were netted from the bed of the canal. The cartridges were all of ·455 calibre, suitable for firing from an army revolver; the bullets matched that which had killed Bella Wright (not that that was much of a clue, considering that ·455 cartridges had been standard service issue since the Boer War, produced in millions by the Webley-Scott company and other government contractors).

The police concentrated their attention on the components of the green bicycle. There seemed no doubt that the machine was the one they had been searching for since the previous summer. It was just possible, of course, that all the publicity had frightened some quite innocent owner of a green bicycle into dismembering his machine and throwing the parts into the canal. But to accept that notion, one had to believe that the self-same person, happening to possess a holster and a number of cartridges (and, presumably, a revolver, though no amount of dredging had revealed it), had discarded those as well.

Pretty unlikely. And made even less credible by the fact that all of the obvious identification marks on the bicycle frame had been scraped away.

However, one identification mark had eluded the scraper's notice. Because the cycle was a BSA de luxe model, known in the trade as a "special-order machine", an extra registration number — 103648 — had been stamped into the pillar of the handlebars.

A telephone call to the BSA factory in Birmingham produced the information that "model de luxe gent's bicycle No. 103648"

Telephone 357 and 862.

LEICESTERSHIRE CONSTABULARY.

£5 REWARD.

At 9-20 p.m., 5th instant, the body of a woman, since identified as that of ANNIE BELLA WRIGHT, was found lying on the Burton Overy Road, Stretton Parva, with a bullet wound through the head, and her bicycle lying close by.

Shortly before the finding of the body the deceased left an adjacent village in company of a man of the following description :—

Age 35 to 40 years, height 5 ft. 7 in. to 5 ft. 9 in.; apparently usually clean shaven, but had not shaved for a few days, hair turning grey, broad full face, broad build, said to have squeaking voice and to speak in a low tone.

Dressed in light Rainproof Coat with green plaid lining, grey mixture jacket suit, grey cap, collar and tie, black boots, and wearing cycle clips.

Had bicycle of following description, *viz.* :—Gent's B.S.A., green enamelled frame, black mudguards, usual plated parts, up-turned handle bar, 3-speed gear, control lever on right of handle bar, lever front brake, back-pedalling brake worked from crank and of unusual pattern, open centre gear case, *Brooke's* saddle with spiral springs of wire cable. The 3-speed control had recently been repaired with length of new cable.

Thorough enquiries are earnestly requested at all places where bicycles are repaired.

If met with the man should be detained, and any information either of the man or the bicycle wired or telephoned to E. HOLMES, ESQ., CHIEF CONSTABLE OF COUNTY, LEICESTER, or to SUPT L BOWLEY, COUNTY POLICE STATION, LEICESTER.

County Constabulary Office,
Leicester, 7th July, 1919.

T H JEAYS & SONS. PRINTERS 7 ST. MARTINS. LEICESTER

41

— out of the ordinary not only because of its green finish but also because it had a back-pedalling brake on the rear wheel — had been supplied to Orton Brothers, bicycle dealers of Derby, in 1910.

Another phone call was made — this time to Derby police headquarters — and within a couple of hours the Leicester detectives heard that, according to Orton Brothers' sales ledger, BSA bicycle No. 103648 had been purchased on Wednesday, 18 May 1910, by a Mr Ronald Vivian Light.

Further inquiries in Derby revealed that, at the time of the transaction, Mr Light was employed as a draughtsman by the Midland Railway and was living in digs close to the marshalling yards. In October 1914, he had given up his job and left the town.

A Leicester detective checked the local electoral register and found the name of Ronald Vivian Light, with an address in Highfield Street, a quiet, tree-lined thoroughfare in a nice part of the town. Ferreting in discreet fashion, the investigators garnered more facts about Mr Light.

The villa in Highfield Street was owned by his recently-widowed mother who was an invalid, cared for by a middle-aged nurse-companion named Mary Webb. Light, who was thirty-four, a bachelor, had been educated at Rugby public school, after which he had gained a civil engineering qualification at the

University of Birmingham. Although, in October 1914, he had told the Midland Railway that he was leaving to join the army, he had in fact returned home, and had remained idle for six months before being commissioned in the Royal Engineers. He had subsequently transferred, as a private, to the Honourable Artillery Company, and had performed active service on the Western Front till August 1918, when, diagnosed as being severely shell-shocked, he was returned to England.

Following his demobilization, Light had again been unemployed for a long while: more than a year. Then, in January 1920 — six months after the death of Bella Wright and a month before Enoch Whitehouse's discovery of part of the green bicycle — he had been appointed assistant mathematics master at the Dean Close School in Cheltenham, Gloucestershire.

As a result of newspaper stories concerning the bargeman's find, two Leicester cycle repairers came forward. It seems a mite less strange that neither man had been prompted to come forward by the prior requests and offers of reward for assistance than that neither of them — nor, the inference is, any other cycle repairers in or near the town — had been quizzed by visiting policemen. Both recalled working on the green bicycle during the early part of 1919; both stated that they had done the work for Ronald Light. One of the repairmen, Harry Cox, said that the last he had seen of the bicycle — and of Light — was on the morning of Saturday, 5 July, when Light, after paying for some repairs, wheeled the machine from the workshop, remarking as he did so, "I am fed up with messing about the town; I am going to have a run in the country." Later that day, Bella Wright's body was found on the country road called the Via Devana.

Superintendent Taylor, the officer in charge of the investigation, decided that it was time for him to take a trip to Cheltenham: to the Dean Close School, which, as he had found out, was an expensive "academy for the sons of gentlefolk". He hoped to learn quite a lot from, and about, the assistant mathematics master.

Observing a nicety of inter-force behaviour, Superintendent Taylor arranged for a member of the Gloucestershire Constabulary to accompany him on his visit to the Dean Close School. When he saw the headmaster, he didn't explain why he and Detective Sergeant Illes wanted a few minutes alone with Mr Light.

Taylor was just as polite, just as discreet, when Ronald Light, having left his class in the charge of a prefect, entered the headmaster's study. Once the headmaster had withdrawn, Taylor explained that he was investigating the murder of Bella Wright. He wondered if Mr Light would mind telling him what had become of his green bicycle.

How Light spoke would be almost as important as what he said, considering that Bella Wright's uncle, George Measures, and his son-in-law had stated that the cyclist who had waited for Bella outside Measures's cottage and then ridden away with her had a "squeaking" voice.

Light's reply — "I never had a green bicycle" — was rendered in a high-pitched, almost feminine voice.

Superintendent Taylor requested Light to think again: had he not purchased a green bicycle from Orton Brothers, the BSA company's agents in Derby, in 1910? Certainly not, Light insisted.

Later, however, he admitted that he had once owned a green bicycle. "I sold it years ago," he claimed.

Ronald Vivian Light

As polite as ever, Taylor said that since he was not satisfied with Light's answers, the interview would have to be continued at Cheltenham police station.

There, Light exclaimed: "What is this stunt?" After saying that he couldn't remember to whom he had sold his green bicycle — "I just can't recall, because I've had so many cycles over the years" — he gave details of two machines that he said he had sold before leaving Derby in 1914. When he was charged with the murder of Bella Wright, he squeaked: "It's absurd!"

A number of identification parades were held, and Light was picked out by George Measures and his son-in-law, by Harry Cox, the Leicester cycle mechanic who said that Light had collected his newly-repaired green bicycle on the morning of the murder; and by two schoolgirls who said that, a few hours before the murder, when they were cycling along a lane near Gaulby, they had been pestered by a man riding a green bicycle.

By the time the committal proceedings began at Leicester Castle, the police had obtained further evidence relevant to the case against Light. It will be remembered that, when the canal was being searched for the missing parts of the green bicycle, the police had fished up a revolver holster and some cartridges — but no revolver. Assuming that Light would claim that he had never possessed a revolver, the police made inquiries among his small circle of friends. One of the friends, a Derby girl named Ethel Tunnicliffe, recalled that in 1916 she had received a letter from Light, who was then in the army, telling her that he was sending her a parcel which she was not to open but to bring to his home in Leicester when he was next on leave. She had done as she was told — and had seen Light open the parcel and take out a revolver.

Equally important evidence came from Mary Webb, the nurse-companion to Light's invalid mother. She said that though a supper-party had been arranged for eight o'clock on the night of the murder, "Mister Ronald" had not returned home till ten. From the time he was demobbed until that night, he had used his cycle almost every day — but he never used it again. "It remained in the back kitchen for some days, then he took it up into the box-room. As well as I remember, it was brought down just before Christmas, 1919. Mister Ronald took it out in the evening. I didn't ask him, but he told me some time afterwards that he had sold it."

You will not be surprised to learn that Mrs Light dispensed

with Mary Webb's services soon after the nurse-companion had testified at the committal proceedings. Mrs Light was too ill to attend any of the hearings, but it was she who paid for the defence. Clearly, she considered that money was no object in trying to save her son from the gallows, for she retained the top Leicester solicitor, a Mr Bigg, who, in turn, briefed the temperamental but brilliant Sir Edward Marshall Hall, KC, to lead the defence at the trial.

Though Light reserved his defence at the committal proceedings, Mr Bigg intimated that, at the trial, the defence would depend upon an alibi.

On the first day of the trial, also held at Leicester Castle, the Attorney-General, Sir Gordon Hewart, sought to pre-empt the defence of an alibi by stressing in his opening speech that there was much eye-witness evidence that placed Light close to the Via Devana shortly before Bella Wright's death.

After only a few prosecution witnesses had given evidence, Hewart was summoned back to London by the prime minister, Lloyd George, to assist in the drafting of proposals concerning the armistice with Germany, and from then on the Crown case was conducted by Henry Maddocks and the young Norman Birkett.

Shortly after Hewart's departure, and taking advantage of it, Marshall Hall dropped a bombshell by announcing that his client admitted that he was "the man on the green bicycle" and that he had thrown the bicycle, the holster and the cartridges into the canal. That meant that Maddocks and Birkett, still struggling to master the larger roles that had suddenly been thrust upon them, had to cobble together a plan of attack that was quite different from the anti-alibi strategy carefully mapped out by their lost leader.

Marshall Hall hardly bothered to cross-examine most of the prosecution witnesses, but he was forceful in his questioning of the two schoolgirls who said that they had been pestered by Light, since their evidence regarding the unwelcome encounter might suggest to the jury that Light was behaving strangely, even frighteningly, shortly before he met Bella Wright. Turning police dilatoriness to advantage, Marshall Hall hammered away at the fact that the girls had not been asked to make written statements until after Light's arrest.

He contested only one small part of the evidence of George Measures and his son-in-law, that being the assertion made by each of them that when Bella had emerged from the cottage, the words spoken by Light were "Bella, you have been a long time." They refused to accept Marshall Hall's suggestion that they had misheard "Hello" as "Bella". The point of the unresolved argument was that if Light was on first-name terms with the girl, they may have met on earlier occasions.

Marshall Hall's greatest success was in persuading the Leicester gunsmith who appeared for the Crown to agree that the fatal bullet might, just might, have been fired from a rifle rather than a revolver.

At the close of the case for the prosecution, Marshall Hall did not exercise his right to make a speech. He at once called Ronald Light to give evidence on his own behalf. Of course, before Light did so, he swore that he would tell the truth, the whole truth, and nothing but the truth.

His high-pitched voice was far from attractive, but at least no one in the dark-panelled courtroom at Leicester Castle had any difficulty in hearing him as he answered his counsel's carefully-phrased questions. It had been his decision, not Marshall Hall's, that he should speak in his own defence. As was Marshall Hall's almost invariable practice when defending in a capital case, he had demanded from his client a signed note stating whether or not he wished to be called; Light had not only responded in the affirmative but had appended a schoolmasterish list of questions that he should be asked and of how he would deal with them — the salient couplet-item of which being the following:

> Will you please ask me to tell the jury in my own words exactly why I did not come forward? I shall say I was dreadfully worried, and for some days was quite dazed at such an unexpected blow, and could not think clearly. When I began to think, I could not make up my mind to come forward, and hesitated for days. I could not give the police any information whatever as to how the girl met her death. If the police and papers had only stated the known facts, and asked the cyclist to come forward, I should have done so, but they jumped to wrong conclusions, and I was frightened when I saw I was wanted for murder.

Wearing a new brown suit paid for by his mother, his dark but greying hair meticulously combed from a side parting, he seemed remarkably composed considering that his life depended on his answers being believed — considering that, if what he said was true, then it was his entire *lack* of composure that had caused him to act suspiciously following the death of Bella Wright and, when questioned by Superintendent Taylor some eight months after the murder, to tell flagrant lies.

Yes, it was quite true, he said, that he had chanced to meet the girl while he was cycling in the country to the east of Leicester; true that he had ridden with her to her uncle's cottage at Gaulby; true that he had been outside the cottage when she reappeared and that, after a conversation with her uncle and his son-in-law, he had ridden away with her in the direction of the Via Devana. . . .

. . . But it was nonsense to suggest that he had murdered her. At a road-junction some distance from the Via Devana, she had said, "I must say goodbye to you here." The last he had seen of Bella Wright, she was cycling towards her home at Stoughton; he had taken the other road and, delayed by a puncture, had reached his home in Leicester at about ten o'clock.

Three days later, he had read in the local paper that the girl had been shot dead on the Via Devana and that the police were seeking "the man on the green bicycle". Now, of course, he realized that he should have gone to the police at once. There were any number of reasons why he had not done so: he was "too confused" . . . he didn't want to worry his mother, who had a bad heart . . . and "It meant unpleasant publicity, which was what I shrank from. I didn't understand what a difficult position I was putting myself in."

And so, first of all, he had hidden his bicycle in the box-room at the top of the house; months later, having filed away marks of identification on the cycle, he had wheeled the machine to the canal, partly dismantled it, and thrown the parts into the water. At the same time, he had thrown away the revolver-holster and the cartridges.

He insisted that he had not owned a revolver since August 1918. In the previous November, when he was sent to France with the Honourable Artillery Company, he had taken his revolver with him. *Only* the revolver — not the holster and the loose cartridges, which for some reason he had left at home. When he was granted early demobilization because of his being shellshocked, "the revolver was taken away from me, with all my other kit, and left behind at the depot at Corby, in Northamptonshire." In any event, Light added, the clothes he was wearing when he met Bella Wright had no pockets large enough to hold a service revolver. Asked what had become of those clothes, he said that he had sold them to someone or other.

Before calling Light to the witness-box, Marshall Hall had told his clerk, "I intend to leave the prosecution nothing on which to cross-examine him." He practically succeeded. The cross-examination was brief — chiefly because Light, as well as being ever mindful of his advisers' warning that he had to effect unawareness of any display of incredulity by Henry Maddocks, refused to budge from the explanations of sorts for every one of his suspicious acts that he had recited, word-perfectly, to the cues of his counsel.

As Marshall Hall called no other witnesses, he had the benefit of the last word (which would not necessarily have been so, had the prosecution been led by Sir Gordon Hewart, one of the two Law Officers of the Crown). In his closing speech, he did his best — which was very good indeed — to confuse the jury: first, by suggesting that the bullet found near the body of Bella Wright was not the bullet that had killed her, and secondly, by theorizing that perhaps the girl had not been murdered but was the victim of a stray bullet fired by a fool engaged in shooting practice up to half a mile away.

When the jury had been absent for more than three hours, the judge, Mr Justice Horridge, recalled them to ask if there was any prospect of their agreeing. The foreman requested another quarter of an hour; but in fact the twelve men returned in only three minutes — with a verdict of Not Guilty. (It was subsequently divulged that, until the judge's intervention, three jurymen were holding out for a Guilty verdict.) Ronald Light fainted and had to be carried from the dock. Thousands of people waited outside the castle in the hope of seeing him — and, presumably, of cheering him — but he made his exit through a side-door and, having borrowed threepence for the tram-fare, travelled incognito to his home in Highfield Street.

That night, he wrote to Marshall Hall: "It seems rather feeble to say 'Thank you' for saving my life, but I feel sure you will understand what I think." Replying, Marshall Hall made it clear that he held Light in low esteem: "Please convey to your mother my sympathetic regards, and you will, I am sure, forgive me if I say that you can best show your gratitude to me by making her life happier in the future than I fear it has been in the past."

The Green Bicycle Case was among Marshall Hall's greatest

Sir Edward Marshall Hall

triumphs. But it was a triumph earned at the expense of justice, of truth. To give just one example of how he knowingly misled the jury, he inveigled the local gunsmith who appeared for the prosecution into saying that the fatal bullet might have been fired from a rifle, and then, in his closing speech, put forward the stray rifle-bullet theory. Yet he knew full well that the bullet could only have been fired from a revolver.

He had thought of calling Robert Churchill, the only real expert on ballistics in the country, as a defence witness — but had abruptly changed his mind upon receipt of Churchill's report that:

> the bullet was fired from a ·455 Webley service revolver, such as was contained in the holster which has been recovered from the canal. . . . It is a revolver bullet unsuitable for any rifle and, by its number of grooves, widths, direction and twist, was fired from a Webley, and could not have been fired from any other make of weapon. . . . The behaviour of the bullet in this case is comparable to what happened in the Moat Farm Murder. In that case, a bullet was fired at close range and, in energy, velocity and penetration, behaved like this one.

The jury were (no other word will do) *conned* into acquitting Ronald Vivian Light. Soon after the trial, a doctor declared that Light was no longer suffering from shellshock — which in some men caused fits and brainstorms, and in a few of them and others (including Light, perhaps), homicidal impulses.

He continued to reside at 54 Highfield Street after his mother's death — and for a year or so following the winter of 1934, when, at the age of forty-nine, he married a Kentish-woman, Lilian Lester.

On 15 May 1975, five months from his ninetieth birthday, he died, apparently painlessly, at his home, 110 Minster Road, on the Kentish Isle of Sheppey; his body was burnt at a crematorium near Ashford, and ashes said to be of it were scattered in a garden of remembrance there; under the terms of a will that he had made in the second year of his marriage, his wife received all of his worldy goods, which were officially valued at slightly more than £10,000.

Certainly, he was lucky not to have had fifty-five years tugged from his life, in the privacy of a gallows-shed. I think you will agree that one may go farther than that, and say that he was among the luckiest murderers who ever lived.

Postscript

There is no indication of Bella Wright's resting-place in the trim churchyard at Stoughton: her parents could not afford a grave-

Ronald Light at home after his acquittal

A recent photograph of Stoughton Church

stone. It seems a pity that the clergyman who conducted the funeral service — and who, as a prelude to his sermon to a tightly packed congregation, said, "I trust that none of you has been brought to the church this afternoon by a sense of curiosity" — did not arrange for a gravestone-financing collection to be taken. Although, in the early 1980s, some persons of Leicester set up a Bella Wright Memorial Fund, and they have since received many contributions towards it, no memorial has materialized — which may mean that its form was decided upon before the fund was started, and remains of greater cost than the total of the contributions. If that is so, it would surely be sensible to use whatever money has been received to obtain whatever less grand memorial it will buy: a simple wooden cross, slight of inscription, would be better than nothing.

Somehow, the frame and front wheel of the green bicycle ended up on a wall in a shop in Leicester. The last I heard, it was still hanging there. Perhaps the proprietor would be willing to donate it to the town's museum — or to sell it to the organizers of the Bella Wright Memorial Fund, who, without much ingenuity, let alone expense, could fashion it into a more fitting memorial than was their intention.

The Puzzle of Rumsey House

Edward Marjoribanks, MP

A FEW days before Bella Wright's violent death, an ailing middle-aged lady, the wife of a solicitor, had died in her bed at Rumsey House, an imposing residence standing in its own grounds at the edge of the Welsh village of Kidwelly, ten miles south of Carmarthen and about the same distance north-west of Llanelli, the town in which her husband conducted his business. Exactly one year later, on 16 June 1920, her husband, Harold Greenwood, was arrested on a charge of murdering her.

Local gossip had undoubtedly led to his arrest. He had married a young and attractive woman, whom he had known for a long time, three months after his wife's death, and had also, in the interval between his first wife's death and his second marriage, proposed to another lady friend, the sister of the doctor who had certified his first wife's death as due to heart failure. This doctor had been called to attend to Mrs Greenwood, who seemed to be suffering from a stomach upset as a result of eating gooseberry tart at Sunday lunch.

The authorities ordered the exhumation of the body, and Dr John Webster, the Home Office analyst, calculated by the Marsh test that there was a little more than a quarter of a grain of arsenic in the woman's body. It was known and proved that Harold Greenwood used a weedkiller, containing a strong solution of arsenic, for his garden. The police approached a girl named Hannah Williams, who had been parlourmaid to the Greenwoods at the date of the first wife's death, and obtained a statement from her that Mrs Greenwood alone had drunk from a bottle of wine on the table at luncheon on the day of her death; that before lunch Greenwood had gone into the pantry cupboard from the garden, and that the bottle of wine which had been on the luncheon-table had disappeared by the following day. Until the very conclusion of the trial, the theory of the prosecution was that Greenwood had polluted the wine in this

54

The Puzzle of Rumsey House

Rumsey House

bottle with arsenic in order to kill his wife, and had watched her slowly die from luncheon on Sunday till 3.15 on the following morning, 16 June 1919.

The brief for the defence was sent to Sir Edward Marshall Hall — his third capital case in the year 1920.[1] Greenwood's case excited the most hostile public prejudice; he was generally assumed to be guilty during his four months' incarceration before trial. Marshall Hall was in a silversmith's shop on the day before he went down to Carmarthen Assizes. "I'm surprised at you, Sir Edward," said the silversmith, an old friend, "for

1. *Editor's Note*
Prior to defending Ronald Light, he had unsuccessfully defended Eric Holt on the charge of having murdered his lover, Kitty Breaks, who had been found dead, with three bullet wounds in her body, on the sandhills at St Anne's, near Blackpool, in the early hours of Christmas Eve, 1919. Upon leaving the dock after sentence of death had been passed, Holt remarked: "Well, that's over — I hope my tea won't be late." The Court of Criminal Appeal dismissed Marshall Hall's argument that Holt, who had been treated for syphilis and was believed by some to be suffering from shellshock, was insane; following a medical inquiry into Holt's state of mind, the Home Secretary refused to recommend a reprieve, and the execution was carried out in Strangeways Prison, Manchester, on 13 April 1920.

55

defending that blackguard Greenwood. You must see he's guilty yourself. However, I suppose it's your job."

"Guilty, indeed!" retorted Sir Edward. "The man's innocent, and I'll get him off — you'll see."

"Very well," said the silversmith, "whether you get him off or not, if you convince me that man's innocent, I'll make you a present of this." As he spoke, he held out an eighteenth-century silver tankard.

Marshall Hill arrived at the Ivy Bush Hotel, Carmarthen, late on a very dark night. Everybody engaged in the case was staying at the hotel, including Sir Edward Marlay Samson, leading counsel for the Crown, and Dr William Willcox, the Honorary Medical Adviser to the Home Office. As Marshall Hall drove down to see Greenwood on the following morning, the streets were lined with spectators — as they were throughout the trial — as if for a royal procession. In the course of the trial, Marshall Hall created an amazing transformation of feeling; at the beginning, as Greenwood was driven to the assize courts, his carriage was given police protection, and he was the subject of angry demonstrations; towards the end, the police witnesses almost needed protection themselves.

It is difficult to select from this trial the essential episodes. There were so many dramatic moments which contributed materially to the result. Marshall Hall himself was a very sick man; he could neither stand up nor sit down without acute physical discomfort, and, for this reason, his conduct of the defence was not only masterly but heroic. But the physical strain told terribly on his nerves, and resulted in frequent outbursts on his part against witnesses, and even in vehement protests at the periodical interventions from the Bench. It was only when his old friends, the experts, were in the box that he exercised restraint.

On the mere facts of the case there were two important witnesses whose evidence it was essential to challenge: the doctor who had certified death, and the parlourmaid.

The latter was a pretty, rather complacent young lady; Marshall Hall sought to show that her whole evidence was coloured by questions put by the burly policeman who had approached her months after her late mistress's death. She altered the details of her story again and again, and finally said that the bottle of wine from which Mrs Greenwood had helped herself at lunch was labelled "Port Wine".

Harold Greenwood with his first wife

"Whoever heard of such a thing?" commented Marshall. "A little touch of the domestic servant."

She also said that she had never known Mr Greenwood to wash his hands in the pantry cupboard before that morning, but she was quite certain he had done so that Sunday on one — or was it two occasions? Miss Irene Greenwood never drank wine, on this occasion or at any time; nevertheless, she, the parlour-maid, had put out two pink glasses, one for Miss Irene and one for her mother.

"Poor little girl! Poor little frightened thing!" Marshall Hall observed in his final speech, and that was undoubtedly the impression created by her on the minds of the jury. She had been led to make statements about details which she could not be expected to remember after the lapse of months, and had tried in vain to adhere to them. But if she was frightened by the big, burly policeman, she was still more frightened by the big, burly counsel for the defence. She seemed to consider herself on her defence for having drunk the remainder of the wine herself.

In answer to the question) "Are you a teetotaller?" she said, "Yes, I am. I am having a name for having drunk it, but I am not drunk today."

Marshall Hall was defending a man's life, and he pressed the girl still further, for her defensive attitude was extremely helpful and interesting to him. She was clearly thinking, not of the prisoner, but of her own position. Finally the judge intervened. "You were shouting at the witness," he said. "I have to see that witnesses are not addressed in a vehement way."

"Why," retorted Marshall Hall, "it is my duty to be vehement."

If this girl's evidence had remained unshaken, it might have gone hardly with the prisoner; but there was another witness for the prosecution whom Marshall Hall was to put upon the defensive — the local doctor who had given the certificate of death. Dr Griffiths had prescribed a mixture of bismuth, and also, according to his evidence at the police court, two morphia pills, which had been administered by a trained nurse to the patient at 1 a.m., after which she was violently sick, and fell into a state of coma, from which she never recovered. It was suggested to the doctor at the police court that these pills might have been the cause of death. Now, a morphia pill contains half a grain of morphia, and a grain of morphia would be a dangerous dose to a woman who, like Mrs Greenwood, suffered from a weak heart. Marshall Hall, when he read this in the depositions, realized that here lay a strong line of defence. If Mrs Greenwood took, under doctor's orders, a drug in a dangerous quantity, and soon afterwards sank into a state of coma — the natural result of such a dose of morphia — from which she never recovered, it would be difficult to attribute her death to her husband, whether arsenic was found in her body months after her death or not. Naturally, Marshall Hall had prepared a heavy cross-examination on this point for the doctor. But an unpleasant surprise was in store for him; things were not to be so easy as that. When the doctor went into the box, he explained that when he had said morphia pills at the police court he had meant opium pills. An opium pill only contains one-fortieth of a grain of morphia, and it would be absurd to suggest that these two pills could have caused death even to a woman with a weak heart.

Marshall Hall was on his feet in a moment, protesting at this apparent change of front, and demanded that his cross-examination should be deferred till the morrow. He did, however, ask the doctor one interesting question that afternoon.

"If you had given her two half-grains of morphia, you would not be surprised that she died before four o'clock?"

"Yes, I would."

Now, this answer was a surprising one, and provided Marshall Hall with all the ammunition which he needed, in view of the doctor's explanation of his previous statement. On the next day the battle was resumed, and the doctor said that opium pills were often called morphia pills.

"Now, doctor," said Marshall Hall, "there is an enormous difference between opium and morphia."

"I know that."

"You said that, in your opinion, there would have been no danger in giving this woman two half-grains of morphia?"

"I meant two half-grains of pure opium."

"I asked you the question last night purposely before the court rose. I asked you if it would have been safe to give this woman two half-grains of morphia, and you said it was perfectly safe. Did you think I meant opium then?"

"Yes."

Marshall Hall spoke slowly and deliberately. "I give every allowance to every witness who says what I don't expect him to say. Have you the smallest doubt whatever that if you, as a medical man, were accurate when you said you gave her two half-grains of morphia after ten o'clock that she would have been dead before four o'clock?"

"If I had given her morphia she would, but I did not give her morphia."

Later Marshall Hall asked Dr Griffiths for the prescription of a tonic given by him to Mrs Greenwood four days before her death. He could only produce a piece of paper which he had copied from his prescription book. He undertook to produce the book itself on the next day. When the time came, he had to admit that the prescription book had been destroyed. It must have been destroyed, he said, when he retired from practice at the end of 1919. But Marshall Hall was able to show from the doctor's own statement that the latter had copied the prescription from the book in June 1920.

"Why was it destroyed?" asked Marshall Hall.

"I don't remember," said the doctor.

The police had taken down a statement from Greenwood in a notebook, and he had signed it. When the statement was read out in court, he said that it differed from the signed one in several particulars. The differences really came to very little but a most unusual scene took place. Marshall Hall saw a piece of paper sticking up from the binding of the book, which indicated that some pages might have been torn out. He flourished his magnifying-glass. The inspector in the box took exception to this, saying that he was positive that the book had been in good order before it passed to Marshall Hall, and adding that he had seen him handling it roughly. Marshall Hall flew into a temper, and demanded to be put into the witness box. The judge calmed him down; but he again became excited when the clerk of assize went into the witness box to count the pages of another police notebook, and found ten more pages in it than in the Greenwood book. However, the incident was only a passing storm, and nothing hinged upon it.

On the fourth and fifth days of the trial Marshall Hall cross-examined the Crown experts. Dr Webster produced a series of glass tubes, or "mirrors", which proved the arsenic present in Mrs Greenwood's body on exhumation. Marshall Hall argued that a very slight mistake in observation or calculation in performing the Marsh experiment would make the most vital difference, and embarked on a long mathematical discussion with Dr Webster, during which the judge made some observations to him.

"I may not know much about the law, but I know something about decimals," Marshall Hall said, and went on with his calculations.

The duel with Dr William Willcox was again a triumph of patience and skill. Marshall Hall hardly received a contradiction from either of these two witnesses; his questions were so cunningly framed that it was hard to disagree with them. When he was putting forward the wildest improbability, he would ask whether such a thing were barely possible, and the doctor would have to agree. An admirer of Marshall Hall's said that his propositions sounded hardly less innocent and unimpeachable than such a question as, "Do you agree with me, doctor, in believing that arrowroot is better for infants than arsenic?" The constant assent by the Crown experts gave the jury the impression that Marshall Hall was winning them over to his views.

Marshall Hall asked Dr Willcox:

"You gave evidence before the magistrates in this case, and expressed the opinion that the cause of death was arsenical poisoning?"

"Yes."

"Is that the opinion you expressed some months ago?"

"Yes."

"Has the evidence you have heard in this case weakened or strengthened your opinion?"

Dr Willcox, who always used a slow, rather deliberate manner, paused very noticeably before replying, "I am *still* of the opinion that death was caused by arsenical poisoning."

This hesitation of the chief expert witness for the Crown was one of the strong points of Marshall Hall's opening speech for the defence.

Even more important was another question and answer: "The utmost deduction that you can draw against the accused here is that something on the borderline of the possible fatal dose had been administered?"

"Approximately the minimum fatal dose had been administered."

And yet again:

"When Dr Griffiths says that morphia pills are often called opium pills, is that news to you?"

"Yes."

Marshall Hall used the suggestion that the arsenic from the weedkiller might conceivably have got on to the skins of the gooseberries which Mrs Greenwood had eaten for lunch; that the arsenic might even have been blown up from the grass by the wind, and that Mrs Greenwood might have inhaled it; he also put to Dr Willcox a number of mysterious and curious instances of arsenical poisoning.

The most dramatic moment of the cross-examination was the result of Marshall Hall's own enterprise. He remembered, as he lay awake in some pain on the night after the local doctor had given his evidence, that the latter had said that he kept both bismuth and Fowler's solution of arsenic in his dispensing-room, and had prescribed bismuth for Mrs Greenwood on the day of her death. An idea occurred to him. The next morning at nine o'clock he was down at the chemist's, and bought two little bottles, one containing bismuth, the other Fowler's solution of arsenic. They were almost indistinguishable in appearance. While Willcox was in the box, Marshall innocently asked him what Fowler's solution of arsenic looked like. "Oh," said the doctor, "it is a reddish liquid."

"Rather like this?" said Marshall Hall, producing his little bottle of bismuth before anyone could stop him. "Yes," said Dr Willcox.

Marshall Hall then showed his other little bottle to the witness and the jury, and suggested that a mistake was quite possible in regard to them. It was in vain for the prosecution to protest that these little bottles were not official exhibits of the court. They had had their effect, and Dr Willcox had been cross-examined as to them.

"If, by some unfortunate mistake, he, in the anxiety and hurry, gave her four teaspoonfuls of Fowler's solution, you would have got all the arsenic you found, or more than you found?"

"Yes."

"And there would be practically no distinction in colour in the mixture, whether the mixture were of bismuth or a solution of arsenic?"

"No; they resemble each other."

He persisted in this suggestion till the trial ended, not as a charge against the ministrations of the local doctor, but as an alternative hypothesis (which he was under no obligation to prove) to account for the presence of the arsenic in the body. It was in the last degree unlikely that the doctor had in fact made such a mistake; but was it not still more unlikely that a respectable solicitor should murder his wife in this brutal manner? Each hypothesis was improbable; the true explanation may have been unguessed, for arsenic can get into the human body in a number of extraordinary ways. But, when one hypothesis postulates murder, it is the duty of the defence to call attention to all other possibilities. The Fowler's suggestion was a brilliant red-herring dragged across the case for the prosecution, and very typical of Marshall Hall's quick and original mind.

It is interesting to go behind the scenes and discover that the long duel between the Crown expert and the defending advocate was only made physically possible by the skill and kindness of Dr Willcox, who throughout the trial gave medical treatment and assistance to Marshall Hall at the Ivy Bush Hotel; if it had not been for this, the latter would never have fought his way through this strenuous case as he did.

Marshall Hall began his opening speech for the defence with

an allusion to the fact that local gossip had been the origin of the case. Adapting the lines from *Othello*, he said:

> Trifles light as air
> Are, to the jealous, confirmation strong
> As proofs of Holy Writ.

He said that he would call two doctors for the defence — Dr Toogood and Dr Griffiths of Swansea — the prisoner, and his daughter, Irene Greenwood. The two distinguished physicians both said that in their opinion Mrs Greenwood had died of a dose of morphia. Greenwood himself went into the box on the sixth and seventh days. Marshall Hall examined him in a most unexpected and dramatic way, only asking him a few questions, of which the last were these:

"Had you anything to do with your wife's death?"

"Nothing whatever."

"After your wife's death, what happened to her private means?"

"They went to her children."

"You have been in prison for four and a half months, and are you now ready to answer any questions my friend may ask relative to his case?"

"Yes."

Greenwood, who spoke very low, survived his long ordeal of cross-examination without breaking down in any important particular. Yet, on trial for his life as he was, the most important witness for the defence was to come after him.

When the case for the prosecution had closed, Marshall Hall had held a long and earnest consultation with the prisoner's daughter, Irene Greenwood, a slim girl of twenty-two, after which he told his clerk that everything depended upon her evidence. Her great nervousness in the witness box showed that she was fully aware of this responsibility; she made a most moving and convincing witness, constantly referring to the prisoner as "my daddy". The great importance of her testimony was that she said that she also had drunk from the bottle of wine from which, as the prosecution alleged, her mother had been poisoned by her father. She gave her evidence with great certainty as to detail. When asked how her memory was so good, she replied that she remembered everything so well because her mother died that day. Marshall Hall afterwards said that she had saved her father's life. As the judge remarked in his summing-up, "If she also drank from the bottle, there is an end of the case."

Marshall Hall's final speech lasted over three hours. It had been very doubtful the night before whether he would be able to make it, but as the prisoner was a member of his own profession, he made a supreme effort. He contended that the case for the prosecution — begun by local gossip, depending for its circumstantial details on the prompted and uncertain memory of a servant girl, and for its scientific justification on the finding in the body of the bare minimum quantity of arsenic necessary for a fatal dose by means of an elaborate and fallible experiment — had been torn to shreds.

"Your verdict is final. Science can do a great deal. These men, with their mirrors, multipliers, and milligrams, can tell you, to the thousandth or the millionth part of a grain, the constituents of the human body. But science cannot do one thing — that is, to find the final spark which converts insensate clay into a human being."

And then the advocate dropped his voice to a whisper, and closed his masterly defence, as he had opened it, with a quotation from *Othello* — the words of the Moor when he stole into Desdemona's chamber:

> Put out the light, and then put out the light.
> If I quench thee, thou flaming minister,
> I can again thy former light restore,
> Should I repent me; but once put out thy light,
> Thou cunning'st pattern of excelling nature,
> I know not where is that Promethean heat
> That can thy light relume.

"Are you going, by your verdict, to put out that light?" he asked quietly. Then he stood erect, and his words rang out loud and clear: "Gentlemen of the jury, I demand at your hands the life and liberty of Harold Greenwood."

After his speech, Marshall Hall was compelled to leave the court. Greenwood was furious, perhaps thinking that his life and mental anguish were more important than any physical pain of his advocate.

During the concluding speech for the Crown, which lasted three hours, Marlay Samson attempted to broaden the prosecution's case by pointing out that the dead woman, besides rinking wine at lunch, had taken tea and brandy, and the oison might equally well have been poured by the prisoner into nose beverages. The motive suggested throughout the trial was Greenwood's physical passion for his second wife; and Samson, n experienced advocate, made a bad slip in referring to the fact hat the lady had not been called to give evidence — a comment rohibited under the Criminal Evidence Act.

Immediately after Mr Justice Shearman's summing-up on the ollowing day, Marshall Hall left, again for reasons of health, in special car, to catch the London train at Cardiff. As he was valking with his clerk on the platform, anxiously speculating on he verdict, a porter came up and spoke to him.

"I see you got him off, Sir Edward," he said.

The jury, whose foreman, by a fortunate chance, was a manuacturing chemist, had acquitted the prisoner after a deliberation of over an hour.

The verdict was an exceedingly popular one; but, although Marshall Hall probably received more congratulatory letters nd telegrams on this case than any other, none came from the risoner himself — the only one of all his prisoners who never hanked him by word or letter. Perhaps his counsel's absences vere still rankling in Mr Greenwood's mind.

Soon after Marshall Hall returned home, he received from his riend the silversmith a parcel containing a tankard, which was nscribed, "I dared you to do it, and you did it." By a romantic coincidence, this piece had been the property of Marshall Hall's grandfather, and bore his name.

Editor's Note

Though I and other compilers of books such as this should — to contradict part of a tailors' expression — "mind the quality", sometimes our choice of naterial is diminished in accordance with the other part of that expression, vhich is "feel the width". Winifred Duke is unjustly neglected, both as a chronicler of crimes and as a transmuter of actual crimes into fiction, and if either of her accounts of the Greenwood case were far shorter than it is, I should probably have sought to use it in preference to that of Marshall Hall's first and best biographer, Edward Marjoribanks, whose underestimation of the reasons for suspecting that Greenwood murdered his wife has the effect — a quaint one, considering how, throughout his book, Marjoribanks tends to overestimate the forensic cunning of his subject — of making Marshall Hall's undoubted triumph appear hardly triumphant at all. If the reader wishes to amplify his knowledge of the Greenwood case, he should seek out a copy of Winifred Duke's *Six Trials* (Gollancz London 1934) — or, better still, the volume on the case, which she edited and introduced, in the "Notable Trials" series (Hodge, Edinburgh 1930).

Towards the end of the Greenwood component of *Six Trials*, Winifred Duke notes "several piquant sequels", including the following:

Early in April 1921, Dr Griffiths sued Greenwood in the County Court in respect of fees for his attendance on the late Mrs Greenwood and the Greenwood family. He claimed forty-five pounds, alleging that there had been one hundred and twenty-five visits and ten consultations from January 1915 to September 1919. The matter eventuated in Greenwood's having to pay.

In March 1922, Greenwood was plaintiff in an action for damages which he took against the proprietor of a waxworks exhibition at Cardiff. He alleged that the defendant exhibited an effigy bearing his name, and purporting to represent him, in a "Chamber of Horrors", amongst convicted murderers and notorious criminals. Greenwood, as an acquitted man, not unnaturally objected to be classed with such undesirable company. He won his case, and was awarded a hundred and fifty pounds' damages. . .

Rumsey House was sold, and Greenwood, with his second wife and younger son Kenneth, left Kidwelly. He settled at Walford, a tiny village near Ross-on-Wye, Herefordshire, and here his last days were spent. One who came slightly into contact with him described him as "a tired, worn out man, who took no interest in anything except his wife and his pony". He changed his name to Pilkington, but his real identity was no secret in the district. He shrank from any social life, and found a dreary solace in cultivating his garden and taking long walks. His financial circumstances were precarious, and his last effort to restore them to some stability was an unsuccessful application for the position of clerk to the Ross Urban Council. His health broke down, and after a trying period of illness attributed locally and elsewhere to "retribution", he died at his house, The Paddock, on 17 January 1929. A nameless, neglected-looking mound in Walford churchyard now holds the answer to the riddle of Rumsey House: who poisoned Mrs Greenwood?

Herbert Armstrong, Poisoner

Edgar Wallace

THE VILLAGE of Cusop, adjacent to the tiny town of Hay, on the borders of Herefordshire and Wales, is not graced by any very distinguished or beautiful buildings. Indeed, one of the best of the houses in the village (and this would have been pointed out to you in the year 1920) is a somewhat plain dwelling known as "Mayfield". It is such a residence as you might expect a country gentleman of very limited income to occupy. It had its garden, its pleasant approaches, and, within the somewhat cramped space of "Mayfield", the apartments were more or less ordinary. There was a drawing-room and a boudoir for the lady of the house, a small room designated "the study", where the master might bring his work home in the evening and pursue his investigations into the troubles of his neighbours, without too great an interference by the noise of the piano which his wife loved to strum.

Herbert Rowse Armstrong was a solicitor, and the Great War, which had drawn this quiet, inoffensive-looking little man into the service of the Army, at the Armistice delivered him back to the admiring village, and to his colleagues of Hay, a fully-fledged major, a rank he was loath to renounce. There are photographs extant, and they were at the moment highly prized by their grateful recipients, showing the Major mounted on a horse, a fine figure of a soldier, and finer since his equestrian exercises did not betray his lack of inches.

Major Armstrong had come to Hay from Devonshire, where, at Newton Abbot, he had practised his profession, without securing for himself that success for which his many qualifications seemed to fit him; for he was a Master of Arts of the University of Cambridge, and something of an authority upon land tenure. And when, having married, he transferred himself to a new sphere of operations, it did not appear likely that Hay, off the main track, away from railway and arterial roads, would give him greater opportunities of achieving success than he had enjoyed in the more populous district of Newton Abbot.

There was in Hay at the time an elderly solicitor, whose partner Armstrong became. The elderly solicitor had an elderly wife, and it is a curious fact that, as soon as Armstrong had settled himself down and learnt the ropes of the business, and had become acquainted with the country gentry, his elderly partner should have died with strange suddenness, to be followed in a few days by his wife. The prosecution did not, at the trial which followed, attempt to establish Armstrong's responsibility for the death of his partner. There were very many reasons why the Crown should concentrate upon the charges which were eventually made against him, without risking the negative result which might follow an attempt to prove further crimes against this remarkable man.

Armstrong became a personage of some local importance when he was appointed Clerk of the Justices of Hay, and in this capacity he sat beneath the bench, advising them on points of law, a kindly yet efficient man, somewhat severe on poachers and on those who broke the law in a minor degree. As a solicitor, he appeared from time to time at the various assize courts. The queer little courthouse at Hereford knew him; he had sat at the horseshoe-shaped table before judges and had instructed counsel, and, generally speaking, performed the duties peculiar to his profession with judgment and skill.

In appearance he was a short but perfectly proportioned man. He had a small, round head, covered with close-cropped, mouse-coloured hair, was small of hand and foot, and had a countenance which was at once benignant and shrewd. His eyes were blue, set deeply in his head and rather close together. The overhanging brows were shaggy, and his prognathic jaw was hidden by a heavy moustache.

Herbert Armstrong was well liked and trusted by everybody with whom he was brought into contact. Cambridge University had given him a finish which made him an acceptable guest at the country houses in the neighbourhood, and although, by reason of his being a stranger, he had the administration of no great family fortune, he nevertheless built up with some rapidity a practice which put him in a position of trust. On behalf of his clients, he bought, sold and negotiated for land, had a finger in

Herbert Rowse Armstrong

clients, he bought, sold and negotiated for land, had a finger in many sales and local flotations, and was looked upon, not only as a safe man, but as a lawyer with a certain social distinction.

His wife, Kathleen Mary, seems to have been of a somewhat finicking disposition. She had rigid views on social behaviour, exacted from her husband's friends the attention and courtesy which were her right, and exercised, if the truth be told, a mild form of domestic despotism which prohibited her husband smoking in the house except in his own room. She had her "afternoons", her select dinner parties, and the etiquette which governs a small village was rigorously enforced. A somewhat difficult woman, all the more so because she had a little money of her own, some £2,500, she in all probability refused to her husband those loans which, to men of his character, come so easy to negotiate.

Nevertheless, they were a happy family from the outsiders' point of view. There were three children of the marriage, and neighbours regarded the Armstrongs as united and good-living people. They were regular attendants at the village church; Mr Armstrong, as he was in the early days, was seldom away from home until the call of war took him to a South Coast town and subsequently to France.

Mrs Armstrong was a little inclined to melancholia. She was a musician of exceptional ability, and would spend hours at her piano, but there was no suggestion that her despondency was caused by any act of her husband or by her knowledge of his misconduct.

To Armstrong the war may have come in the nature of a pleasant relief. It took him from his restricted activities to a larger and wider world, pregnant with opportunity, to new faces, new interests, and, incidentally, to new ambitions.

It was whilst he was quartered on the South Coast that he met a lady who was subsequently to play a sensational part in his life. Her name, well known to the press, has never been divulged publicly, and I do not propose deviating from the very charitable attitude which the Press of the day adopted. It is no secret, however, that Madame X was a middle-aged lady possessed of much property, and with whom Armstrong became acquainted some time in 1918. He was an attentive friend, and there grew up between these two people a friendship, which seems to have been wholly innocent as far as the lady was concerned. She knew he had a wife "in delicate health", and she formed the impression that his marriage was an unhappy one.

Armstrong's behaviour seems to have been perfectly proper, and the friendship, stimulated by exchanges of letters, developed into a tacit understanding that, if the "delicate health" of Armstrong's wife took a serious turn, the Major, after a decent interval, would appear to claim the fulfilment of a promise which was never actually asked and never given.

Doubtless this little, middle-aged man, with his iron-grey moustache, was a dapper figure in uniform, well likely to raise a flutter in the heart of a lady who had passed her fortieth year. In course of time Armstrong was demobilized, came back to Hay, and plunged into arrears of work, taking up the threads from his assistant, and being welcomed, on his first appearance as clerk to the Hay Justices, with many encomiums on his public spirit and courage.

Whatever appearance he might make to those who did not probe too deeply beneath the surface, there is little doubt that Armstrong was something of a profligate in a mean and sordid

ay. It is not permissible to tell the evidence which the police
unearthed of his amours; but undoubtedly, in the argot of the
village, he "carried on", though of this Mrs Armstrong was
ignorant, as also was an elderly lady who lived with the family, a
Miss Emily Pearce, who was devoted equally to the husband and
the wife, and kept a maternal eye upon the children. Miss
Pearce seems to have been everything from housekeeper to
nursery governess. She was the kind of family friend which is
almost indistinguishable from an upper servant.

Outside of his work, Armstrong had only one hobby, and that
was gardening. Though he employed an odd gardener, he
himself supervised the work, and helped mow the lawn, trim the
rose bushes, and generally assisted in beautifying his limited
estate. He made several purchases of weedkiller, and on two
occasions had bought a quantity of arsenic, both in its commercial and its chemical form, for the purpose, as was claimed and
as undoubtedly was the fact, of destroying the weeds which
flourished exceedingly and had taken a new lease of life since his
personal supervision had been removed by the war. There is no
suggestion that the weedkiller was employed for any other

*Broad Street, Hay, at the turn of the century. Subsequently, Mr Martin's
office was in the lowest building on the left, and Major Armstrong's
directly opposite.*

71

purpose than that for which it was purchased. Armstrong
attacked the enemies of his lawn with great vigour, and grad
ually brought his garden back to the state in which he had left it

He found something else on his return from the war. A new
solicitor had established himself in Hay, and was taking a fair
share of the work which country disputes and land conveyance
provide. This Mr Martin was married to a lady who was the
daughter of the local chemist, and Armstrong must have known
of his existence before he put his uniform on, but at any rate
when he did know, there was nothing unfriendly in his attitude.
Indeed, he seemed anxious to do all that lay in his power to
make the path of the new man as smooth as possible, and even
went to the trouble of securing for him a commissionership of
oaths. In this he was probably not altogether unselfish, for there
was no commissioner of oaths nearer than Hereford, and it
frequently happened that the remoteness of this official was an
embarrassment to Armstrong himself.

Whatever may have been his object (and it is not incon-
ceivable, even in an innocent man, that he should have
combined courtesy with profit), the Major was on the most
friendly terms with his younger rival, and assisted him to the
best of his ability whenever such assistance was needed. In
course of time, as was natural, they represented opposing interests, one of which demanded from Armstrong the return of
certain monies which had been paid to him on account of
property in the sale of which he was interested.

Long before this happened, Armstrong was faced with a
domestic crisis. His wife had grown steadily more and more
morose. Her interests had become more self-centred. She was
infinitely harder to please than she had been, and exaggerated
the most petty irritations into events of tremendous importance.
Amongst other victims of her rigid code had been the unfortunate Mr Martin, who had been guilty of the unpardonable
solecism of appearing at one of her afternoon parties in *flannels*.
To call on Mrs Armstrong in flannels was an offence beyond
forgiveness. Martin was blacklisted, and became, from the point
of view of this woman, whose mind was obvious a little
deranged, a social outcast.

So acute was the form her malady took that Armstrong consulted the family doctor, Dr Hinks, and it was decided, after taking

Mrs Armstrong

a second opinion, that this unfortunate lady should be transferred to a lunatic asylum at Gloucester "for observation". She was admitted and examined by the medical superintendent, who found her suffering from a mild form of peripheral neuritis. Since it was not a case of mania, and the symptoms were of a more or less elusive kind, she was given a certain measure of freedom, though the doctor at Barnwood Asylum, on the strength of certain delusions and incoherence of speech, had accepted her as insane.

It was on 22 August 1920 that Mrs Armstrong was admitted to this institution, where she remained for four months. During the period of her detention she wrote a number of very sane and clearly expressed letters to her husband, in which she begged him to bring her home for the sake of her children. There is little question that to Mrs Armstrong the children were a first consideration.

Armstrong paid several visits to Barnwood, and, finding her health had improved visibly, after Christmas he took steps to have her removed to his house. She returned on 22 January

1921, so much improved in health that both Armstrong and the family doctor were delighted — at least, Armstrong "displayed a great deal of satisfaction". Evidently this development was not at all in accordance with Armstrong's expectations. Whether the sharp attack of illness which had left her with these delusions, that had subsequently brought her to Barnwood, was the result of poison, is a matter which can never be known with any certitude. In all probability the man had already begun his "experimenting". He had in his study a quarter of a pound of white arsenic, and one may assume that the first illness of Mrs Armstrong was due to the administration of this deadly poison.

With her return to "Mayfield", his plans underwent a change. She had made a will, leaving practically everything to himself, and revoking an earlier will which made such a distribution of her property that he would benefit to a very small extent. He was in some financial difficulty, but the determining factor in his action was Mrs Armstrong's "difficulty". He was weary of her, her primness, her rigid sense of propriety, her faculty for making enemies.

Herbert Armstrong, in short, had grown sick and tired of excessive respectability — and in his hatred of his cramped and too well-ordered life you may well find the primary motive for his terrible crime. It is extremely doubtful that the small sum of money, some £2,000, which would pass into his keeping on his wife's death, had anything to do with his determination to get rid of her. This is a view which may be contested; but as one who followed the case very carefully from its beginning to its tragic finish, that is the conclusion I formed, and that, I believe, is also the view of eminent counsel engaged in the case on either side. His wife had become an incubus, a daily trial to him. He decided upon taking the step which was to lead him to the gallows.

A week or so after her return from Barnwood, Mrs Armstrong was taken violently ill following a meal. The family doctor was called in, and prescribed certain medicine. Mrs Armstrong was put to bed, a nurse was engaged, and she made a fairly good recovery. There was no suspicion in the mind of the doctor that his patient was suffering from arsenical poisoning. He thought that it was a return of her old trouble, and treated her for peripheral neuritis, being strengthened in his diagnosis by the recovery which she made.

She was hardly well before a second attack followed. Armstrong received from his magisterial colleagues the sympathy to which he was entitled, and one of his friends sent him up some bottles of champagne. This fact did not emerge at the trial, but it is possible that the agent through which Mrs Armstrong received the dose of arsenic which ended fatally was champagne. Probably Armstrong himself opened the bottle and gave his wife a glass. Unfortunately, at the trial this point was never cleared up, by reason of the fact that there was not one of the principal witnesses for the Crown who could clearly remember who opened the bottle and who gave its contents to this wretched woman. And so there was no reference to champagne at all in the evidence which was taken at the Hereford Assize Court.

This is a curious fact: that Armstrong was convicted without any proof being put in that he administered with his own hands food or drink of any description whatsoever; and there were many, cognisant of all the facts, who believed that this would be a fatal bar to a conviction, and the foundation of the optimism which was shown by the defence is also to be found in this curious circumstance. Armstrong was eventually convicted, not because he was proved to have given his wife poison, but because he had accessibility and the opportunity for so administering it. But for the haziness of witnesses' memories on this point, the conviction of the Major would have been a foregone conclusion.

On the night before her death, when she was weak and exhausted as the result of arsenic administered to her a day or two days previously, Armstrong gave to his wife a glass of champagne in which he had dropped five or six grains of this tasteless and colourless alkaloid. She drank the wine, being refreshed by the draught, and although she was weak, talked sanely and rationally of her illness and of the house and its management. In the middle of the night Dr Hinks was sent for, and arrived to find her *in extremis*. She died on the morning of 22 February 1921, and the doctor certified that she had succumbed to natural causes.

The sympathy of the village and the countryside went out to this lonely man, left with three small children: the funeral was attended by every local notability, and the distress of the bereaved widower at the graveside was commented upon. Armstrong, in his quiet, self-repressive way, bore himself manfully.

"In many ways I am glad that her sufferings are over," he told a friend. "The best and truest wife has gone to the Great Beyond, and I am left without a partner and without a friend."

Through the summer and the autumn that followed, a tribute of flowers lay upon the sepulchre of the murdered woman. He himself took the choicest roses to adorn the grave. He was, he said, so run down by the tragedy that he sought leave of absence and went abroad, having communicated with Madame X that the trials of his sick wife were at a merciful end. Armstrong's itinerary was a curious one, for he not only visited Italy, but took a trip to Malta, for no special reason except that he had always been interested in that romantic island.

On his return to "Mayfield", Madame X was invited to stay with him, and there is a possibility that the advent of the lady who was a potential Mrs Armstrong caused a little heartburning in certain quarters. Others may have considered that they had a prior right to the fascinating Herbert Armstrong.

Armstrong does not appear to have wasted very much of the money which came to him from his wife's estate. That money was practically intact at the moment of his arrest. But he does seem to have drawn very heavily upon funds which were entrusted to him to complete certain purchases of land. There arose a triangular correspondence between himself, Martin the solicitor, and a land agent living in Hereford. Perhaps "triangular" is hardly the word, in so far as it implies that Martin was concerned with the Hereford land agent. But certainly the negotiations which should have been completed hung fire, and there came from Martin a peremptory demand, on behalf of his client, that the money deposited should be returned. What was the cause of dispute between Martin and the land agent at Hereford has not transpired. After a visit to Hay and on his return to Hereford, the land agent died very suddenly.

One day Martin met Major Armstrong in the village, and reminded him that he had not received a satisfactory reply to a letter he had sent concerning the money and the property which was the cause of the dispute concerning them. Armstrong smiled; he had a quick, inscrutable smile that lit his face for a second and died as instantly, leaving him expressionless.

"I think," he said, "there is a great deal too much letter-writing between us, and the best thing you can do is to come up to tea with me and we will talk the matter over."

"Mayfield"

Mr Martin, probably remembering the coldness of his reception when last he put his foot across the threshold of "Mayfield", demurred to this suggestion, but eventually agreed. That afternoon he went up to "Mayfield", was most graciously received by Armstrong, who led him to the drawing-room, where a tea-table had been laid. There was a cake-basket, one of those wicker affairs which carry three tiers of cakes and bread and butter, and, in this particular case, a plate of buttered scones. The tea was poured out, Armstrong handed a cup to his visitor and chatted pleasantly, and a little ruefully, of his failure to meet the demands of his legal friend, and then:

"Excuse fingers," said Armstrong, and handed a wedge of hot buttered scone to his guest. That scone had been sprinkled with the tasteless white powder which had removed Mrs Armstrong from the world. Martin ate it to the last crumb, drank his tea, and, after a more or less satisfactory talk, drove back to his own house in Cusop.

It was not until he was taking his dinner that night that he began to feel ill, and then so alarming were the symptoms that he was put immediately to bed and Dr Hinks was summoned.

Whatever Dr Hinks's views were about this sickness, so strangely resembling that which had preceded Mrs Armstrong's death, Martin's father-in-law, Davis the chemist, held a very decided opinion. It was part of his duty as a pharmaceutical chemist to understand, not only the properties, but the actions of various poisons, and to know also something about their antidotes. His son-in-law's sickness was obviously caused by arsenic. He immediately conveyed his suspicions to Dr Hinks, and that practitioner accepted that possibility, an attitude which undoubtedly saved Martin's life.

It is impossible for a leading man in a tiny place like Hay to be taken seriously ill without the news becoming public property; and when, a few days after, Martin, very white and shaky, met Armstrong, the Major was intensely sympathetic.

"You must have eaten something which disagreed with you," he said (very truly), "and I have a feeling that you will have another illness very similar."

Martin probably registered a silent vow that, if he could help it, that second illness should not occur. He, with Dr Hinks, had sent a certain fluid to London for analysis, and when the analyst's report came, showing a considerable trace of arsenic, Scotland Yard was notified.

In the meantime there was another curious happening. Mr and Mrs Martin received one day a box of chocolates, and, upon eating one, Mrs Martin was taken ill. The fact that these chocolates, which contained arsenic, could not be traced to Armstrong, resulted in that aspect of the man's villainous activities being dropped at the trial.

Armstrong was growing desperate. He made another futile attempt to induce Martin to pay a further visit, and, when that failed, asked him up to his office for tea, an invitation which was declined.

The mentality of such people as Major Armstrong is puzzling, even to the expert psychologist. One supposes that they are mad, that they are paranoiac in the sense that they have to an excessive degree the delusion of their own infallibility. Certainly Armstrong must have realized, from the repeated refusals of Martin to deal with him, that he was under suspicion; and a normally minded man, even though he were not a Master of Arts and a clever lawyer, even if he had not the assistance of a large experience in criminal cases, would have taken immediate steps to remove every trace of his guilt and to cover himself against the contingency of exposure. Armstrong went about his work in the usual way; he was to be found in his place when the local court assembled, exchanging smiles with the presiding justices, who knew nothing whatever of the suspicion under which their clerk lay, and assisting them to deal with the peccadilloes of local wrong-doers. He was corresponding with Madame X, and at the same time was conducting an illicit love affair, of which evidence was plentiful in the village of Cusop.

Scotland Yard, having all the facts in its possession, including the statement made by Dr Hinks as to the symptoms of Mrs Armstrong, was necessarily compelled to act with the greatest circumspection and caution. The man under suspicion was not only a lawyer, who would be conversant with every move in the criminal game, but he held a high position. It was impossible to conduct such an inquiry as would have been set on foot supposing the suspected man were living in London. Even the advent of two strange men would have set tongues wagging, and Armstrong would have been warned that all was not well; whilst, if those strangers were reported to be inquiring about his movements, then the task of bringing him to justice was rendered all the more difficult.

The officer in charge of the case was favoured by the fact that the nights were long and dark. He and his assistant were in the habit of arriving at Hay by motor-car long after shops had closed and the people had dispersed to their several homes, pursuing their inquiries in secrecy and returning towards midnight to their headquarters at Hereford. Martin was seen and cross-examined, a statement taken of his visit to "Mayfield" and the subsequent attempts of Armstrong to induce him to make a further call; the chemist who supplied the arsenic displayed his books; Dr Hinks showed his casebook and gave particulars of Mrs Armstrong's illness; whilst one of the nurses who had looked after that unfortunate lady up to her death was also interviewed, under a pledge of secrecy.

On New Year's Eve, 1921, the police were in possession of sufficient evidence to justify an arrest, not on a charge of murder, but for the attempted murder of Martin. The Home Office had been consulted, and permission to exhume the body of Mrs Armstrong had been tentatively given, to be followed later by the actual order which only the Home Office authorities can issue and which was, in fact, issued once Armstrong was under lock and key.

When he reached his office that morning, he was followed into the room by the two detectives in charge of the case, Chief Detective-Inspector Crutchett and Sergeant Sharp, together with the Deputy Chief Constable of Hereford, Alfred Weaver, an old friend of Armstrong's. He must have realized, as the cross-examination grew closer and closer to Martin's illness, that he was more than under suspicion, but he did not by any sign betray either his guilt or his apprehension. He did, however, volunteer to make a statement, and this was taken down in writing by Sergeant Sharp.

But he was so confident of his own ability to hoodwink the police, so satisfied that, occuping the position he did, no charge could be brought against him without his receiving sufficient warning, that he never dreamt that the open arrest would be followed by a closer one. The normal course that would have been taken, had he been under suspicion, was for an application to be made to the local justices for his arrest, and it is certain that he banked upon receiving this warning, never dreaming that Scotland Yard would move independently of the justices, and that the first intimation he would receive would be the arrival of the detectives.

After his statement had been read over to him and signed, Crutchett said, "Mr Weaver now has something to say to you."

Weaver then arrested Armstrong on a charge of having attempted to murder Martin by the administration of arsenic. He replied, "I am quite innocent," and was then asked to turn out his pockets. All his papers were put into a parcel. Later, as his room was being searched, he made an attempt to get at them, but was sternly told to leave them alone.

He was conducted to the local lock-up, which he had so often visited and to which he had been instrumental in consigning so many petty breakers of the law. It was not until several days later that the papers from his pockets were examined, and a tell-tale packet of arsenic was found. This act of indiscretion on his part had been little short of madness. He must have carried the arsenic in the hope of Martin's accepting one of those invitations he had so frequently issued, never dreaming that this damning proof of his villainy would go far to hang him.

"What is this, Major Armstrong?" asked the inspector.

"That is arsenic." Armstrong's voice was cool, his nerve unshaken.

"Why do you carry this arsenic in your pocket?'

"I use it to kill the dandelions on my lawn," he said, and elaborated this story later.

From the little cell he heard the church bells of Hay ring in the dawn of a New Year through which it was fated that he should not live. In the morning he again appeared in the court he knew so well, but this time a stranger sat at the clerk's place, and the bewildered justices, in sorrow and consternation, gazed upon their friend standing in the dock, wearing his British-warm overcoat and smiling affably at the friends whom he recognized in the court.

The position was an incredible one. The first few moments in that tiny court-house were poignant in their tragedy. Armstrong was committed on remand to Worcester Prison. Again he was brought up, formal evidence given, and again he was remanded. In the meantime the police and the Home Office authorities had exhumed the body of Mrs Armstrong, and in a nearby cottage Sir Bernard Spilsbury, the Home Office authority, performed his gruesome task, removing the portions of the body which were to be sent to the government analyst. Armstrong came up before the court one morning to learn that there was a second charge against him, namely, that he did "feloniously and wilfully and with malice aforethought kill and murder one Katharine Mary Armstrong on 22 February 1921, at Cusop, in the county of Hereford, by poisoning her with arsenic".

The court proceedings, and those at the coroner's inquest which followed, will always be remembered by the journalists who were present. The court was so tiny, and the incursion of reporters so great, that the most extraordinary methods were employed to cope with the situation. Tables were extemporized from coffin-boards, and upon these the representatives of the great London dailies wrote their accounts of the proceedings.

It so happened that at the time of the preliminary inquiry, the Assize Court was in session, and it seemed that the man would be compelled to wait for six months before he was brought to the bar of justice. But Mr Justice Darling announced that he would hold a special assize for the trial of Armstrong, and this was formally opened on Monday, 3 April, at the Shire Hall,

Hereford, after the man had been committed on both charges: that of the attempted murder of Martin, and of killing his wife.

Armstrong's attitude throughout the preliminary inquiries had been taciturn and confident. He had followed every scrap of the evidence with the keenest interest, but had said little or nothing, and I think he was the most confident man in the court when he was finally committed for trial, and knew that he was leaving the neighbourhood in which he had lorded it so long, and where he had lived for so many years in the odour of sanctity and the approval of his fellows.

His vanity supported him, as it has done with so many poisoners — for men who destroy life in this dreadful manner are so satisfied that no evidence other than that which they might offer themselves can be of value in securing a conviction, that they are certain up to the very last that they can escape the consequences of their ill-doing. There seems never to have been, in the history of poisoners, a single instance of a man confessing his guilt.

Such was the public interest in the trial, and so serious a view did the law authorities take of this case, that the Attorney-General, Sir Ernest Pollock, later Master of the Rolls, was sent down to conduct the prosecution, the defence being in the hands of Sir Henry Curtis Bennett, a brilliant advocate who had conducted the prosecution of all the spies caught in England during the war.

On a cold day, with snow blowing through the open windows of the court, Herbert Rowse Armstrong stepped lightly into the dock and bowed to the thin-faced man in the judge's box. He was as neatly dressed as ever — brown shoes, with fawn-coloured spats, brown suit and brown tie perfectly harmonized. He had been brought over by motor-car from Gloucester Gaol that morning, had interviewed his counsel, and now, with an assurance which allowed him to glance round the crowded courthouse and nod to his friends, he listened to the cold, dispassionate statement of his crimes.

He was in a familiar setting: he knew most of the court attendants by sight or name; in happier circumstances he had exchanged views and words with the Clerk of the Assizes; he had even appeared to instruct counsel before the judge who was now to conduct the trial. He sat back in his chair, his arms folded, a motionless and intent figure, following the evidence of every witness, the blue eyes seldom leaving their faces. Even at that hour he was satisfied that the evidence which could be produced would be insufficient to secure a conviction, either for murder or attempted murder, and he expressed to the warders, who had to bring him every day the long journey from Gloucester, his faith that the case for the Crown was so ill-constructed that the trial could not but end in his acquittal.

"If this case were tried in Scotland," he told them, "there could be no question that 'Not proven' would be the verdict."

Sir Ernest Pollock put the case fairly and humanely against him, and it was not until Armstrong himself went into the box that the full weight of the law's remorseless effort began to tell against him. In the witness-box Armstrong was a suave, easily smiling and courteous gentleman. His soft, drawling voice, his easy manner, his very frankness, told in his favour; nor did the cross-examination of the Attorney-General greatly shake the good impression he made. But there was a man on the bench wise in the ways of murders, who saw the flaws in Armstrong's defence. When Mr Justice Darling folded his arms, and, leaning forward over his desk, asked questions in that soft voice of his, the doom of Herbert Rowse Armstrong was sealed. They were merciless questions, not to be evaded nor to be answered obliquely.

Firm to the very last, Armstrong met the dread sentence of the court without any evidence of the emotion which must have possessed him.

The clerk of the court asked, in halting tones:

"What have you to say that the court should not now give you judgment to die according to law?"

Armstrong almost rapped out the word: "Nothing!"

Though his guilt had been established on evidence which was good and sufficient for the twelve men who tried him, he was not without hope that, on certain misdirections, he would secure a reversal of the verdict at the Court of Appeal. But this court, which exercises its powers of revision very jealously, saw no reason to interfere with the course of the law, and on 31 May, Derby Day, Armstrong met his fate.

During his period of incarceration in Gloucester Gaol he had occupied the condemned cell, adjoining the execution shed, which was, in fact, a converted cell opening into the apartment where condemned men spent their last weeks of life. The disadvantage of this arrangement was that almost every sound in the death chamber could be heard in the condemned cell, and Armstrong, who knew Gloucester Gaol — knew too the proximity of his cell to the place of his dread end — must have been keyed up to the slightest sound. It was necessary that the executioner should try the trap whilst Armstrong was at exercise. He arrived, however, too late for this to be done overnight, and it was not till the following morning that the drop was tested.

At seven o'clock Armstrong, who had been up an hour, was invited by the warders to take a final walk in the exercise yard, an experience unique for a man under sentence of death. The sky was blue and cloudless, the morning warm and balmy, and he strolled about in the limited space allotted to him, showing no evidence of the terrible agony which must have been in his soul. After nearly an hour's walk he was conducted back to the condemned cell, where a minister of religion was already waiting, and within a very short time he had paid the penalty for his crime.

The Armstrong murder is historic from the point of view of the lawyer, since he was condemned on evidence which was entirely circumstantial. But, as Sir Ernest Pollock pointed out at the trial, in a poison trial direct evidence is practically impossible.

"In this case," said Sir Ernest, "we know that Mrs Armstrong died from arsenical poisoning. This body of evidence which will be called before you will be directed piece by piece, circumstance by circumstance, pointing to a conclusion that it was the prisoner at the bar who killed his wife.

"She died from arsenical poisoning. Who had the means, who had the opportunity in August and in February, who had the motive to administer the poison?

"You find the means with the prisoner. You find the opportunity — the one man who was at 'Mayfield' both in August and in February. You find the motive in the will referred to."

Though there was no proof of the administration of poison, and the evidence of motive, so far as Mrs Armstrong's fortune was concerned, was perhaps the weakest that was ever put against any man on the capital charge, nobody who knew Armstrong, and who was brought into close touch with his life, will doubt that he was guilty.

Before Ellis, the hangman, pulled the bolt, the slight figure standing on the drop said something that was indistinguishable. One present thought that it was a confession of guilt — more likely it was a last protest of innocence.

Armstrong had refused an offer of £5,000 which I had made to him a few days before for a complete confession of his crime.

Postscript

On 22 April 1922, the weekly magazine *John Bull* published an article, ostensibly by Harold Greenwood (see page 54), entitled "Armstrong's Fight for Life":

Many brilliant pens have been at work during the past fortnight depicting the salient features of the Armstrong trial. There is, of course, a magnetism about a murder trial; drama enters naturally into it; and everybody is fascinated to watch the long drawn out struggle between the Crown and leading Counsel for the Defence, ranging around the silent figure who for the most part can only sit helpless in the dock awaiting an issue which for him means liberty or — death.

But when I read these brilliant descriptions of the trial, I feel that in one sense they fall short of the reality. They are, of necessity, written from the *outside*. Only the unfortunate creature who has himself been "the man in the dock" during such a tremendous ordeal as that arising from a charge of murder can begin to understand the *inward*, hidden drama concealed from superficial observers.

If the stuffy and inconvenient Court House at Hereford — which I have visited professionally on several occasions — be substituted for the still more vilely ventilated and poky Assize Court in Carmarthen Town, I could very well imagine that the dreadful experience I passed through some fifteen months ago was being repeated as a sort of ghastly nightmare.

It will readily be understood that, try as I will, I cannot help making a mental comparison between these two trials which are so remarkably similar in their characteristic details.

When I read that the prisoner in the dock appeared "calm", "stolid", "animated" or "smiling", I recall how unreal and futile such phrases seem when read after the ordeal is over. I had a bundle of newspapers to look through on the day following my acquittal — and they taught me a lesson. For as a lawyer I have frequently defended men who claimed they were innocent. Mostly I had been led to form my own opinion to a large extent by the appearance of the accused in the dock. Facial calmness or agitation, and the composed or distressed attitude of the prisoner, is a dangerous index of the guilt or otherwise of any person.

For consider. The majesty of the Law may well be described as a terror of evildoers: it may also be a frightful menace to the innocent.

While this Armstrong drama unrolls its slow length like a legal kinema played out in an incredibly dingy and dusty setting, I go back in memory to my own experience.

To be arrested, safely caged up, to become the centre of universal comment, to know that one's business, built up with such care, is daily falling to ruins, to be cut off from the world of home and friends, and to be faced with the most atrocious charge that can be laid against any man — that of subtle, secretive poisoning of a wife; that is sufficiently agonizing.

But there is another aspect, perhaps more dreadful.

It is the business of the Crown, when once a prosecution has been decided upon, to press the case with the utmost industry. And remember, the Crown does not stop for money. Inquiries are made regardless of cost; expert evidence is paid for without the need of economy; witnesses are found and maintained by the Crown. In short, the case against the accused is built up without the necessity for stinting money.

But the position of the defendant is quite different. He is, literally, fighting for his life. "Skin for skin, all that a man hath will he give for his life," said patient Job. And when a man finds himself faced with a murder charge, not the least part of his torment is one of ways and means.

Owing to our antiquated assize system, there is a possibility that the accused may spend several months in gaol. There is no hope of bail. Week after week he waits and waits for the ordeal, knowing that by some means, even if it ruin him, he must raise sums of money for the building up of the defence, the briefing of counsel, the maintaining of witnesses during the trial, and the costly evidence of experts to rebut the evidence given by the Crown's "star" medical and scientific men.

I spent several months in Carmarthen Gaol. I was racked with anxiety as to how the ways and means of my trial could be found. And then when the day came that I took my place in the dock before a battery of curious eyes, my "careworn appearance" was adversely commented upon in some quarters. I dwell upon this to let the unthinking realize what the prisoner has been passing through before he stands up to plead.

Then, should he falter, he is exposed to the fear that this may be written down as a consciousness of guilt; or should he by an iron effort face his judge and jury with a show of calmness, he is "jaunty" and "coolly composed". Well indeed have I learned the lesson that the demeanour of a prisoner is but little to go upon.

Only those who have been the man in the dock, too, can realize the awful sensation of listening to leading counsel for the Crown "opening the case". A helpless, suffocating sense of impotency, and doubly so when the prisoner is a lawyer.

It sounds black — black to the point of certainty. The lightest action assumes a sinister appearance; a chance word becomes ominous; letters are found to foreshadow violence; *motive* is harped upon. This is legitimate, of course, from a forensic point of view. Our Crown lawyers are scrupulously fair, but their business is to prosecute, and "with the utmost rigour of the Law".

86

Herbert Armstrong, Poisoner

When the Attorney-General in Hereford Court went on in his silken tones constructing the case against Major Armstrong, he did it with a fairness that was beyond reproach — but with a forensic skill that was unutterably deadly.

And I know what the prisoner felt! Helpless, trapped, overborne. He steals a glance at the jury and sees that every word is telling. That is almost the worst moment in the trial.

My refuge during the trial was the knowledge of the scrupulous impartiality of the judge. And at Hereford I was struck with the skill and wisdom with which Mr Justice Darling held the balance between the great advocates on either side.

The jury of necessity are swayed backwards and forwards by the skill of contending counsel. I remember that when a telling point was made by the Crown against me, I simply dared not look at the jury.

Then, too, there is the ordeal of going into the box. Many a time in former days I have urged a man to go into the witness-box, and have drawn an adverse conclusion if he has hesitated. I have changed my views upon that point now.

It is an ordeal that can never be realized except by those who have been through it. After being worn out with some days of unparalleled strain in the earlier stages of the trial, the prisoner "goes into the box". The eyes of the crowd watch every motion, the twitch of his face, and the fluttering of his hands. He knows that he will be exposed to a pitiless hail of questons from an expert in the art of interrogation. If he answers too fully he will be admonished to be more "direct"; if he replies briefly, a raised eyebrow or the inflection of a voice, the darting of a meaning look by counsel at the jury, may influence their minds.

For my part I was told afterwards that I seemed perfectly "cool and composed". In fact I was on the verge of a breakdown, only sustained by the knowledge that if I did not keep my head I was lost. For weeks afterwards I felt the strain of that ordeal. It was, of course, a perfectly fair cross-examination. But those who talk lightly of the prisoner's attitude under examination should bear in mind facts such as I have been describing.

And then comes the suspense of waiting for the verdict.

The judge's summing up has preceded this, of course, and I suppose to a lawyer this is more painful than can be described. For a trained legal mind can appreciate exactly the effect upon the jury. As minute by minute the cultured, measured voice flows on, hope seems to evaporate. And so at last the jury are dismissed to deliberate, the judge seeks his private room, and the court buzzes with expectation.

The prisoner is taken below to wait. Ah! That waiting. Never can I forget those moments like eternity while the jury deliberated upon my fate. The attendant policemen were kind and considerate, but they were only policemen. After all the months of racking anxiety, I really felt that those minutes of suspense were more than I could bear. Then suddenly there was a fresh bustle of excitement and I found myself being ushered up the dock stairs again.

It seemed an eternity while the Clerk of Arraigns was interrogating the middle-aged foreman of the jury. How slow, how impossibly deliberate he seemed! Until amid a deathly hush I heard him murmur: "Not Guilty!" Then the dock doors were open and I was free again. But I draw a veil over that.

I have followed very carefully the Armstrong drama, and naturally I can write about it from a feeling heart. It does seem to me an injustice that the accused's counsel does not have the last word with the jury. Of course, if the accused does not go into the box, calls no witnesses, and puts in no documents, he has this advantage; but on the other hand an adverse opinion must be formed by the jury if a prisoner does not give evidence upon his own behalf.

It is a fearful, unbelievable thing to be tried for your life. But terrible though the ordeal was, I am perfectly certain that British justice is scrupulously fair to the accused. Nevertheless, only those who have been charged with murder can realize the exact nature of the ordeal.

The Origin of the "Gigman"

H. M. Walbrook

THE MURDER on the night of 24 October 1823 of William Weare, outside a lonely cottage in Gill's Hill Lane, near Elstree, Hertfordshire, makes one of the most memorable stories in the annals of human wickedness. There was nothing in the tragedy itself to give it this prominence. Its brutality and its sordidness, extreme as they were, can yet be paralleled easily enough.

The three men chiefly implicated in the murder — John Thurtell, Joseph Hunt, and William Probert — were all morally among the lowest of the low, and their wretched victim was little better. Thurtell himself, the actual murderer, was the son of well-to-do, highly respected, and religious parents in Norwich, and earlier had held a commission for two years in the Marines. On his return to civil life he deteriorated into being a follower of race-meetings and prize-fights, a bully, a swindler, and a ruffian generally. Hunt also had some respectable connections by marriage, and was a good singer, but degenerated into a haunter of gambling-hells, a liar, and a coward; while Probert, a huge fellow with the soul of a villain and the courage of a rabbit, was as vile as the rest. The ill-fated Weare was an ex-waiter who had made money by all sorts of swindling, and was reputed to carry his "fortune" about with him inside his shirt, distrusting banks as deeply as he distrusted humanity in general. In short, never did a crime lift a shoddier crew into the limelight of public fame.

Yet the story and its *dramatis personæ* seemed immediately to captivate not only the sensation-loving public, but also some of the finest minds of its time. Thomas Carlyle, seizing on a grotesque sentence in a morning newspaper's account of the trial, quoted it again and again for years after, and, as I shall show later on, gave it a sort of immortality. George Borrow gave a remarkable picture of Thurtell in *Lavengro*. William Hazlitt introduced the same individual under a very slightly disguised name into one of the most vivid of his essays, the one called

JNO. THURTELL   JOS. HUNT.   WM. PROBERT

"The Fight". Sir Walter Scott poured his scorn on the maudlin crowd who visited the fatal garden of the cottage in the Hertfordshire lane and "treasured up the leaves and twigs of its hedge and shrubs as valuable relics".[1] Other elements, which I shall refer to presently, also helped to make the story remarkable; but its outstanding memorial is undoubtedly the curious fascination it cast upon the minds of these and other great artists in phrase and line.

The cottage near Elstree belonged to William Probert, whose wife lived in it with her young children, two of her sisters, and from time to time a couple of servants, while the owner spent most of his time in London and elsewhere, finding and defrauding his victims. Thurtell had a grudge against his friend Mr Weare: "He owes me three or four hundred pounds," he confided to Hunt, adding that he was "going to get it". Accordingly, it was arranged that on 24 October he should take Weare down to Elstree for "some shooting", kill him, and seize the money he had in his shirt. That Friday morning Thurtell and Hunt went to a pawnbroker's in Marylebone and bought a couple of pistols, which the former pocketed. Hunt also bought a sack and a rope, and handed them over to his friend as likely to be useful. In the

---

1. *Editor's Note.* Sir Walter's scorn seems to have been hypocritical. Four years after the crime, when driving from London to Scotland, he made a diversion to Elstree to see the cottage (by then half-destroyed by souvenir hunters) and other landmarks of the case.

afternoon, Thurtell, in a gig, called for Weare at his rooms in Lyon's Inn, a now-vanished Inn of Chancery attached to the Inner Temple, lying between Wych Street and Holywell Street, off the Strand. He found him ready and waiting, with a change of linen in a green carpet-bag, a double-barrelled gun for the "sport" that had been promised him, and a backgammon-board with men and dice for the evening pleasure of the party. In high spirits, off the pair started for Elstree. Meanwhile Hunt and Probert had also started on the same journey in another gig. They were all to meet at the cottage. Apparently Probert and Hunt expected that, by the time they arrived, Weare would have been "dispatched", as Thurtell had the pistols with him.

They were not disappointed. On their arrival about eight o'clock, Thurtell met them, and informed them that he had "done the trick". He proceeded to describe how, at the first shot, Weare had jumped out of the gig and "run like the devil up the lane, singing out that he would deliver up all he had won off me if only I would spare his life; but I jumped out of the gig and ran after him, I got him down and began to cut his throat, as I thought, about the jugular vein, but couldn't stop his singing out. I then jammed the pistol into his head. I saw him turn round; and then I knew I had done him. I thought at one time he would have got the better of me. Those damned pistols are like squibs; they're of no use."

To all this Hunt calmly replied: "I thought one of those pistols would have killed him dead; but you had plenty of tools." After which they went to where the body was still lying, hid it in the sack, proceeded to the cottage, apparently in great good humour, and supped off some pork chops which Hunt had brought down with him from London.

After supper Thurtell presented Mrs Probert with the long gold watch-chain which he had taken from his victim, and Hunt favoured the company with a couple of songs. When the lady had retired, Thurtell handed six pounds each to his accomplices, with the words, "That is your share of the blunt," after which they held a long discussion in whispers — little guessing that their hostess, who had become suspicious, was on the staircase outside listening over the balusters. Presently Thurtell and Hunt rose and went out.

By and by, from an upper window Mrs Probert saw them coming back along what was called the "dark lane", dragging

H. M. Walbrook

THE SCENE OF THE MURDER, with the Gig in the Lane.

omething heavy in a sack. Needless to say it was Weare's body. The lane led to a pond in Probert's garden. They pushed the body into his pond, having previously weighted the sack with stones. On the following Sunday evening a game of cards was proposed, and was vetoed by Thurtell on the ground that it would be "setting a bad example to the children". On Monday a wandering labourer found a blood-stained knife; also a pistol smirched on the barrel with what looked like human brain-matter. Late that night Thurtell and Hunt drew the body from Probert's pond and took it in a gig to a brook a short distance off, on the north side of Elstree, where they sank it again. On the following day Probert was taken into custody; on the Wednes-day Hunt and Thurtell were arrested in London; and on 1 November the three were committed to St Albans Gaol on a coroner's warrant to await their trial at Hertford on 4 December.

By this time the whole press was ringing with the case. From *The Times* downwards, the newspapers of the country made as free with the characters and records of the three prisoners as if they had already been tried and proved guilty. Other conspi-racies to murder were freely attributed to them, and all the gossip and scandal of the gambling-hells and the public-houses in regard to them were printed and commented upon in a spirit of the rankest sensationalism and the most reckless contempt of

The cottage near Elstree

93

court. As Eric R. Watson says in his essay on the subject,[2] the case of John Thurtell was the first in our annals of what is called "trial by newspaper". It was also perhaps the worst. So universal became the popular prejudice against the prisoners that an application was made on 4 December, before Mr Justice Park in Hertford, for a postponement of the trial. Said counsel in addressing his lordship:

> In this very town where Justice is to be administered, the public mind has been polluted; hundreds of placards and bills have been circulated; facts have been distorted; wrong views have been presented to the minds of those persons who are to form the jury on this important trial; and who can say what effect this may have on the fate of the unhappy ones at the bar?

The cottage in Gill's Hill Lane had become a place of popular pilgrimage, with men at the gates doing a roaring trade selling printed vituperations of the accused.

On the south side of the Thames a still grosser defiance of justice had been perpetrated. At the Surrey Theatre, a melodrama called *The Gamblers* was produced, with the murder as its subject, in which persons were introduced representing Weare and Thurtell, and of which the identical gig in which Weare had been driven to his death, with the actual horse which drew it, were further features. This shameless exhibition attracted crowds and caused extraordinary excitement; with the result that here again an application was made to the court (before Chief Justice Abbott) and the play was ordered to be withdrawn. Reference to this scandalous production was made in the application at Hertford for a postponement of the trial. Said one of the counsel in supporting the plea: "I blush for England and for Englishmen that when the murder was represented they did not hiss the actor off the stage for exhibiting a man as guilty who is as yet unconvicted." And in sanctioning a postponement of the trial to 6 January, Mr Justice Park, whose conduct of the proceedings now and hereafter was distinguished by a notable dignity, addressed some memorable words to the newspaper editors of that day:

> Trial by jury is the palladium of English liberty, and this palladium ought above all things to be preserved pure and uncorrupted. If such

2. *Editor's note.* Introduction to *Trial of Thurtell and Hunt*, in the "Notable British Trials" series, Hodge, Edinburgh 1920.

a licentious pruriency exist among the public to run after something new, and if publications which appear to have such enormous circulation are to poison the sources of justice whenever the
editors think fit, the palladium of English liberty is endangered.
Justice has been impeded and retarded. This is a thing which
ought not to be tolerated; and I do most earnestly hope and trust
that those gentlemen who have erred on this occasion, though
without any bad intention, will bethink them of the cruelty committed by such conduct, and of the deep injury they may inflict on
society by doing that which has a tendency to pollute and corrupt
the fountains of public justice.

After this the newspaper agitation died down; but the public
mind was made up on the guilt of the prisoners, and the fate of
all three seemed a foregone conclusion.

On Tuesday, 6 January 1824, the trial opened at Hertford in a
court crowded to excess. A fanfare of trumpets accompanied
the entry of Mr Justice Park; then came the three prisoners:
Thurtell charged as guilty of the murder, and Hunt and Probert
as accessories before the fact. An early sensation came with the
announcement of the prosecuting counsel, Mr Gurney, that it
was not his intention to offer any evidence against Probert. That
worthy had, in fact, completed his infamy by offering to bear
testimony against his associates. His offer had been accepted,
and by the judge's direction he was acquitted and removed from
the dock. The story against the two remaining prisoners was
then set forth with great skill and precision by Mr Gurney, after
which came the evidence of some forty witnesses for the prosecution, each contributing his more or less telling fact or facts,
with Probert and his wife heading the list, and stripping the last
rag of covering from the guilt of the actual murderer and of the
man who sat cowering beside him.

The second and concluding day of the trial brought with it a
memorable display on the part of Thurtell. Called upon by the
judge to make his defence, he proceeded to deliver an oration in
every way so eloquent that, while probably failing to shake the
conviction of a single listener, it thrilled the whole court. The
report of it fills more than twenty pages of the report of the case
in the "Notable British Trials" series, and its combination of
impudence and cleverness still makes it admirable reading. Its
chief points were: (1) that the evidence against himself was
either circumstantial or bribed, and therefore entirely inade-
quate, and (2) that the actual murderer of Weare was the man

who had turned King's evidence, William Probert! Of the many remarkable passages in the speech, here is a characteristic one:

> Gentlemen, my entry into life was under circumstances the most auspicious. I was reared by a kind, affectionate, and religious mother, who taught my lips to utter their first accents in praise of that Being Who guides the conduct of your hearts and that of the learned judge upon the bench. My youthful steps were directed by a father conspicuous for the possession of every good quality, but above all for his unaffected piety. On leaving my parental home, I entered the service of our late revered monarch, who was emphatically styled the father of his people. For years I had the honour of holding his commission and served under his colours, and I may justly take the credit to assert that I never disgraced the one nor tarnished the other. I have done my country some service. I have fought and bled for her, and in her cause have never feared to draw the steel against an open foe, against my country's enemy. But to raise the assassin's arm, and that, too, against an unsuspecting friend! — believe it not! It is horrid, monstrous, and incompatible with every feeling of my heart and every habit of my life.

As it happened, there was no record of his ever having had to "draw his steel" against an enemy of his country, but the point was obviously a good one to make in addressing a jury. Then came a self-rebuking, self-pitying description of his subsequent addiction to gambling, his misfortunes (all, of course, due to others!) in the commercial world, his bankruptcy, and his scandalous treatment by the press in connection with "this deed of horror, at which humanity stands aghast". Then, with arms uplifted and the air of a great tragic actor, he concluded as follows:

> Gentlemen, I have now done. I look with confidence to your decision. I hope your verdict today will be such as you may ever after be able to think upon with a composed conscience, and that you will also reflect upon the solemn declaration which I now make — So help me God, I am innocent!

Says a spectator of the scene: "The solid, slow, and appalling tones in which he wrung out these last words can never be imagined by those who were not auditors of them."

Through the long and deadly summing-up of the judge he sat calmly, and while the death-sentence was being pronounced, he ostentatiously helped himself to a pinch of snuff.

Two days later he was hanged in front of Hertford Gaol in the

resence of a multitude. Charles Lamb, in a letter to his friend,
ernard Barton, wrote these words:

> It is just fifteen minutes after twelve: Thurtell is by this time a good
> way on his journey, baiting at Scorpion perhaps; Ketch is bargaining
> for his coat and waistcoat! the Jew demurs at first at three half-
> crowns but, on consideration that he may get somewhat by showing
> 'em in the town, finally closes,

nd, for a fortnight after, the dissecting-room in St Bartho-
omew's Hospital was crowded to suffocation by spectators
atching Dr Abernethy dissecting the body of the wretched
an.

The man Hunt, who had also been found guilty and sentenced
o death, was reprieved at the last moment and transported to
Australia, where he was reported in 1837 to be living as a
gentleman's servant" in Bathurst, New South Wales. One can
nly hope that his master found him satisfactory. As to Probert,
is treachery to his associates did him little good in the end.
hunned by all as the bearer of a double infamy, he rapidly sank
ower and lower, and a year later he was arrested on a charge of
orse-stealing, tried, found guilty, sentenced to death, and, in
ccordance with the savage law of those times, hanged in front
f Newgate Gaol.

William Cobbett in his *Rural Rides* tells us how in the winter of
823–24 all the world was talking and writing about Thurtell, and
is curious how the echoes of the crime have persisted to the
resent day. A sentence in a London newspaper, the *Morning
Chronicle*, describing Probert as a man who always "maintained
n appearance of respectability and kept a gig", appealed keenly
o Carlyle's humour, and was the origin of the many allusions to
gigmanity", "gigmanic", and "gigmanism" which appear in his
ritings as synonymous for sham respectability. When Dickens
n 1843 was writing the forty-second chapter of *Martin Chuzzle-
it*, with its description of the drive of the murderer Jonas and
is destined victim through a night of thunder, lightning and rain,
e evidently had in mind the earlier drive in which a villain in real
fe conveyed the man he was about to slay from London to
lstree. As late as the 1890s most people had heard the quatrain:

> They cut his throat from ear to ear,
>   His brains they battered in,
> His name was Mr William Weare,
>   He lived in Lyon Inn,

which had earlier so entertained Sir Walter Scott. In *The Dic-
tionary of National Biography* a place is found for a Life of Joh
Thurtell. And in the year 1923 the centenary of the crime wa
celebrated by a local "pageant", in one of the scenes of whic
the blood-stained phantom of the murdered man appeared fron
behind a hedge in a white shirt. But nothing that has bee
written about the murder of Mr Weare sticks so queerly and s
unforgettably in the memory as the vision of his slayer, fres
from his brutal crimes, declining to play cards on a Sunda
evening on the grounds that to do so would be "showing a ba
example to the children".

The Frozen Footprints

Albert Borowitz[1]

THE FARMHOUSE tenanted by Dietrich Wessels stood back from the Jamaica Plank Road (now Jamaica Avenue) in rural New Lots, Long Island, which adjoined on the east a thickly settled section of Brooklyn called East New York. The house was in the lower part of the lot, in the south-east corner. The major portion of the farm was planted with cabbages and other vegetables that Wessels sold in the metropolis, but the rear of the lot was dotted with piles of hard-corn stalks that would soon be cleared off by burning.

The weather in New Lots had been variable at the onset of winter in 1875. Sunday night, 12 December, was clear and mild, but on Monday a storm covered the ground with an inch or two of snow. By Tuesday some of the snow had melted but the ground remained frozen.

It was early on Tuesday afternoon that Wessels's labourer, Martin Segellern, discovered the girl's body. Her arms outstretched, she lay on her back, fused to the ground by her own frozen blood, near a stack of corn stalks about four hundred feet from the farmhouse and an equal distance from the road. Her knees, stained with mud as if she had knelt before the murderer, were raised; her upturned face showed a wide gash that swept from the middle of her throat to her right ear-lobe. On her right cheek there was a deep stab-wound, and her left palm was cut where she had possibly seized her assailant's weapon. The girl's face, hair and upper body were dark with clotted blood. About twenty years old, she was bareheaded and respectably dressed in a pearl-coloured underdress and black alpaca skirt; a red-and-black striped shawl lay nearby.

---

1. The author of, among other books, *The Thurtell-Hunt Murder Case: Dark Mirror to Regency England*, Louisiana State University Press, Baton Rouge and London, 1987.

Wessels, summoned from the house by his terrified labourer, kept his wits about him. The farmer did not touch anything, except that decency required him to pull down the girl's skirt that had rucked up far above her knees. Losing no time, he called promptly at the East New York police station, where he informed Roundsman Thomas Herbert of the discovery. Herbert's searches at the scene were unfruitful, but detectives who arrived in mid-afternoon were more successful: they found a bloody knife thrust among the corn stalks. At first glance the weapon resembled an ordinary sailor's sheath-knife, but closer examination revealed that it had a round scimitar point much like the knives used by cigar-makers. Coroner Henry Simms took possession of the weapon and ordered the girl's body carried to the station house for identification.

When the body was brought to the station, the horrors of the murder began to mount. Removing the shawl that had been thrown over her head to conceal the wounds, the police found that the flesh around the neck-wound had been eaten away by field-mice and that the girl's face was decomposing. It was also obvious that she was several months pregnant.

Theories and speculations abounded among the throngs that besieged the station house, anxious to identify the victim. The initial suggestion that the girl had been butchered in a foiled rape attempt seemed refuted by the fact that her garments showed no sign of rough handling. Many Brooklyn-area residents thought they knew her — as a woman who had visited a fair at a German Catholic church on Sunday or as a servant in a New Lots household. Police also checked out a liquor-dealer's statement that she had visited his store recently, looking for the mother of a notorious scoundrel who had been arrested on many occasions for theft and robbery.

About noon on Wednesday, three men visited the coroner's office and asked to see one of the coroners. Neither was in, but a reporter from the Brooklyn *Daily Eagle*, who recognized the visitors as "Russian Poles", asked what they wanted. Showing the reporter a New York newspaper, one of the men pointed to an advertisement for his missing sister and said in broken English that he feared that she might be the murder victim. The brief newspaper item stated that Sarah Alexander, a young Jewess, had disappeared on Sunday from her home at 30 Essex Street in Manhattan's Lower East Side. Her brother, J. P. Alexander, a peddler, explained that the description given of the dead girl's appearance and clothing in the New York papers seemed to fit his sister's description. She was about nineteen and had been in America for about a year and a half. When she first arrived she had lived with the family of a cousin, Israel Rubenstein, who, with another relative, Jacob Shemansky, had accompanied Alexander to the coroner's office. Rubenstein kept a dry-goods store at 83 Bayard Street on the Lower East Side. Sarah had stayed there about ten months, but when her brother started to keep house had moved in with him. She had been a seamstress but lately was out of work.

Last Sunday at about 1.00 p.m. Sarah had left her brother's home to go to the Rubensteins' apartment on Bayard Street. Rubenstein, his wife, and his son by an earlier marriage, Pasach Nathan Rubenstein, were at home. She had left there at about four o'clock and had never been seen again.

The *Eagle* reporter accompanied the three men to the morgue. The body had not yet been transferred there from the police station, and while they were waiting the newsman interviewed the three men. Alexander told him that Sarah was very religious and attended the Ludlow Street Synagogue every Sabbath. Careful about her morals, she never went out with young men and in fact had no male acquaintances outside her family. Since she was not in the habit of staying out at night, he believed that someone must have waylaid her.

Israel Rubenstein had a melodramatic addition to make to young Alexander's story. Confirming the hours of Sarah's visit on Sunday, he stated that she was all alone when she left to go home. It was only on Monday morning that he learned of her disappearance when her brother came around to see if she was there. Shortly after his visit, Israel's son, Pasach Rubenstein, startled him by recounting a horrible dream he had had last night about Sarah. Her figure appeared to him in his sleep, and told him that she had been murdered ten miles out of the city; she pleaded for him to bury her.

Although Sarah's relatives were very anxious about her, they did not pay any attention to Pasach Rubenstein's dream. The reporter, though, was intrigued. He wanted to know more about the prophetic dreamer. Pasach Rubenstein, he was told, was a jewellery peddler who worked out of the back of his father's dry-goods store on Bayard Street. He was the oldest of three married sons; his wife was in Europe but was due to arrive soon in New York. The reporter concluded that he must have thought a great deal of Sarah. She had apparently been a frequent visitor to the Rubensteins' home; while she was still living there, Pasach Rubenstein was severely ill and she had insisted on nursing him night after night, sleeping only in short spells. When he recovered, he paid a lot of attention to her, explaining that she had been kinder than a sister.

This innocent view of the cousins' relationship did not commend itself to the reporter or the police. The girl's pregnancy suggested that "an illicit intercourse was established between her and Rubenstein". Such a discovery would be extremely damaging to the cousins — but to make matters worse, Pasach's wife was on her way to New York. It was true that he had taken conspicuous part in the search for Sarah, but when the New York papers published a description so compelling that the girl's other relatives were sure she was the murder victim, her devoted Pasach did not come to the morgue to inspect the body.

When the three relatives viewed the body, they immediately identified Sarah. Other identification followed quickly. The police produced several witnesses who on the previous Sunday had ridden on the 5.08 p.m. Broadway (Brooklyn) streetcar from the South 7th Street Ferry, including passengers Edward Buckholtz and Augustus Taylor, and conductor Henry Lee. Most of them identified Sarah as a passenger on the horse-drawn car. Taylor said she was travelling with a thin dark-featured man with a prominent nose, black straggling side-whiskers and a beard and moustache; he wore a "slouched" hat. Taylor was certain Sarah was the girl he saw in the car. She wore a shawl over her head, but he did not regard that as remarkable because he knew that Polish women seldom wore hats. He supposed that the man with her was her husband, and thought they had had a little "miff" because they sat apart and had paid their own fares. The man kept turning from one side to the other in his seat and never faced anyone in the car, looking instead out of the window. They rode to the corner where the streetcar passed the Jamaica Plank Road and got off there.

Inspector Waddy went into the room adjoining the morgue, where Pasach Rubenstein's father was sitting. In order to determine whether Taylor's description matched that of Pasach, he told the old man that he thought one of his sons had been there a minute before and proceeded to describe him in Taylor's words; Israel Rubenstein replied that the visitor must have been

his son Pasach. Inspector Waddy, satisfied with the accumulat-
ing evidence, sent Detectives George Zundt and David Corwin
to Manhattan to arrest Pasach Rubenstein.

When they arrived at the Bayard Street store, they asked after
Pasach but did not identify themselves. Mrs Israel Rubenstein
told them he had left but would return. Zundt stayed on in the
store, pretending to be interested in purchasing a pair of gloves,
and managed to avert suspicion until Pasach came back, running
in from the street as if pursued. When Zundt ordered him to
accompany him to the Brooklyn morgue to view Sarah's body,
Pasach tried desperately to persuade the detective that his
identification was unnecessary. Weren't his relatives already at
the morgue, he asked? When Zundt remained adamant,
Rubenstein tried another tack: he ran into the back room and
brought out a pair of earrings which he asserted were identical to
those he had given Sarah. Zundt confirmed that the dead girl
was wearing similar earrings, but threatened to take Pasach by
force when he persisted in his refusal to come along.

When the suspect was brought to the morgue, the post-
mortem was still in progress; the examination showed that Sarah
was about five months pregnant. After the doctors had finished
their work, they covered her body with her shawl that had such a
distinctive pattern and brilliant colours that it could be easily
remembered by anyone who had once seen it. Brought into the
dissecting room by Zundt, Rubenstein immediately confirmed
to Coroner Simms that he knew the girl; he shrank back against
the wall, apparently wanting to keep his distance from the
corpse. Simms, however, was unsatisfied by the instant recogni-
tion, since Sarah's feet lay towards Pasach and the height of the
marble slab prevented him from seeing her face. The coroner's
commands did not induce Pasach to come closer, and finally
Simms caught him by the collar and marched him up to the slab.
Pasach, though nodding continuously, still said nothing — but
he turned towards Simms just as the coroner removed the shawl,
disclosing the nearly severed head. He cried out in terror and
pulled himself loose of the coroner's grasp; jumping backwards
from the slab, he threw up his hands to hide the body from his
sight.

Detectives Zundt and Corwin searched Pasach in the private
room of Patrick Campbell, superintendent of the Brooklyn
police. In his pockets they found several rolls of money amount-
ing to $750, and watches, chains and precious stones value at

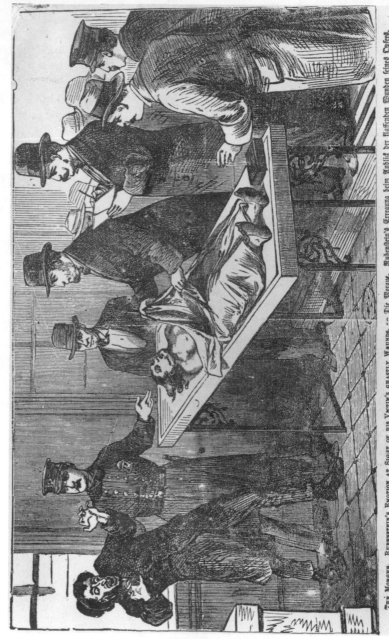

THE MORGUE. RUBENSTEIN'S EMOTION AT SIGHT OF HIS VICTIM'S GHASTLY WOUNDS. — Die Morgue. Rubenstein's Erregung beim Anblick der klaffenden Wunden seines Opfers.

Courtesy of the Brooklyn Historical Society

$2,000. They ordered him to undress and searched each article for blood. As an undergarment, Pasach wore a "chest preserver", a piece of thick cloth with a hole in the centre for his head and panels hanging down over his back and breast. On the front of this garment, near the neck, was a red stain. When the detectives took the "chest preserver" to the window for closer examination, the naked Pasach ran up to them, crying out in protest: "No, no! Medicine — medicine!" The garment was turned over to Dr Warner Shepherd for microscopic and analytic examination.

The results were disappointing to the police, for the stain was not of blood.

But Patrolmen Thomas Clifford and William Folk had greater success with the prisoner's boots and the dead girl's shoes. On Thursday, 16 December, both pairs were taken up to Wessels's cornfield and were found to fit a double track of footprints that led from the fence along Jamaica Plank Road to the vicinity of the murder site. Yellow mud on the boots appeared to match that of the field and to be quite unlike the mud on the streets of Brooklyn or lower Manhattan. The depth of the mud on the boots was similar to that of the larger footprints, and patches on the soles of the boots were plainly imprinted in the tracks.

Even more significant evidence had already been found on Rubenstein's boots. Patrolman Clifford, when he took the boots from the prisoner, had observed a scaly substance clinging to the shank of one of them. Chemistry professor Asahel Eaton discovered that the substance contained a piece of woollen fibre similar in texture to the fringe of Sarah's shawl. Eaton also found a piece of corn-husk adhering to the fibre, and determined that both the husk and the fibre were encrusted in dried blood; he also cut a radiating drop of blood from the top of one of the boots.

Superintendent Campbell questioned the prisoner, with Detective Zundt acting as interpreter. Pasach tried their patience with his meandering answers and protestations of innocence, but finally gave an account of his movements on Sunday. He had risen at 6.00 a.m. and gone to the synagogue. He stayed there until 8.00 a.m., came back to his house and breakfasted, and at 9.00 a.m. went down to Maiden Lane, intending to see a man on business. He would not identify the man, but claimed that he did not turn up. After dinner at 12.30, Rubenstein went out again, this time to see a man named

Jarmulowski on Canal Street and to walk to 32nd Street to collect a commission from William Jacobs, for whom he had sold a chain. He returned home before dark and found Sarah Alexander there. She poured him a cup of tea, and was still there when he left for evening services at the synagogue. After the services, he paid some visits on Division Street and arrived home at 8.00 p.m., when he went to bed.

To test Pasach's alibi, Campbell sent Zundt to Bayard Street to question Pasach's stepmother and sisters; the Superintendent asked an *Eagle* reporter to accompany the detective and to take notes. Zundt and the reporter found Mrs Rubenstein in a little back-room on the first floor which gave off a strong aroma of cloves; about a dozen women and twice as many children were gathered round Pasach's stepmother, "a portly dame in a black velvet sacque and a wig". Zundt spoke to her in English; he hoped that if she thought that he could not speak German, he might overhear confidential comments between her and her relatives. She told Zundt that Pasach was home all day on Sunday and was not out in the afternoon as much as half an hour. She said that Sarah Alexander came to the house at 1.00 p.m. and left at 4.00 p.m. — but, contradicting Pasach's statement that the girl had poured out tea, said that Sarah had not seen Pasach because she was upstairs and he was down in the store. Still another account of Pasach's Sunday was furnished by Mrs Rubenstein's daughter Annie. She confirmed that Sarah was at Bayard Street between 1.00 p.m. and 4.00 p.m., but told Zundt that Pasach was not home at all while she was there and that he had come in at about six o'clock. This early interview of the Rubensteins followed the same bewildering pattern as the alibi evidence that would be offered by the defence at the trial; the friends and relatives of Pasach gave inconsistent accounts of his movements on Sunday, and none of them confirmed his own version of his whereabouts, at least as it was reflected by Zundt's translation. Still, the insistence of the Rubenstein household that Pasach had made only brief excursions on Sunday posed a problem for the investigation; Zundt had ascertained that a round-trip between Bayard Street and the murder scene, via Manhattan's Grand Street ferry and the streetcar to New Lots, required more than four hours.

In the meantime, the police sought to forge an important link in the case against Rubenstein. At about 9.30 a.m. on Thursday, Detectives Zundt and William Butts, on orders from

Campbell, went to New York City with the bloody cigar-knife in their possession, hoping to find a cutler or storekeeper who had sold the weapon. By 2.00 p.m. the detectives had visited over a hundred places on Manhattan's Lower East Side without result. Although becoming footweary, they persisted, calling at a factory of a man named Eckhoff on Essex Street. After a casual glance at the knife, Eckhoff told them it was a special make and that Gustave Simon of 138 Division Street was the sole manufacturer. That address rang a bell in Zundt's mind: it was in the same area of Division Street that Rubenstein claimed to have visited on the Sunday of the crime. The detectives went immediately to Simon's address and found both him and his thirteen-year-old daughter Augusta on the premises. Without hesitation, Simon identified the knife as his, saying that three rivets in the handle were a feature peculiar to his cutlery; but he thought it must have been stolen or sold without his knowledge since it was flawed and therefore unfinished. He told the detectives that a great many Jews made purchases in his place and that he could not remember any particular customers among them.

Augusta had left the store during this conversation, but that evening, after her father reported the detective's inquiries to her, she told him that she had sold the knife to a Jewish man on last Monday week. She subsequently furnished the details of the transaction to the police. Her father and she had both been in the store, but she waited upon the man. She showed him quite a number of finished knives, but he threw them all to one side and was about to leave when he saw the rough, unfinished knife lying at the far end of the counter. Augusta told him it was a reject, but he said it would suit his purpose and bought it for twenty cents.

When the prisoner was escorted into the room where Augusta was being questioned, she nodded immediately to Zundt. He insisted that she look more closely. She had been crying from fright, but obediently dried her eyes and after an intent look "of fifteen seconds" assured Zundt that Pasach was the man who had bought the knife. The prisoner refused to lift his eyes.

So far as the Brooklyn *Eagle* was concerned, the statement from Augusta Simon completed the net of circumstantial evidence against Pasach Rubenstein for a murder that the newspaper predicted would prove one of the most extraordinary in the annals of local crime. The *Eagle* had been struck at the outset by Rubenstein's retelling of his bloody dream:

The supposition here is that, having committed the murder, he was unable to sleep, and after remaining for a time in his bedroom he sought relief by making a partial confession, like [the eighteenth-century English schoolmaster-murderer] Eugene Aram, in the narrative of a dream.

Adding to the sense of strangeness was that the defendant and victim, and most of the witnesses, were Eastern European Jews who lived in a milieu closed to the experience of the general community. Irresponsible and exploitative sectors of the press slanted their accounts to appeal to anti-foreign and anti-semitic prejudice, but the Brooklyn *Eagle* struggled to be fair without being able to divest itself of the combination of suspicion and gullibility that even the well-meaning bring to the observation of "out-groups". The ambivalent feelings of the *Eagle*'s editorial staff was evident in an article appearing the day after Rubenstein's arrest:

> In this connection it is not improper to say that such crimes as the one charged to Rubenstein are exceedingly rare among people of Hebrew descent. Whatever their shortcomings may be, strong affection for each other cannot be denied them, and a humaneness of heart that makes the shedding of human blood repugnant to an inexpressible degree. The law against murder was first given to the Jews and they have been distinguished among civilized people for their observance of it.

The *Eagle* reported that the prisoner faithfully performed his religious duties in the Raymond Street jail; with great curiosity, they watched him bind phylacteries to his left forearm and forehead, and overheard prayers that fell strangely on American ears.

The newspaper also reported the burial of Sarah Alexander at the Bayside Cemetery on the Jamaica Plank Road as if revealing to the world for the first time the exotic rites of a never-never land. No services were held over the body, and Sarah's brother and sister and two friends were the only people who followed her to the grave. The undertaker told the reporter that the Jewish religion forbade any services over those who meet a violent death. The day before, the undertaker and mourners had arrived at the morgue without a coffin; after consultation, they had gone to a carpenter's shop, and a rough box of plain wood had been hurriedly made and brought to the morgue. The *Eagle* stated that, in accordance with Mosaic law, the body was left unwashed so that the blood of the murder victim would show. The undertaker placed a white shroud over Sarah's body, dressed her in white muslin, and threw a white veil over her face. The undertaker begged the police to allow him to put the bloody clothes in the coffin, as required by tradition, but the police refused, explaining that they would be needed at the trial.

In the six weeks between his arrest and trial, Pasach Rubenstein had great difficulty in adjusting to prison life. He would not eat food prepared by the prison staff. Soon after his commitment, his sister brought him a basket of food, but Inspector Waddy would not permit it to be given to him for fear that it

Sarah Alexander and Pasach Rubenstein
Courtesy of the Brooklyn Historical Society

contained poison. Ultimately Pasach agreed to take the prison fare, but for the most part subsisted only on bread and water. Although his health visibly declined, the prison doctors were not alarmed. In fact, the main concern at the Raymond Street jail was that Pasach might attempt to cheat the gallows by suicide.

As the trial approached, journalists speculated about the motives for the New Lots murder. Although the expected arrival of Rubenstein's wife had given him a pressing reason to terminate and hide a guilty love affair, reporters hunted for more arcane roots of violence in the mores of the little-known immigrant group. On 20 December, the Brooklyn *Eagle* informed its readers that the crime had long been in contemplation and was not committed in hasty impulse. It was rumoured that as long ago as 12 November, Rubenstein had entered into an agreement to pay a "poor Israelite" $45 to assume the guilt of whatever sins Pasach might commit. The *Eagle* had been informed that such a contract was allowed by the Talmud, but greatly doubted that this could be so. In any event, the *Eagle*'s report continued, the man who had contracted to assume Pasach's future guilt reneged because of the objection of his wife, and his breach of contract came before "two rabbinical tribunals of Polish Jews". According to the *Eagle*, one rabbi, on a curious Talmudic hypothesis, decided against Rubenstein, but the second compromised the matter by allowing the scapegoat to retain his fee on condition that each day he recited a certain number of prayers on Pasach's behalf. The *Eagle* had no doubt that the crime to be vicariously atoned for was the murder of Sarah Alexander, and it opined sententiously that such a transaction was a strange thing to take place in a progressive country like America in the nineteenth century of the Christian era. The *Eagle* mentioned another related theory for the avowed purpose of expressing disbelief. It was said that Sarah Alexander, filled with religious remorse over her adulterous pregnancy, was a consenting party to her own murder: she went to the lonely "field of blood" near a cemetery where many of her people lay buried so that she might expiate her sin by the hand of her lover. The Brooklyn *Daily Sun* elaborated this hypothesis by suggesting that the murder was in fact the result of a suicide-pact, but that Pasach's failure of nerve had spared his own life. Despite its readiness to propagate these wild conjectures, the *Eagle* ultimately kept its vision of the death scene unclouded; the uplifted hands of the victim and the wound in her palm were mute evidence that she had not acquiesced in the brutal assault.

The trial of Pasach Rubenstein began at the King's County Court House in Brooklyn on Monday, 31 January 1876, with Justice Calvin E. Pratt presiding and Winchester Britton leading for the prosecution. Rubenstein had been fortunate in securing the services of one of the most eloquent advocates of the period, William Augustus Beach. Then sixty-seven, Beach had participated in many *causes célèbres* of New York; he had, for instance, represented the plaintiff in the adultery proceedings against the famed Brooklyn minister Henry Ward Beecher, and had appeared for the State in the 1873 trial of Edward Stokes for the murder of railroad robber-baron Jim Fisk. Beach's command of a vast and subtle vocabulary was the result of conscious effort which had begun with the study of tables of synonyms that his mother had placed in his hands. Though he was at his persuasive best in arguing to juries, "he could talk as sweetly to the echoing groves, with no other auditors than the dumb creatures around him, as he could in the crowded court-room, with a surging mass of people hanging with breathless interest on every word that he uttered".

The first major skirmish of the trial was signalled on the third day, 2 February, when the chemistry professor, Asahel Eaton, took the stand to explain his tests of the defendant's boots and clothing. He testified that the black splotch taken from the shank of one of the boots was dried blood, intermingled with particles of corn fibre and a piece of woolly fibre about half an inch in length; he had also detected blood on the inside of both sleeves of Rubenstein's coat. The police had asked him to compare the yellow mud taken from the crevices of Rubenstein's boots with soil specimens from the cornfield and from New York City streets, and he had found that the mud from the boots corresponded closely to the New Lots soil, which had small granules of quartz which were not found in the city.

Cross-examining, Beach established that the piece of corn husk Professor Eaton had examined microscopically was not more than an eighth, or possibly a tenth, of an inch long. The witness had identified the fibre as corn husk solely on the basis of prior experience; he had not compared the fibre with other husk; nor could he, despite Beach's insistence, explain to the jury the physical characteristics that distinguish corn husk from other vegetable fibres. Beach also attacked the witness's failure to subject the dried blood to chemical tests to confirm that it was human blood. Unruffled, Eaton explained that human blood could be distinguished from that of certain other animals whose blood corpuscles were much smaller, such as the ox, the sheep or the pig, but that once blood had dried, the difficulty of analysis was increased.

The prosecution's six witnesses who were aboard the 5.08 p.m. Broadway streetcar in Brooklyn on the night of the murder proved far less convincing than Professor Eaton. Although they identified Sarah Alexander without difficulty, they varied in their perception and memory of her male companion, and only one of them, Lizzie Koch, had picked Rubenstein out of a police line-up at the Brooklyn jail. Louisa Kerr was equally confident that Pasach was not the man in the car, who "had curly hair and did not look so old as the prisoner".

The prosecution recovered momentum, however, with the testimony of Sarah's brother, J. P. Alexander. He stated that, while Pasach assisted him in the searches for his sister on the day after her disappearance, he had told the distraught Alexander that "loafers might have dragged her away into a country place and killed her". Beach could not shake this recollection on cross-examination, but obtained the startling admission that Alexander had searched for his sister at a brothel on Elizabeth Street, a strange place to expect to find a girl whose morals the state had presented as beyond reproach.

The fourth day of the trial was its dramatic peak. Early in the session, Beach succeeded in casting some doubt on the allegation of the State that Pasach Rubenstein's wife was due to arrive soon from Europe. In cross-examination of S. Jarmulowski, a broker for a steamship line (and possibly the man Pasach claimed to have visited on Canal Street on 12 December), Beach demonstrated that the defendant's wife had long hesitated to make the crossing. Although Rubenstein had purchased a ticket for his wife's passage in November 1875, he had previously obtained a refund on a ticket bought for her in September 1874 when she refused to depart during the six-month period that the ticket was effective.

This minor mystery was soon forgotten with the appearance of a "surprise witness" for the prosecution, Solomon Kramer. A licensed peddler from Williamsburg, Brooklyn, he had met the defendant in the way of trade without knowing his name, and had conversed with him in a streetcar on 9 December. Then on Sunday, 12 December, at about 4.30 p.m., as he was passing the toll-gate in Jamaica Plank Road on his return to East New York from a funeral at Cypress Hills Cemetery, he met Rubenstein and a girl wearing a shawl. He asked Rubenstein where he was going, and Pasach replied that he was looking for a place for his cousin. Kramer laughed, saying that it was not customary to look for a place so late in the evening. He then told the girl he would find her a place and, when he asked for her residence, she gave the Alexanders' address at 30 Essex Street. The couple continued on their way and Kramer saw Rubenstein go over the fence at the Wessels farm and walk on towards the cornfield. Soon he heard a noise and the girl crying: "Fire, fire; help, help; my life is gone." Kramer claimed that on the following Tuesday, while travelling near New Lots, he was informed of the murder and observed the dead girl lying in the field. Still, it was only on the previous Friday, 28 January, that he had gone to the jail with Detective Zundt and had identified Rubenstein.

Beach subjected Kramer to a blistering cross-examination, emphasizing his long delay in contacting the authorities and demanding the details of the funeral Kramer claimed to have attended at Cypress Hills. Asked why he had not answered the girl's cries, Kramer replied: "I was scared, I kept on walking; you are not very safe out there in that part of the country about getting licked; it is a pretty dangerous place out there, and if they get somebody at night, they generally give them a licking; I am a nervous kind of man."

When the defence opened its case on 7 February, Beach paraded witnesses to undermine Kramer's doubtful story. A number of fellow-members of a fraternal society placed Kramer at a lodge-meeting late on Sunday afternoon. Functionaries of cemeteries bordering Jamaica Plank Road gave evidence indicating that the funeral described by Kramer had not taken place on 12 December. Several witnesses described him as unworthy of belief under oath, and his own brother Adolph said that Solomon had "a screw loose." His story of attending the funeral alone made no sense, Adolph explained, because the Jewish religion required a complement of ten men. Adolph had seen a paper setting out a summary of his brother's evidence before the trial; he understood that a young girl had prepared it in Detective Zundt's house.

The impeachment testimony was so overwhelming that the prosecution ultimately renounced Kramer, advising the court that it would not rely on his statements. The *Eagle*, in summar-

izing Kramer's disreputable role in the trial, strongly condemned his imposture but was more willing to blame the prisoner's friends than Detective Zundt for flimsy testimony:

> He came in like a feeble-minded, humpbacked ghost, and told his
> damning story. Then he slid off the witness stand, sneaked round
> the back of the jury box and disappeared. But he left behind him a
> powerful effect on the jury and the audience. By and by, the defence
> handled him in merciless reprisal, and showed clearly that he lied.
> He was intended for surprise, and he was one — to the prosecution
> most of all. . . . It is thought not impossible that Kramer was
> employed by the prisoner's friends to play a nice little game. . . .
> The old man was put up to give the evidence he did, only with a view
> to benefit the prisoner by having it proved beyond a peradventure
> that he lied.

With Kramer disposed of, Beach was able to return to the
main prepared lines of his defence. Dr Joseph Weiner
buttressed Beach's claim that Pasach was not in strong enough
health to have overpowered Sarah. Weiner had attended
Rubenstein in April and May and found him to be suffering
from an incurable onslaught of Bright's disease. Although he
had principally attended to his patient's kidneys, he has also
observed that Rubenstein had trouble with his lungs and had
been spitting blood.

The major emphasis of the defence was on alibi evidence. A
jewellery manufacturer, Arnold Kohn, testified that Pasach had
been in his office between three and six on the afternoon of
Monday, 6 December, the time at which little Augusta Simon
stated she had sold the murder knife to a man resembling the
defendant. Kohn fixed his memory of the date of Pasach's call by
reference to a cheque payable in gold, received from Rubenstein the same day. Pasach and he had left the office together,
the manufacturer asserted, and returned together to Bayard
Street, where Kohn had collected a $2.00 balance due to him
from the defendant.

Female members of the Rubenstein family, while differing in
details, agreed that Pasach, except for short intervals, had been
at home during the late afternoon and early evening of the fatal
Sunday. Two of the girls had gone to a wedding that afternoon
on Hester Street and when they returned in the evening Pasach
was at home, watching the women playing lotto.

Beach reinforced this family testimony with the evidence of
neighbours that they had seen Rubenstein in the Lower East

Side on the evening of the crime. Perhaps the most impressive witness of all was sixteen-year-old Dora Rubenstein, a cousin of the prisoner's family. When she finished work at 8.00 p.m. on Sunday evening, her employer sent her to Bayard Street to ask Pasach to fetch him a ladies' watch. Arriving at Pasach's home after a ten-minute walk, she found him in the front room observing the lotto game. Her employer followed her to the stand to confirm her errand. The *Eagle* referred to Dora as "singularly attractive", and opined that there was no suspicion in the mind of anyone who heard her that she was telling anything but the truth. Still, the newspaper's reporter added, the child's story went for nothing in the face of the damning evidence provided by "those miserable old boots, with the mud and the sand and the corn husks". It was "not that the jury believed Dora less, but the boots more".

Towards the end of the defence case, Pasach Rubenstein took the stand and testified briefly through an interpreter. In a barely audible voice he said that he was suffering from weak lungs, felt feeble, and had fainted the day before in court. Asked whether he had murdered Sarah, he raised his hands, crying, "Oh no!" In cross-examination, the district attorney began to question the defendant about his movements on 12 December, but when Pasach appeared physically unable to continue testifying, quickly broke off his interrogation.

In its rebuttal case, the prosecution dealt a last blow to the beleaguered defence. Beach had questioned several witnesses about a young shoemaker named Nathan Levy who lived at 83 Bayard Street, hoping to suggest that Levy had been on intimate terms with Sarah and might therefore be guilty of her murder. In support of this theory, several witnesses swore that while Levy had once worn a full beard, he had shaved off the hair at the sides of his face since the murder. On direct examination, Levy stated that he was eighteen and had never had occasion to use a razor. Beach's ineffectual cross-examination ended the defence dismally:

Q. Did you ever light the gas for her?
A. No; I only lighted the gas on our floor.
Q. Did you ever call her your girl?
A. No.
Q. Or anything like that?
A. I am engaged for the last year.

- Q. Wait one moment; answer the question; did you ever call Sarah Alexander your girl?
- A. No, never.
- Q. Do you say that you have not cut your whiskers or changed them?
- A. No, never. I have only had my hair cut, but nothing done to my face.
- Q. Have you never cut your beard with shears?
- A. No, I never had any. What is the use of shears there?

William Beach's summation for the defence was a masterpiece of his forensic art. Beginning with a traditional caution regarding the difficulties of appraising circumstantial evidence, Beach at the same time acknowledged with delicacy that circumstances of secret crimes, if logically established, do not lie.

"They are the sentinels of God," he told the jury, "stationed by his wisdom around the footsteps of guilt. In every case of crime, were it not for the imperfection of our vision and the infirmities of our powers, there are surrounding circumstances planted by the finger of God, surely revealing the offender."

Beach launched his attack on the prosecution's case with a challenge to the reliability of Detective Zundt, whom he accused of overzealousness in turning out "such a pupil as Solomon Kramer", and of mistranslation of the defendant's accounts of his movements on the day of the murder. He also emphasized that the prosecution had not established a murder motive, since there was no evidence that Rubenstein had seduced his cousin. It was clear that the death of the girl, who was "remarkably well developed in muscular power", was accomplished only after a severe struggle, and that the defendant, suffering from tuberculosis since the previous June, did not have the physical power to overcome her resistance.

Having attempted to weaken the very foundations of the prosecution, Beach turned to the circumstantial evidence of the footprints He asserted that their comparison with the boots was made for the first time on Thursday, when the thaw had changed the character of the original impressions. He dismissed Professor Eaton's analysis of the boots with contempt. The witness had identified the blood visually, without the aid of chemical analysis, and could not be certain that it was human blood or, if it was, that it had not been caused by a nose-bleed or haemorrhages from the defendant's diseased lungs. Beach offered the jury the alternative theory that the condition of Pasach's boots could be fully accounted for by his tramping through the muddy streets of New York City, where there were corn husks from mattress factories and blood from butchers' shops. Twenty times a day, he argued, Pasach had walked through his father's store, crammed with woollen fabrics with fibres like those found on his boots.

Beach attributed Rubenstein's remarkable dream to his sensitive temperament, and underscored instead the evidence that Sarah's brother had searched for her in houses of prostitution; she was proven, he averred, "to have been a night-wanderer at improper hours in the streets of New York, with unknown companions".

The defence counsel ended his argument with a summary of testimony that supported Pasach's alibi both on the murder night and at the time of the purchase of the knife. Directly confronting the possibility that the jury would discount the alibi testimony as given by Pasach's friends, relatives and co-religionists, Beach made an eloquent attack on religious prejudice:

> You may consign them all to a common grave of infamy. Discredit them if you will, because they are relatives and Jews, but it would be wise to reflect upon the justice and policy of such arbitrary condemnation. . . . You may slaughter reputation by the wholesale, but the equal and just administration of the law will not be promoted. It recognizes no distinction of race, or caste, or faith. Its courts are equally open to the Jew and the Christian. If the Jew is charged, and may not purge himself by the testimony of his brother, his condition under this boasted government of law is most deplorable.

In response, District Attorney Britton sought to defend the evidence regarding the footprints and the defendant's boots. It was colder in the country than in New York and Brooklyn, and the thaw in New Lots had not been deep enough to obscure the murderer's tracks. The yellow mud found in the crevices of Rubenstein's boots was observed by Patrolman Clifford when the boots were taken from the prisoner, and could not, as Beach had suggested, have resulted from the subsequent police experiments in the cornfield. Supporting Professor Eaton's microscopic examination of the fibre found on Rubenstein's boot, Britton ridiculed Beach's argument that his client "travels along where they kill chickens, gets a clot of blood on his boot, goes somewhere else and gets a piece of corn husk on that very spot, goes somewhere else and gets a piece of shawl also on that very spot".

Britton made the best he could of the unpersuasive identification testimony given of Sarah's companion on the streetcar. Lending new elasticity to the requirement of proof beyond a reasonable doubt, he said that when five strangers testify in court and two of them are certain that the prisoner is the man seen before, two of them uncertain, and one of them thinks he is not the man, "it is pretty safe to say he *is* the man".

The hunt for Sarah in an Elizabeth Street whorehouse did not, Britton argued, put her reputation in a bad light. Her brother feared that she had been abducted there against her will.

Turning at last to the alibi testimony offered by the defence, Britton launched into a defamatory tirade against Polish Jews. "They are dirty, ignorant, uncultivated, have no school education except what is obtained from their religious teachers, they are oppressed and despised by surrounding races. There they are isolated, having their own customs, their own laws and their own peculiar faith, and as a consequence, they become intensely clannish; they can live nowhere but among their own class; they discard from their minds as a natural result that broad fellowship which goes out to the whole human race." When Beach's associate counsel John Mott entered a mild protest that there was no evidence in the case of the characteristics or peculiarities of the Jewish people, Britton responded acidly: "I suppose, if I were talking about Napoleon Bonaparte, you could say that there was no evidence in this case of his existence."

Presiding Justice Pratt delivered an even-handed charge to the jury. While Pratt was speaking, "Mr Beach sat with those large, ox-like eyes fixed steadily on the judge — enough to make an ordinary man feel nervous, to say the least. But the judge never wavered." Regarding the alibi evidence, the judge stated that it was the duty of the jury to assume, if they could, that every witness intended to tell the truth. The judge had not intervened in the interchange between Britton and Mott regarding the prosecutor's slurs against Polish Jews, but he left no doubt concerning his views on the issue:

> It is true, as stated by the counsel for the prisoner, that the law throws its shield around every person charged with crime. It respects no person, age or condition; the high, the low, the rich, the poor, the white, the black, the Jew, the Gentile, when they come to

the bar of justice, are entitled to the same consideration, the same proof, and the same measure of justice; all are alike under its protection and amenable to its demands.

The jury retired, and after an hour and twenty minutes rendered a verdict of guilty of murder in the first degree. The prisoner was brought forward to the rail and asked whether he had anything to say as to why sentence should not be pronounced. The Brooklyn *Eagle* describes the scene that followed:

He raised his hands, threw back his head, fixed his gleaming eyes on the judge, and cried, in a piercing tone: "I don't want to give up my blood."

Then, with his eyes flashing, his white teeth glistening between his pallid lips, and his whole frame quivering with almost ferocious energy, he suddenly placed his hands to the sides of his head, and drew forth his hair, which was rolled up behind his ears.

Holding the long, wavy locks which descended from his temples in each hand, and shaking them towards heaven, he almost shrieked:

"This is my witness, before Jehovah, that I never put hand on a woman! I am innocent, and you will find it out. I can show where I was all that day! This is my witness!"

The *Eagle* reporter was stunned by Rubenstein's outburst, seeing it as a manifestation of the violence of which he was capable:

When he sat down, a glimpse of the Rubenstein who was in the cornfield at East New York, rather than the Rubenstein at the prison and the court-room, seemed to have been revealed to the spectators. The scene over, Rubenstein relapsed into [his former weak condition] and the chances are that death in the prison, rather than on the scaffold, will overtake him. Law and justice have, however, been vindicated.

Despite the valiant efforts of William Beach, it is difficult not to agree that justice was done by the jury if not by the district attorney's argument. After the passage of a century, however, the joy that the *Eagle* found in retribution can be tempered with sympathy for Rubenstein. It seems doubtful that he committed the crime to avoid the wrath of his wife, who appeared to be in no hurry to join him in New York. In view of his failing health, the elimination of his pregnant lover could not have won him any substantial worldly benefit. The fact that Sarah's brother searched for her in a brothel may indicate that the girl's morals were not all that they seemed, and the New Lots murder might therefore have been a crime of jealousy. More likely, though, the ailing Pasach could not, even for the brief period of life that remained to him, face the religious guilt and communal shame that would have followed the birth of Sarah's child.

Rubenstein's execution was set for 24 March 1876, but was deferred. On 8 May, a writ of error and a motion for a new trial were set down for argument before the General Term of the New York Supreme Court. The following day it was reported from Raymond Street jail that Rubenstein had died of pulmonary tuberculosis (which the prison authorities had somehow never diagnosed), hastened by abstention from nourishment and nervous prostration. The Brooklyn *Eagle* had the last word, saying of the pending appeal that "a Higher Court has cognizance of the case, and the appeal to human ears will avail nothing".

The Tragedy of Amy Robsart

Louise Swanton

"NONE BUT but the brave deserve the fair" might well have been the motto of Robert Dudley, future Earl of Leicester. Not only was he one of the handsomest youths of a day that abounded in splendid-looking young Englishmen, but, evil as he seems to have been from childhood, he was yet a remarkably courageous man.

According to tradition, he first met the girl who was to become his wife when he was on his way to suppress a rising known in history as Kett's Rebellion. He passed by Siderstern, the beautiful castle of Sir John Robsart in Norfolk, and there, while being hospitably entertained by one who was still a stranger to him, he was so enchanted with the loveliness of his host's daughter that he decided to marry her.

That lovely Amy Robsart was probably equally attracted by the handsome youth may be taken for granted. For one thing, the young soldier came of a family far more famed in the annals of England than were the Robsarts, and there was an aroma of sinister romance about him. Both his father and his grandfather had been executed for high treason, and it was probably known to the girl that he had been a friend and playfellow of the Princess Elizabeth in whom the whole of England was beginning to take an intense interest.

But whether Amy knew the little there was to be known at that time concerning Robert Dudley, we cannot doubt that her father, Sir John, went to the trouble of making close inquiries concerning the young man who came asking for his daughter's hand in marriage. Amy was a very great heiress, for her father had no other children, with the exception of an illegitimate son named Arthur Robsart, who played a certain role in her tragically brief life and sad death. Her mother had been a widow when she married Sir John Robsart, and Amy had two half-brothers and two half-sisters named Appleyard.

Sir John was Steward of Castle Rising, and a great personage in his way, and when it became clear to him that his daughter and young Dudley were so violently attracted the one to the other as to make a marriage not only probable but desirable, he brought the girl to Sheen, where Edward VI then held his court. It was there that the wedding took place on 4 June 1550, the bride being then eighteen, the bridegroom a year older. The marriage was made the occasion of a splendid festival, as was noted by the young King in his diary:

> Sir Robert Dudley, third son of the Earl of Warwick, married today Sir John Robsart's daughter, after which marriage there were certain gentlemen that did strive who could first take away a goose's head which was hung alive between two great posts.

It was a brutal age; men, and women too, were hideously cruel not only to animals but to one another. It was quite an easy matter to hire an assassin to do away with one's enemy, and everyone in the court world feared poison. Indeed, to the timorous this terror of the poisoned cup shadowed the whole of their day-to-day life. Wise folk warned each other against drinking any kind of liquid not prepared by a trusted hand. The greater the position, the greater the danger run by its possessor. To give an example: the Duke of Norfolk had a devoted body-servant who alone was allowed to have anything to do with his food.

But at the time that Amy Robsart became Lady Robert Dudley, neither she nor her youthful husband could have felt afraid of sudden death, for though they were an important young couple, neither stood in anybody's light.

Sir John Robsart, who apparently adored his daughter, gave the young couple Siderstern. This is proved by more than one letter which was written by Lord Robert to the steward there.

Time went on, and Amy grew even more beautiful. Like so many lovely women, she spent a great deal of her thought and time over her dress. Never was feminine, or, for the matter of that, masculine apparel more splendid or more costly than in those days. It was quite a usual thing for a lady's gown to be thickly embroidered with precious stones and pearls; but though the Lady Robert Dudley spent great sums each year in adorning herself, she seems never to have been in the slightest difficulty for money. Soon her father died, and so she became even wealthier than she had been before.

There was, however, one terrible sorrow in her life. She intensely wished to have a child — and her husband naturally desired an heir. But they remained childless.

In those days, what we now call a quiet, peaceful life was out of the question, even for so fortunate a young woman as was Amy Robsart, and she had only been married three years when her husband was put in the Tower for having taken part in the Lynn Rebellion. Amy, though then only twenty-one, proved that she was a woman of great spirit and courage. She left her country-seat, after having made all arrangements for the carrying on of her husband's business, and, hurrying up to London, obtained, with a great deal of difficulty, leave to go and see him in his prison.

Eventually Dudley was released, and once more the young couple took up their residence in the country, where they lived in great state and in apparent amity, though later certain people declared that they had not even then been on good terms the one with the other.

At last there came a day, great in the annals of English history, which must have been marked with a black stone in the annals of poor Amy Robsart. On 17 November 1558, Queen Elizabeth ascended the throne, and at once the maiden sovereign showed her old playfellow the greatest favour. Indeed, one of her first acts as Queen was that of making Robert Dudley Master of the Horse, and immediately afterwards he was created a Knight of the Garter. In one of the few letters written by her which survive, Amy Robsart speaks of her husband as being "sore troubled with weighty affairs". This really meant that Queen Elizabeth could hardly bear him even then out of her sight, and very soon Her Majesty's passionate interest in this, the best-looking and the cleverest of the younger men of her court, began to attract the attention of all the foreign envoys, and also aroused the greatest anger among the Queen's own nobles.

The ambassadors and foreign envoys were delighted to get hold of something so exciting and so scandalous to write home about, and among them all by far the most lively chronicler was the Spaniard, Quadra. It is to his dispatches that we are indebted for many a piece of gossip.

The Queen was so familiar with Dudley, even in public, that those about her were shocked and surprised, and it began to be whispered throughout the court that if only Lord Robert could get rid of his wife, he might well aspire to the position of Prince Consort — or even King Consort, Quadra early formed a bad opinion of the favourite, and in one of his letters he wrote: "Lord Robert is the worst young fellow I have ever encountered. He is heartless, spiritless, treacherous, and violent. Every day he presumes more and more, and it is now said that he means to divorce his wife."

The same rumour seems to have reached the Duke of Norfolk, who wrote to a friend: "Lord Robert shall never die in his bed unless he gives over his preposterous pretensions."

Evil gossip soon spread, even among the humblest folk of the realm, and a certain Anne Dowe of Brentford was solemnly tried and sent to prison for having been heard to say that the Queen had had a child by Lord Robert Dudley. The great statesman, Cecil, Lord Burleigh, threatened to resign if Her Majesty insisted on treating Dudley with such marked favour. Though no one said anything in the presence of the Queen, it was openly declared that Dudley was not only master of the business of the State, but of the person of the Queen, and Cecil did not hesitate to tell the Spanish Ambassador that he could not help suspecting that they — meaning his sovereign and her lover — were thinking of destroying Lord Robert's wife.

There was secret talk of getting rid of Dudley by poison, and his sister declared to Quadra that there was a plot to poison her brother and the Queen at a splendid banquet which was to be given to the sovereign by the Duke of Norfolk's son. Quadra wrote home with evident enjoyment: "In Lord Robert it is easy to recognize the future King; but I am mistaken if the English will stand so crooked a business. There is not a man or woman who does not cry out on the Queen and on Lord Robert with disgust and indignation." More and more serious grew the scandal, and at last Dudley entirely gave up going to Norfolk, where his wife lived a sad and lonely life.

But in the summer of 1560, Elizabeth having then been nearly two years on the throne, Lord Robert suddenly informed his wife that he wished her to move to Cumnor Place, a splendid country house near Oxford, which had been, before the Reformation, the principal country seat of the Abbot of Abingdon. Amy seems to have gone there unsuspectingly. When she first saw Cumnor she must have thought it a more attractive place for her to live in than her Norfolk home, if only because it was nearer London and the court. It was a beautiful place, famous for its lovely gardens and capacious fishponds, and at that time belonged to Dr Owen, Queen Elizabeth's body physician. It was taken from him by Anthony Forster, a creature and hanger-on of Dudley's. His official title was Comptroller of the Household.

Probably because she was herself a woman of great wealth, Amy Robsart lived at Cumnor in considerable state; she had a great many servants, some of whom were devoted to her. But she was also compelled to harbour under her roof not only Forster, but also a man called Verney, who was another of Dudley's creatures and already noted for doing his dirty work. As a kind of lady-in-waiting there was Mrs Owen; also Mrs Oddingsells, Forster's mistress. After a short time Amy seems to have become exceedingly uneasy. She doubtless heard some of the rumours concerning her husband's connection with the Queen, and a cruel or over-candid friend may have told her that, were she only out of the way, Lord Robert might aspire to be virtual King of England.

As an old ballad — which must have been written soon after her death — put it:

Now nought was heard beneath the skies,
The sounds of busy life were still,
Save an unhappy lady's sighs
That issued form that lonely pile.

No more thou com'st with lover's speed
Thy once beloved bride to see,
But be she live or be she dead
I fear stern Earl's same to thee.
Last night as sad I chanced to stray,
The village death-bell smote my ear,
They winking aside and seemed to say
"Countess, prepare — thy end is near."

Meanwhile, on 4 September of that same year, 1560, the Queen told one of the foreign envoys that Lord Robert's wife was exceedingly ill, indeed dying, if not dead. She was, as a matter of fact, quite well. The envoy, himself a shrewd man, in the secret dispatch in which he put on record the Queen's curious confidence, observed that he did not think that even in the case of poor Amy's death, Her Majesty would marry Dudley.

By the evening of the 8th, four days after the Queen had said Lady Robert Dudley was ill, Amy Robsart was lying dead at Cumnor Hall.

Sunday, 8, September, was a fine day, and early on, according to later reports, the wife of the Queen's favourite sent off all her servants to Abingdon Fair. That some of the household must have remained at home is obvious from the fact that Amy Robsart and Mrs Owen dined together; but there is no record of what happened after dinner, and when the servants came back from the fair they found their mistress lying dead on the floor of the hall at the foot of the great staircase. It was apparently assumed that she had slipped and, falling down, struck her head, and so killed herself.

It is said that within three days there was no village in England where the terrible news was not known and being eagerly discussed, the theory of death by accident being scornfully dismissed, and Dudley named as the contriver of his wife's death.

Now let us consider how the news reached the court. Amy Robsart was found dead, as we know, on the evening of the 8th, a Sunday. On Monday, the 9th, Dudley was in attendance on Queen Elizabeth at Windsor, when he was told that one Bowes, whom he probably knew as a member of his wife's household, desired to see him on urgent business.

He left the Queen's presence and was at once told of his wife's death. Not only did he seem prostrated with horror and with grief, but he exclaimed to those about him that he felt sure she had been done to death, and that he would be accused of having compassed her destruction!

It was thought by those at court that he would at once leave for Cumnor, but instead of doing that, he contented himself with sending messengers to his wife's various relations in Norfolk, and he wrote a singular letter to a friend and cousin named Thomas Blount. In this letter he mentioned the malicious talk which he knew a wicked world would spread about him, and most solemnly did he enjoin Blount to open an inquiry into his wife's death. He begged him to hasten to Cumnor, there to see the coroner, and to help the latter in choosing a jury composed of discreet and substantial men, adding that the body was to be viewed by them. He asked Blount to give him a true and long report of the whole matter, and, especially, to tell him whether in his opinion Amy's death had come by evil chance or by villainy. He ended his letter, "Your loving friend, and kinsman much perplexed" and in a postscript explained that he had asked his brother-in-law, Appleyard, also to attend the inquest.

It is impossible to tell whether this letter was written in sincerity, or whether Dudley wished Blount to read between the lines. Be that as it may, Blount, instead of going straight to Cumnor, put up at an inn at Abingdon, in order that he might hear what ordinary folk were saying concerning the event. On arriving there, he went down into what we should now call the coffee-room and proceeded to listen. But he heard very little; even the landlord, whom he seems to have cross-examined, declared that while some were disposed to say well, others were disposed to say evil. Blount then went off to Cumnor Hall, and from there wrote a long letter to Dudley, but which contained practically nothing new as to Amy's death. On the other hand, it is in this letter that we find the first mention of Anthony Forster as being involved in the tragedy. He was, as we know, Dudley's Controller, and some people believe to this day that he killed Amy Robsart with his own hand. Blount also mentioned Mrs Oddingsells, whom he described as "the widow that liveth with Anthony Forster".

Now it is significant that, with the exception of Blount's letters to Dudley, every document concerning the inquiry into Amy Robsart's death was destroyed. But there seems no doubt that some of the jury were inclined to consider Forster guilty; and, years later, Appleyard, who was at the inquest, admitted that he had "covered her death for Leicester's sake". Whether he did this for Leicester's or the Queen's sake, the fact remains that he was loaded with favours, both by Her Majesty as well as by the man whom this death had freed, for the rest of his life.

Once the inquest was over, Amy was quietly buried in Cumnor churchyard; but a little later her body was re-buried in St Mary's Church, Oxford, with the greatest pomp and a splendid ceremonial.

Meanwhile, all through England there was murmuring — not only against Dudley but against the Queen. A famous preacher

— the Master of Sherborne Hospital, and a Canon of Durham — actually addressed a letter to two members of the Queen's household, in which he boldly said that "here in these parts semeth unto me to be grievous and dangerous suspicion and mutterings of the death of her who was the wife of my Lord Dudley". He asked the two gentlemen to whom he wrote, Sir Francis Knollys and Sir William Cecil, whether there could not be further inquiry into the mysterious matter.

A story which became widely current told how a certain Dr Baily of Oxford had been asked that very summer to prescribe a potion for Lady Robert Dudley, and that without seeing her. He refused to do this, saying bluntly that he might after be hanged, "to give a colour to the sin of those who ordered the potion".

It was further declared that when Lord Robert's own chaplain, Dr Babington, was preaching Amy's funeral sermon, in Oxford, he tripped when commending to the prayers of the faithful "that lady so pitifully *murdered*," instead of saying "slain".

Queen Elizabeth, though it is clear that she was delighted that her favourite was at last free, was evidently made uneasy by the indignation Amy Robsart's death had aroused. She sent for the foreign envoys, and smilingly informed them that she no longer thought of marrying an Englishman, but intended to choose a foreign potentate for Prince or King Consort. Not a single one of them was deceived by her ruse, and they all wrote home saying that within a very short time the Queen's forthcoming marriage to Dudley would be announced.

All the time-servers crowded eagerly round the favourite, and he received many letters of condolence. To give an example, the English Ambassador in Paris sent him a very moving epistle — but though he wrote most pathetically of "the cruel mischance late happened to my Lady, your late Bedfellow, to your discomfort", he wrote at the same time a secret letter to Cecil imploring him to try and stop the Queen from marrying Dudley. Indeed, his exact words were that if the marriage came to pass "our Sovereign will be discredited, contemned and neglected, our country ruined, undone, and made prey". He was not even content with doing that, for he also wrote a letter to a friend of his who was English Ambassador in Spain, saying that though it might be believed in England that Lady Robert had by mischance broken her neck, it was openly declared by the French that her neck had been broken for her. He did not add what is undoubtedly true — that the French court believed that Queen Elizabeth had secretly married Lord Robert immediately after Amy's death.

Although the Queen had not married Dudley, she behaved as if they were already married lovers. That Dudley fully believed he was going to become Prince Consort is proved by a curious circumstance: namely, that his brother-in-law, Sir Henry Sidney, sought out the Spanish Ambassador, Quadra, and told him in confidence that Amy Robsart's death had been a natural one, and that the Queen and Lord Robert were now lovers intending honest marriage. He further declared that he himself had examined into the whole circumstances of Lady Robert Dudley's tragic end, and that he had satisfied himself that she had been killed by falling down the stairs.

To that Quadra replied that, though it might be quite true, Lord Robert would encounter great difficulty in making people believe it; he added significantly that if the lady had been murdered, God and man would both punish so abominable a crime. Sir Henry Sidney, in no way turned from his purpose by Quadra's words, then astounded him by hinting that if the King of Spain would uphold Elizabeth in this matter of her marriage to Dudley, she might seriously consider, in exchange, re-establishing the Roman Catholic religion in England.

Four months after his wife's death — to be precise, on 13 February 1561 — Dudley himself sought out Quadra and proposed the same bargain, and two days later Elizabeth sent for the ambassador and had a most strange conversation with him; from what we know of her nature, it is impossible not to believe that the record which survives of their talk is substantially correct.

She began by saying that though she could not deny that she had a strong regard for the many qualities she saw in Lord Robert, she had not yet resolved to marry either him or *any* man. Even so, she felt day by day and more and more the want of a husband, and there were times when she could not help thinking that her people would prefer to see her married to an Englishman rather than to a foreigner — but that she was open to persuasion.

Now Quadra was impressed both by the bargain which had been half-proposed to him as to the restoration of the old faith, and also by the Queen's strange confidences, and in June, being alone with the two lovers in a barge, he said to the Queen that he wondered why Her Majesty did not shake off the tyranny of those about her and, while restoring the true religion and good order, marry whom she pleased.

Nothing came of this advice, though Elizabeth went on being extremely intimate with Dudley. Then, after having gone to a good deal of trouble to make Quadra understand how far removed were her private apartments from those of the favourite, she suddenly declared that Dudley's rooms were not healthy, and caused him to be moved to a storey of the palace just above her own apartments.

But the weeks lengthened into months, the months into years, and though the Queen heaped favours on the now Earl of Leicester, she would not make him Prince Consort. Small wonder that he grew morose and, though in the full enjoyment of immense material prosperity, more and more revengeful towards those whom he thought had done him an ill, even in the distant past. He remembered for years any injury done him, and accordingly all those at Court became exceedingly afraid of him. No one dared assail him openly, but everyone in secret spoke ill of him, and a certain judge observed, "If I should commit to prison everyone who spoke evil of Leicester there would have to be as many prisons in London as there are dwelling-houses."

Leicester had an exceptional knowledge of poisons, and it is believed that he caused the death of Throckmorton, the ambassador who, while writing so touching a letter of condolence to him on the death of Amy, had written at the same time two other letters deprecating the thought of his marriage to the Queen. Throckmorton died just after he had been to dinner with Leicester; when he was seized with frightful pains, he called his household round him, informed them that he had been poisoned by the man with whom he had just dined, and declared him to be "the wickedest, most perilous and perfidious man under Heaven".

More than one man waited till he was on his deathbed to say what he thought of Leicester. Thus one, when dying, declared: "He will be too hard for you all — you know not the beast as well as I do!"

Women were his great preoccupation and interest in life. A friend of Leicester's wrote: "His Lordship has a special fortune in that when he desires any woman's favour, whatever person standeth in his way has the luck to die quickly." This "luck" is said to have befallen Lord Sheffield, with whose wife Leicester was for some time in love. He was so powerful that when one of his creatures, an Italian called Julio, who was supposed to be a master of the art of poisoning, committed bigamy, his patron quarrelled with the Archbishop of Canterbury, and declared that Julio had a right to as many wives at once as he liked.

At last growing weary of the shilly-shallying ways of the Queen, he secretly married Lady Lettice Devereux. After a while, one of his enemies told the Queen of this. She fell into a terrible rage and talked of sending him to the Tower — but then contented herself by banishing the new Lady Leicester from Court.

However, fate was lying in wait for Elizabeth and Dudley. Twenty-four years after the death of Amy Robsart, there was printed in Belgium a strange and terrible book called *Leicester's Commonwealth*. This indictment of the man who had been Amy Robsart's husband, what would now be called a fearful libel, was believed to be the work of the Jesuit, Father Parsons, helped maybe by Cecil, Lord Burleigh. On the title-page was the text from Job: "The Heavens shall reveal his iniquity, and the earth shall rise up against him."

Many copies of the book were smuggled into England and were read there with such absorbed excitement and interest that the Queen in Council made a pronouncement that "The books and libels against the Earl of Leicester are most malicious, false and scandalous, and such as none but an incarnate devil himself could dream to be true". But in spite of the fact that all the coasts of England were watched, so that copies should not get into the kingdom, *Leicester's Commonwealth* was soon a "best seller". Innumerable manuscript copies of the work were made; at the present time, there are many more manuscript copies that have survived from far-off date than there are volumes of the printed book.

The writer was a master of English and of invective, and it may be doubted if there was ever such a vindictive attack written on any human being. Not only is Leicester described as being "full of dissimulation, hypocrisy, adultery, falsehood, treachery, rebellion, treason, cowardice, atheism and what not", but he is plainly accused of having murdered his wife.

The anonymous writer tells at length the story of Amy's death, declaring that at first Leicester had intended that she

should be poisoned, and that Verney should carry out the fell design. Dr Baily of Oxford was to be the actual instrument, and as he refused, Leicester left the manner of her death to the discretion of her murderer.

But the author of *Leicester's Commonwealth* did not go into such detail as did a subsequent author, Ashmole, who, though he took a great deal of material from the "Commonwealth", either invented certain passages or heard what he put in them from old people who survived to his day. According to him, Amy was stifled in bed: after this had been done, the murderer broke her neck and flung her downstairs, hoping that the world would accept her death as a mischance.

Leicester, however, was not without his defenders. His sister's son, Sir Philip Sidney, wrote an answer to the "Commonwealth", but this work is worthless from the point of view of proof, for it does not attempt to refute the statements in the book. Nearly a hundred years after the first publication of the "Commonwealth", the work was reprinted, and again was widely read. Strangely enough, a serious attempt was made by the government, even then, to suppress the book. But in our own century a fine edition of *Leicester's Commonwealth* has been printed, with an excellent introduction by the Librarian of the Lambeth Public Library.

It was Sir Walter Scott who, in his novel *Kenilworth*, made alive for millions of readers the beautiful and moving figure of Amy Robsart. But the book is not in any sense history. Sir Walter altered indefensibly the character of Forster, and Kenilworth did not become the property of Lord Leicester till years after Amy's death.

Even so, Amy owes her present fame to Scott. In France, Germany and Italy, she is a heroine of romance. An opera has been written round her tragic story, and she is enshrined in many a heart to whom even our great Queen Elizabeth is but a name.

A Ritual Murder

Rayner Heppenstall

IN THE small village of Uruffe in the Lorraine province of north-eastern France lived the Fays family, modest folk with daughters aged nineteen and seventeen, and twins aged nine. The elder daughter, Régine, worked at the glassworks in Vannes-le-Châtel, nearby and not very much larger. By the late summer of 1956, it could no longer be concealed from Madame Fays that Régine was pregnant. She refused to say who was the father. No doubt it was some young man at the glassworks, though in a neighbourhood like that not even young workmen were anonymous. The Fays were good Catholics and collectively amiable. It was a Catholic village, with a calvary by the roadside not far out. The *curé*, Guy Desnoyers, was a man in his early thirties, of peasant stock, remarkable neither for spiritual fervour (his sick, saintly predecessor had died at the altar) nor for intellectual distinction, but always active in good works, organizing amateur theatricals, choir outings and even excursions to the remote seaside. All doors were open to him. He was welcome at every table.

Not that the breath of scandal had quite failed to touch him in the past. A girl from the glassworks, for instance, had gone away to somewhere in the south of France to be cured of fatty anaemia or sprue, one symptom of which is a protuberant stomach. At the same time, the priest had been absent from his parish. An older woman said that the girl had in fact been pregnant and had gone away to have either the baby or an abortion and that he was the father. He had threatened her with proceedings at law, and she had withdrawn the allegation. When it turned out to be true that the girl had borne a child, a diocesan emissary had appeared from Nancy, but reported back to his bishop that the culprit had evidently been not the priest himself but a cousin of his who had been staying at the presbytery. The scandal had died down. It was clearly a good-natured community. The *curé d'Uruffe* had been lucky in his parishioners.

For he was the father of Régine Fays' unborn child. She would not divulge the fact, but neither would she go away or have an abortion. He was afraid that the child might conspicuously resemble him. Régine was already eight months gone. On Sunday, 2 December 1956, he announced to his flock that there would be no church services for a few days, as he felt in need of rest and, after a visit to Nancy the following day, proposed to stay for two nights with his brother at Haplemont. The following evening, he drove over from Nancy to meet Régine Fays by the calvary. She got into the car, and they turned along the Baudricourt road, stopping again less than a mile and a half from the village. The girl again refused to go away and have the baby elsewhere. Why should she, since her family were prepared to make it welcome? He wanted to absolve her. She said she had forgiven him, but he could keep his absolution. The crime would no doubt have been even more "ritual" than it was if he had given her absolution, for we may suppose that he would then have shot her while she was kneeling. Instead, she got out of the car and said she would walk home. As soon as her back was turned, he took a 6·35 mm automatic from the glove compartment, and she was less than two yards in front of him when a bullet entered her head. The priest turned back and switched his lights off.

In the dark, on the frozen verge, the rites were performed. Later that evening, the telephone rang in a house at Haplemont. The call was from Uruffe. The caller, a young woman, wished to speak to the Reverend Father Desnoyers, the subscriber's brother, Guy. The caller was Régine's friend, Michelle, none other than the girl whose child by the priest was growing up elsewhere. Régine had gone out at 6.00 p.m. Now it was 10.00 p.m., and she had not returned. The Fays were out of their minds with worry. Would he come? He got out the car and drove to Uruffe, where he called on the mayor and obtained permission to ring his church bell as though for a fire. A hundred villagers turned out. Their parish priest and the mayor split them up into search parties and sent them off in various directions. Father Desnoyers telephoned for a doctor from Vaucouleurs to come to Madame Fays, whose heart was weak. Then he took Michelle into the car and himself drove slowly along the Baudricourt road. It was 2.30 a.m. There was something untoward on the grass verge. He reversed. There, in the headlights, lay a young woman's body, its clothes stripped off, the belly ripped open, near her a baby, pierced to the heart, its face a mass of blood.

The two got out of the car. We do not know whether the girl shrieked. We do know that the priest took off his cloak and spread it over the dead mother and her dead premature child and also that, after he had done this, he put his hands under the garment and moved the child's body closer to the mother's. We know that he said, "Let us pray!" and himself knelt and that he distinguishably recited the *De profundis*. We do not know just how quickly others were on the scene, but we know that it was not long and that they included the doctor from Vaucouleurs and Monsieur Fays. The priest said: "Poor Régine, I hope she had time to prepare herself for death." He told her father that he was sure it could not be suicide. He said that he must now go and break the news to her mother, but the doctor intervened. It was *his* duty, he said. Madame Fays was his patient, and her heart might not stand it.

There seems to be some little doubt also about the point at which, and to whom, Desnoyers first intimated that he knew something about the matter but that he was bound by the seal of the confessional. This could only be taken to mean that he knew who the father of Régine Fays' baby was and that that man would turn out to be the murderer. At daybreak, he was in his presbytery, being questioned (it was he, after all, who had found the bodies) by a warrant officer of the *gendarmerie*, to whom one of his men presently brought a spent cartridge found at the scene of the crime. In the absence of a ballistics *expertise*, it could at least be said that this was of 6·35 calibre and that it was for a weapon of that calibre that the priest held a licence. He admitted his responsibility. He also produced a knife and said that the handkerchief with which he had wiped it would be found in the graveyard at Haplemont.

It was noon, and the angelus was ringing, when Guy Desnoyers, *curé d'Uruffe*, in an ordinary suit and open-necked shirt, handcuffed, was ready to leave his presbytery for the last time. As the door opened to let the *gendarmerie* and their prisoner out, a villager of good sense, standing outside, begged them not to come out for a moment, as the children would just be leaving school. They waited and then took him to the town hall. The examining magistrate, who had driven out from Nancy, was a woman. The priest made a statement on oath. He had extracted the child from its mother's womb to baptise it.

Then he had stabbed it from the back and slashed the face to remove anything tell-tale from its features. Even Marcel Jouhandeau,[1] who, I should have thought, would be sensible to just such details, does not say or surmise with what water the sacrament was performed. There would be some in the car's radiator, of course. The priest might have brought water with him, ready blest, in a bottle. He might, with the heat of his fingers, have melted sufficient hoar frost off the grass. At any rate, the child's soul was safe. And Desnoyers had not, he was careful to insist, severed the umbilical cord, though if that is either a theological or a legal point, it escapes me.

The bishop's palace in Nancy issued a statement which, in the United Kingdom, would have exposed the bishop to proceedings for contempt of court.

> Public opinion has been deeply shocked to hear of the tragedy which has just occurred in a parish of this diocese. This monstrous act defies understanding. Human justice must now follow its course.
>
> We share the grief of a family so fearfully tried, and, from the bottom of our heart, we must express a deep sense of humiliation that such a crime should have been commited by one of our people.
>
> In the face of deeds which beggar human imagination, Christians, nevertheless, are not left without resource. It remains a comfort to us that, before God and man, we may still confidently pray for the victim and ourselves expiate this man's guilt.

The Canon who conducted Régine's and the baby's funeral service pointed out that among the Apostles there had been Judas and that the shame of this act struck not only at the priesthood and the Church but at the whole human race. The Fays family set up a tombstone over the grave. Upon it, their daughter was described as having died murdered by the vicar of her parish.

At Nancy, in January 1958, the former parish priest of Uruffe was tried before a jury of nine, the number of jurors at a French criminal trial having been raised by two in a recent promulgation, to be embodied in the new Code de Procédure Pénale which, the following year, would supersede the old Code d'Instruction Criminelle, encumbered with a hundred and fifty years' amendments. The priest was defended, *ex officio*, by the

1. Author of *Trois Crimes Rituels*, Paris 1962.

leader of the Meurthe-et-Moselle bar association, from which it may be inferred that no prominent criminal defence lawyer had been willing to accept a brief on behalf of a defendant so universally execrated. As he pleaded guilty, there would in effect have been no trial in a British court, but, although the expression *plaider coupable* has come into use, it means little in France, where the whole case must be heard and the accused defended. This, I am bound to say, strikes me as more reasonable than our own rule. It is not at all uncommon for a man to confess to a murder he has not committed, and it is at least conceivable that, in the United Kingdom, he should be found guilty (and that some of his predecessors may have been hanged) entirely on the basis of such false admissions, whether these were prompted by hysteria, exhibitionism, a remarkable death-wish or (now) a taste for prison, or by a firm determination to shield someone else.

Among the murderous priests in French criminal history, we may be sure that *le curé d'Uruffe* will not be forgotten. The most famous of his predecessors are, I suppose, Fathers Mingrat, Delacollonge, Verger, Auriol, Boudes and Bruneau, whose crimes were committed between 1821 and 1894. All but Father Verger (whose vow greatly bothered him) had recklessly broken their vows of celibacy, though only Fathers Mingat and Delacollonge murdered the women with whom they had sinned. The only two to be executed were those who had murdered other priests, in Father Verger's case his archbishop, in Father Bruneau's the elderly vicar to whom he acted as curate (in English and indeed in Anglican terms, for in French the parish priest is the *curé* and any assistant he may have his *vicaire*). Though it did not affect their position before courts of law, this may have made a great difference to Catholic jurors. A priest may, it appears, be deprived *a divinis* only if he denies the doctrine or defies the authority of the Church. Verger had been suspended from his priestly functions before he stabbed Monseigneur Sibour in a Paris church, and, as he struck, he shouted a controversial anti-Marian slogan. When he came up for trial and sentence, he was therefore no longer a priest. The position of Father Bruneau is perhaps more obscure, but no doubt to murder your immediate superior in the hierarchy shows some lack of obedience. Like Fathers Mingrat, Delacollonge, Auriol and Boudes, Father Desnoyers remained both orthodox and submissive. His bishop could not quite disown him. As he proclaimed in his last words from the dock, he remained a priest.

His orthodoxy had, indeed, been made quite plain by the sheer horror of his actions. He had wished to absolve the mother before he shot her, and he had ripped the child from her womb in order to baptise it before it died. Throughout his trial, he had held a crucifix in his hands. The prosecution demanded his head, of course. The jury refused it by finding extenuating circumstances.

There are, it seems, certain types of case in which a reprieved murderer's fellow-prisoners are always anxious to remedy the law's omission. In British prisons, child-murderers are said to stand in particular danger. "They'll get him," it is said, "as surely as a cat will get a canary." That, one understands, is why Hindley and Brady were long kept in a kind of solitary confinement and are so glad to see Lord Longford. At Loos, where the former parish priest of Uruffe began his life sentence, the matter was no doubt further complicated by the notorious anti-clericalism of the French industrial proletariat. At any rate, he was considered to be in danger of his life at Loos and was moved to St Malo, where he was made librarian.

The Peasenhall Case

William Henderson

THERE ARE many remarkable features connected with the murder of Rose Harsent and the subsequent trials of William Gardiner for the crime. An almost impenetrable atmosphere of mystery surrounds the case from beginning to end, and there are certain psychological considerations which are more attractive than those arising out of most murders.

The story opens in the pleasant little Suffolk village of Peasenhall, which lies north of Ipswich, near the old town of Saxmundham. Here William Gardiner occupied a double-fronted cottage in the Main Street. He was married, with a family, a reliable workman who held the position of foreman of the carpenters employed at the Peasenhall Drill Works, where agricultural implements were manufactured, and who had represented his employers at the Paris Exhibition. A dark, swarthy-complexioned man of heavy build, he was said to be descended from Huguenot ancestors who had taken refuge in our eastern shires. He was, to all appearances, a deeply religious man; an active member of the Primitive Methodist Congregation at the neighbouring village of Sibton, where he acted as assistant steward, treasurer, Sunday-school superintendent, and choirmaster. Laborious days in the workshop and innumerable evenings sacrificed to chapel business had established him in a position of honourable distinction in Peasenhall.

An insight into his character is given by his solicitor, who says that, during nine months' association with him, Gardiner invariably told the truth; his honesty and reliability as a workman were established beyond dispute; and, notwithstanding his excessive claims to familiarity with the Almighty, he was a truly religious man. So far as his domestic relations were concerned, he had provided and maintained a comfortable home for his family, and in that home he was the dominant figure. Upon the whole, he was a man with a good character and an excellent

Peasenhall

record — a man not greatly liked, but regarded with respect by all who knew him.

The character of Rose Harsent, on the other hand, was not above reproach. She was a domestic servant employed at Providence House,[1] Peasenhall, an attractive girl of East Anglian type, something of a village belle. It would be unjust to call her a loose woman, but the attentions of a number of admirers among the young men of the village had not been altogether free from certain gross accompaniments. Moreover, the cruder side of her amorous adventures was not entirely distasteful to her, for she treasured in her box a number of indecent verses which had been sent to her by an ardent swain, whose indiscretion subsequently caused him considerable discomfort. There is no reason to suppose, however, that before she became acquainted with Gardiner she had transgressed the ultimate limit of modesty, and living as she did in a part of England not notably celebrated for a particularly high standard of moral purity, she was probably a fair specimen of the girlhood of her district.

It was doubtless in the Sunday school and choir that Gardiner first became friendly with Rose Harsent. They possessed sufficient tastes in common to afford the basis of an acquaintanceship, for both were interested in chapel affairs and particularly

1. *Editor's Note.* Now called Stuart House.

140

in the chapel music. It may be assumed that they would often return together to Peasenhall after the evening choir practices at Sibton.

The acquaintance, which began innocently enough, nevertheless held from the beginning a certain element of danger since it pandered to the vanity of both parties. They both felt flattered by it, she by the attentions of such a prominent and highly respected member of the small community, and he by the unsophisticated admiration of a young girl with considerable physical attraction. Moreover, the development of an "eternal triangle" situation would not be retarded by the personality of Gardiner's wife, a frail, faded little woman of about forty years, whose married life had been fully occupied with her housework and the bearing of children to a healthy and vigorous spouse.

It is impossible, except by the aid of the imagination, to trace the growth of Gardiner's alleged liaison with Rose Harsent. They were often together, and under circumstances which would afford opportunities for misconduct. Indeed, it was not long before rumour was rife in the district about the nature of their friendship. Spicy stories were freely circulated, and eventually the scandal was made the subject of an inquiry by the chapel authorities, under the auspices of Mr John Guy, superintendent minister of the Wangford Circuit of the Primitive Methodist Church.

At this inquiry, a definite charge was made against Gardiner by two young men named Wright and Skinner, who deposed that on the evening of 1 May 1901, they saw him follow Rose Harsent into an old thatched building called the "Doctor's Chapel", which stood a little way back from the main road, opposite the Peasenhall Drill Works. Expecting, as Skinner subsequently admitted, to "hear something indecent", they approached to within a few feet of the "chapel", and first heard some laughing and rustling going on inside. Then a woman's voice called out "Oh, oh," and, according to Skinner, who remained there after his companion had gone away, the same voice later asked, "Did you notice me reading my Bible last Sunday?" The man said, "What were you reading about?" and the woman replied, "I was reading about like what we have been doing here tonight; I'll tell you where it is," naming a chapter and verse of Genesis. Finally she said, "I shall be out tomorrow night at nine o'clock. You must let me go." This story was absolutely denied by Gardiner at the inquiry, and by Rose

Harsent later, and the result of a rather unsatisfactory investigation was entirely negative.

An interesting glimpse of Gardiner's character is afforded by his behaviour under this ordeal. As soon as Skinner's story became public, he called the latter, who was employed at the Drill Works, into his room and demanded an apology, which, however, was not forthcoming. He also wrote two letters to Rose Harsent. Whether he was innocent or guilty of the charge, these letters indicate that he was no weakling. The first reads:

> Dear Rose, — I was very much surprised this morning to hear that there is some scandal going the round about you and me going into the Doctor's Chapel for immoral Purposes so that I shall put it into other hands at once as I have found out who it was that started it. Bill Wright and Skinner say they saw us there, but I shall summons them for defamation of character unless they withdraw what they have said and give me a written apology. I shall see Bob tonight, and we will come and see you together if possible. I shall at the same time see your father and tell him. — Yours, &c.,
>
> WILLIAM GARDINER

The second letter reads:

> Dear Rose, — I have broken the news to Mrs Gardiner this morning, she is awfully upset but she say she know it is wrong, for I was at home from ½ past 9 o'clock so I could not possibly be with you an hour so she wont believe anything about it. I have asked Mr Burgess to ask those too Chaps to come to Chapel tonight and have it out there however they stand by such a tale I don't know but I dont think God will forsake me now and if we put our trust in Him it will end right but its awfully hard work to have to face people when they are all suspicious of you but by Gods help whether they believe me or not I shall try and live it down and prove by my future conduct that its all false, I only wish I could take it to Court but I dont see a shadow of a chance to get the case as I dont think you would be strong enough to face a trial. Trusting that God will direct us and make the way clear. — I remains, yours in trouble,
>
> W. GARDINER

It is difficult to decide whether these are the resentful letters of an injured man, containing as they do his expression of trust in God and threats of legal proceedings against the slanderers, or mere camouflaged "instructions for the defence" written by a guilty man to his accomplice, notifying her that he is going to present a brazen front to the charge and warning her that she must do the same. If the truth of the matter lies in this latter interpretation of the letters, then they surely do credit to Gardiner's intelligence, for the closest scrutiny yields no indication that they are such.

Even at the present day, village communities like Peasenhall tend to be dominated by the local church or chapel, whose culture and methods of thought, not less than their religious doctrines, permeate the social lives of the inhabitants. But this feature of village life was considerably more marked at the start of the century than it is today, and whether Rose Harsent's mysterious lover was Gardiner or some other person of a similar class, one can well imagine that their relations were characterized by an incongruous mixture of religion and sensuality. If Rose had fostered her amour on excerpts from the book of Genesis, their study of the Bible had doubtless extended to the exquisite love song of Solomon, and they were probably familiar with the sensuous words of the psalmist: "Behold thou art fair, my love; behold thou art fair; thou hast dove's eyes, thy teeth are like a flock of sheep that are even shorn, thy lips are like a thread of scarlet. Thy two breasts are like two young roes that are twins which feed among the lilies. How fair and how pleasant art thou, oh love, for delights." But the "delights" are apt to pall and the piquant charm of illicit pleasure sometimes becomes flat and stale.

If intimacy did exist between Gardiner and Rose Harsent before the investigation by the chapel authorities, it might have been expected to cease after the inquiry. He was no flippant Don Juan, but a man of sound fundamental qualities whose worthy object in life had been to attain respectability in his village; and, obviously, further relations with the girl were fraught with the gravest danger to the position that he cherished. Yet it was the contention of the prosecution at his trials that the girl maintained her hold over him even after the inquiry, and that he persisted in his intercourse with her so as to become the father of her expected child.

At any rate, we know that Rose Harsent was pregnant during the spring of 1902. She was then in the employment of Deacon and Mrs Crisp as general servant at Providence House, a picturesque, gabled building with a walled garden, situated in the main street of Peasenhall within a short distance of Gardiner's cottage. In the face of impending trouble, it may be assumed that all the glamour of the early romance had faded, to be replaced by something quite different — by anxious discussions

Providence House

and bitter recriminations between the girl and her secret lover, whoever he may have been, and by innumerable, futile plans to avert discovery until, as the months passed, the girl could not conceal her condition much longer.

These were distressing circumstances in which Rose Harsent now found herself, but her sufferings were minimized by the comparative coarseness of her nature, and her lapse from virtue would not be likely to condemn her to social ostracism among her class; but, for the unknown man, if he was of some note in the village, the penalty would be far more severe. And as the magnitude of the threatened disaster impressed itself upon him — his public humiliation, the ruin of his home and probable dismissal from his employment — the resolve to murder the girl might well take shape in his mind. Other less criminal methods having failed to achieve their object, it was absolutely necessary for his self-preservation that she should be got out of the way. Brooding on the matter, the character of Rose Harsent may even have assumed an uglier aspect. It would not be difficult for him to imagine that she had been his temptress. Then why, indeed, should he suffer for the sin of a scarlet woman? The master touch to this line of thought would be that he was performing a religious duty in destroy-

144

ing Rose Harsent, since her wiles might be the downfall of many other men!

In the evening of 31 May 1902, a violent thunderstorm broke over the Peasenhall district. Thunder crashed, lightning flared, and a torrential downpour lashed the fields and roads. That night William Gardiner might have been seen by a chance passer-by standing at the door of his cottage, apparently watching the storm. But from where he stood could be seen a steady light that for some minutes showed at the window of the room in which Rose Harsent slept. This light was a signal to her secret lover.

Rose Harsent's bedroom and the kitchen were situated in an outlying part of Providence House, and communicated with each other by means of a separate staircase. That afternoon, the postman had delivered a letter addressed to "Miss Harsent", the last of a series handed in by him, all enclosed in buff-coloured envelopes of the same kind as those in use at the Drill Works. This letter, which was afterwards found, was as follows:

> D R, — I will try to see you tonight at twelve o'clock at your Place if you Put a light in your window at ten o'clock for about ten minutes. Then you can take it out again. Dont have a light in your Room at twelve as I will come round to the back.

Shortly after ten o'clock in the evening, Mrs Crisp said goodnight to Rose and retired to her bedroom. Like other inhabitants of Peasenhall, she was disturbed by the storm, and some time in the middle of the night she was startled by hearing a scream and a thud, as if someone had fallen. She did not, however, make any investigation. By four o'clock in the morning the storm had abated, and the remaining hours of darkness were quiet and peaceful.

The first morning of June dawned brightly. At about eight o'clock William Harsent went to Providence House to take some clean linen to his daughter. On entering the kitchen, he was shocked to find the dead body of Rose lying in a pool of blood. He gave the alarm immediately, and the police were called.

Rigor mortis had set in. It was impossible to say when the girl had died. The body lay with the head near the stairs and the feet towards the kitchen door. There was a punctured wound in the breast caused by an upward thrust of an instrument having a sharp point and blade, and the throat had been slashed across from ear to ear by two distinct cuts inflicted with such force that the windpipe was severed. On the right cheek were a bruise and a small superficial cut, and there were numerous semi-circular cuts about the hands such as would be caused by warding off blows. The dead girl was lying flat on her back; she was dressed only in her nightgown and stockings. The nightdress was burned, particularly at the lower part, and there was considerable charring of the flesh about her thighs and buttocks. On the floor close to the body was a lamp with a detached oil-container and a broken glass, and the room was permeated with the smell of paraffin. Beneath the body was a copy of the *East Anglian Daily Times* — delivered, it was later alleged, by Rose Harsent's brother to William Gardiner a few days previously. No knife or other weapon was found, but near the girl's head was a broken bottle which had contained paraffin and which had a label on it, bearing the words, "Two to three teaspoonfuls, a sixth part to be taken every four hours — Mrs. Gardiner's children."

Strangely enough, the first impression formed by those who followed Harsent, and viewed the body, was that the girl had committed suicide. Some colour was lent to this by the fact that no footmarks were to be seen in the blood that lay upon the floor. But it does seem extraordinary that such a theory could have survived the most cursory examination. It was negated by the fact that either of the throat wounds would have proved fatal; and, therefore, if the deceased had inflicted the first it would have been impossible for her to inflict the second. Moreover, the cuts upon the hands were quite inconsistent with suicide, indicating as they did an attempt by the girl to protect herself. And how, if the girl had taken her own life, were the signs of burning to explained away? To put the matter beyond doubt, there was the absence of the knife or similar weapon by which the wounds were caused. It has indeed been suggested — somewhat foolishly — that they might have been self-inflicted by the broken paraffin bottle, and we have learned from a reliable source that there was, in fact, surgical evidence available to the defence to support this theory. A broken bottle, which is a deadly weapon, might easily be used in a suicide, but the jagged or lacerated edges of the wounds inflicted by it are quite different from the clean incisions of a knife such as extended across the throat of the dead girl.

Still more astonishing, there were people who believed that Rose Harsent's death had been accidental. The leader of this

D R

I will try to see you tonight at 12 oclock at your Place if you Put a light in your window at 10 oclock for about 10 minutes then you can take it out again. dont have a light in your Room at 12 as I will come round to the back

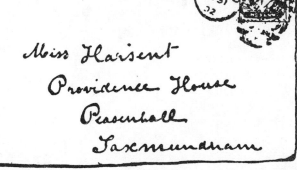

Miss Harsent
Providence House
Peasenhall
Saxmundham

select band was a local clergyman, and his theory is explained in detail in Max Pemberton's interesting story of the Peasenhall Case.[1] "An unknown man" it is supposed,

> desired to see the girl secretly. He wrote and made an appointment with her at midnight, telling her to put a light in her bedroom window that he might know it was safe for him to come. He gets a pair of india-rubber shoes from somewhere, and creeps up the road to the window of her kitchen. There a horrible spectacle is revealed — the girl lies dead at the foot of the steep flight of stairs, the lamp she carried is shattered, the paraffin has caught fire and is already burning her body. The man is horrified and flies. He is not a murderer, but his intrigue with her has undoubtedly been the cause of her death.

In support of his view, he continues,

> Just before twelve o'clock Rose Harsent took the lamp in one hand and the glass bottle in the other and began to descend the steep flight of stairs leading to the kitchen. Halfway down, perhaps, her foot becomes entangled in her long nightdress and she pitches headlong down the stairs into the kitchen. It was at this moment that Mrs Crisp, the deacon's wife, heard the thud and the scream, and, but for her husband's persuasion, would have gone to the kitchen to see what was the matter. Rose Harsent, thus falling, if fall she did, naturally thought first of the lighted lamp she carried and did her best to save it. She stretched out her arm to prevent its breaking; and so we find it upon the floor in three pieces — the unbroken glass farthest away from the body; the reservoir near, and then the holder. The paraffin, naturally escaping from it, ran back to the rill worn in the stone at the stairs' foot, as rills are always worn in the stones of these country cottages. There it caught fire and, for a little while, burned briskly. Meanwhile the poor girl herself had forgotten the glass bottle in her other hand, and upon that she had fallen with all her weight. It cut her throat and killed her.

It is hardly necessary to comment on this amiable theory, the product of a vivid imagination.

There were other fantastic explanations, and the usual "confession" from an ill-balanced individual, without which no murder case seems to be complete. In point of fact, there were three such missives received during the course of the Peasenhall trials, none of which had any bearing on the case.

1. *Editor's Note.* "The Unsolved Mystery of Peasenhall", in *Great Stories of Real Life*, edited by Max Pemberton, Newnes, London 1929.

Important evidence would almost certainly have been discovered if the police had arrested their man immediately. But, with all the facts pointing to murder, and enough evidence in their possession to warrant an arrest, their minds were apparently so obsessed with the theory of suicide that it was not until three days after the tragedy that the step was taken. They had the evidence of the bottle that Mrs Gardiner had owned, of the newspaper alleged to have been delivered to Gardiner's house, and of the scandal which the chapel authorities had investigated.

Moreover, other testimony was soon forthcoming. A young gamekeeper named James Morriss, who had passed through the main street of the village about five o'clock on the morning of the murder, declared that he noticed a series of footmarks leading from Gardiner's cottage to Providence House. He was aware of the stories that had circulated in the village concerning Gardiner's relations with Rose Harsent, and he seized this opportunity to do some amateur detective work. He traced the footsteps, and found that they led close up to the gate of the house and back again to the cottage. Examining the marks carefully, he came to the conclusion that they had been made by rubber-soled shoes with bars across their treads. Morriss gave this evidence at the inquest. A juryman made a sketch of a shoe sole and the witness drew lines across it representing the bars. It was discovered later that Gardiner possessed a pair of rubber-soled shoes which, the prosecution afterwards alleged, would correspond exactly with the imprints that Morriss had seen.

Gardiner was taken into custody on 3 June, and both he and his wife made statements to the police which were free from serious contradiction. He said: "On Saturday I drove to Kelsale at 2.30. I got home about 9.30, had my supper, and stayed at the front door because of the storm. We went into Mrs Dickenson's about eleven o'clock. I left Mrs Dickenson's with my wife about half-past one, went to bed, and did not go out until 8.30 next morning."

The only noticeable discrepancy between this account and that given by Mrs Gardiner was that she stated that she went to Mrs Dickenson's first and that he came shortly after. If the prosecution had been able to ascertain the exact time of the murder, this variation might have been of the greatest importance.

The first trial of William Gardiner opened in November 1902 at Ipswich, before Mr Justice Grantham. Mr H. F. Dickens,

KC,[3] and the Hon. John de Grey conducted the case for the Crown, while Mr Ernest E. Wild and Mr H. Claughton Scott were for the defence. Tremendous interest was aroused by the trial, and many notable people came to hear the proceedings. When the time came for the accused to give his evidence, he made a most favourable impression in the box. "We saw," wrote Max Pemberton, "a finely built man, with clear eyes and hair so black that, as was said, he might have been of Spanish origin." His attitude is thus described in a contemporary issue of the *East Anglian Daily News* (which newspaper, by the way, made itself largely responsible for the money required to have Gardiner adequately defended):

> The accused went from the dock into the witness-box, and, after stroking his raven-black moustache and beard for a moment or two in a rather nervous way, pulled himself together, and stood somewhat unsteadily, with one hand resting on the ledge in front of him — often raising it to emphasise his statements — and the other held close to his side. He spoke in a clear voice, raising it occasionally at the request of counsel, so that the jury might hear, and the quietude of his demeanour was the subject of general amazement.

The statements he made to his own counsel were not shaken, to any marked extent, in cross-examination. While he was obviously anxious, he was never flustered, and gave his answers without hesitation.

On the fourth day Mr Wild wound up an exceedingly skilful defence by a remarkable speech: but the effect of this eloquence on the jury, it was thought, must have been dispelled by the summing-up of Mr Justice Grantham, which was unquestionably against the accused. There was intense excitement when the jury retired to consider their verdict at a quarter past four in the afternoon. They returned at half-past six to reveal that they were in disagreement and wished to know what inference they were to draw from the fact that there was no blood on the accused's clothing. The judge said that that fact was in the accused's favour, but that guilt had been clearly established in other cases where there was no blood found upon the clothes. If the other evidence was not conclusive, these facts would serve the accused; but if this evidence was conclusive, the absence of blood ought not to affect the evidence of guilt. The jury retired

1. *Editor's Note.* A son of Charles Dickens.

again, and it was not until twenty minutes to nine that they returned. The foreman intimated that they had not been able to reach a verdict. Mr Justice Grantham then asked if there were any questions that he could answer, and a juryman stood up to say that there were no questions which he wished to ask. It was he who was in disagreement with the others. When asked by Mr Justice Grantham if he thought time might be of value to him in considering the question, the juryman said: "I have not made up my mind not to agree if I was convinced that the prisoner was guilty, but I have heard nothing to convince me that he is guilty." The applause in court which followed this statement was quickly silenced. As there was no prospect of an agreement, the jury was discharged.

The second trial also resulted abortively, but the position here was the exact reverse of that at the first hearing, eleven jurymen being for acquitting Gardiner and one for condemning him. The trial again took place at Ipswich, and the same counsel were engaged, with Mr Justice Lawrence this time on the bench. The evidence was patiently gone over again, and again the summing-up inclined towards a conviction. After a little over two hours' absence on the fourth day, the foreman of the jury led his men back to intimate that there was no possibility of their reaching an agreement.

Speculation was now rife as to whether the accused would again be tried, and it was confidently expected locally that he would appear at the next Suffolk Assizes. The power of ordering a further prosecution no doubt existed, but its enforcement was discretionary, and on this occasion the discretion was wisely exercised. Five days after the trial, the accused's solicitor received the following telegram from the Director of Public Prosecutions: "*Rex* v. Gardiner — just lodged *nolle prosequi*. — Sims, Treasury, London." On the same day the governor of Ipswich Prison received an order to release his prisoner.

It is said that Gardiner's first act on being informed of this was to fall on his knees and thank God for his deliverance. In the evening this much-tried man stepped forth from the prison, his appearance much altered by the removal of his black beard and whiskers. Within a few hours, he was a passenger on the night-train to Liverpool Street Station, London, and after many months of public notoriety his identity became obscured in the city's millions.

*   *   *

As nothing of importance occurred during the first trial which was not covered during the second, our discussion of the evidence will be confined to the latter.

There was no direct evidence against the accused. Only the murderer knew what had actually happened in that blood-stained kitchen, and the Crown had to depend on a cumulative case of circumstantial evidence. In pointing this out to the jury, Mr Justice Lawrence said:

> If a man came to the witness-box and said he saw A shoot B through the head with a pistol, A would be tried for murder, and that would be direct evidence. And the only question you would have to consider would be: Can we trust this man who has said he saw A shoot B? In direct evidence only one question arises: Do you accept the statement of the person who gives the evidence? Let me give you the plainest and simplest case of circumstantial evidence and the most familiar one in the textbooks. Suppose you saw a man rush into a room with a naked sword, and you afterwards saw him coming out with it covered with blood. Supposing that in that room there was a man who was found to be struck in the back or in a place where he could not strike himself. That would be circumstantial evidence. First, you would have to say whether you were satisfied that the witness saw A go into the room, and then, if you believed that, the next question would be: What presumption does that give rise to in my mind? Circumstantial evidence is evidence which gives rise to a presumption. First, you have to say whether you accept the fact, and then, secondly, what is the reasonable inference to be drawn from the presumption? There are cases in the textbooks in which it is shown that circumstantial evidence is of greater value than direct evidence.

Sir Michael Foster, in comparing the value of the two kinds of evidence, has said, "Witnesses sometimes lie, facts never." There is much truth in that, but, at the same time, it should be remembered that a tribunal may have extreme difficulty in ascertaining the correct inferences to be drawn from the facts. This is a weakness of circumstantial evidence which has often been exploited to good purpose by the defence.

Look, for instance, at this case of Gardiner. A broken bottle, which has contained paraffin, is found in the kitchen near Rose Harsent's body, and the label on it bears the words "Mrs Gardiner's children". Here, it would seem, is a piece of circumstantial evidence of the greatest importance which cannot be contested. What does it prove? From the point of view of the prosecution, it supports the view that the accused has filled the bottle with paraffin at his home and taken it with him to Providence House for the purpose of using it to burn the body of the dead woman. Regarded in this light, the evidence of the paraffin bottle assumes a damning aspect. Yet, when the defence come to deal with the matter, it is put forward as the strongest proof of Gardiner's innocence! They say that, if he were the guilty man, he might just as well have left his visiting card on the body of his victim. It is one of the earliest lessons to be learned in defending criminals that apparently glaring pieces of evidence like this can be countered by the argument that no one but a maniac would provide such evidence against himself. And that contention may not always be met successfully by the answer — although it is an established fact — that however clever a criminal may be, he usually assists detection by at least one act or omission of unaccountable stupidity. A host of instances of this immediately come to mind — the package of arsenic kept for months by Herbert Rowse Armstrong, the preservation of incriminating letters by Mrs Thompson of Bywaters and Thompson notoriety, and the open use in their workshop of surgical instruments stolen at the time of the murder of Police Constable Gutteridge by Messrs Browne and Kennedy.

Let us begin our examination of the evidence given at the trial by scrutinising the incident of the meeting at the "Doctor's Chapel", from which Gardiner's alleged association with Rose Harsent dates. It was early realized by the advocates that this was the key to the whole position, and in his opening speech Mr Dickens fenced round and guarded this part of his case with meticulous care. He suggested that Skinner's story was too extraordinary to have been invented, and pointed out that there was no antagonism between the two young men and the accused. The fact was stressed that, in spite of the threat of legal proceedings against them, the young men would not apologize; and an elderly man named Henry Rouse would be called to support this view that Gardiner was more than friendly with Rose Harsent.

He had seen them walking together in the month of February 1902, and had also detected familiarities taking place between them as they sat in the choir while he was preaching at Sibton Chapel. The answer to this, in Mr Wild's opening speech, was that his client had been the victim of village gossip; and the fact that he had retained all his offices of honour at the chapel after the inquiry was proof that the charge had been fabricated. The jury heard Wright and Skinner tell their story, and though Mr Wild bombarded it with heavy artillery, the young men were not much shaken. Then Mr John Guy, superintendent minister of the Wangford Circuit of the Primitive Methodist Church, before whom the inquiry at Sibton was held, appeared to support their testimony. Mr Guy said that it was as the result of a letter received from Rouse, stating that there were certain rumours abroad relating to the conduct of Gardiner, that he decided to hold the inquiry. He admitted that Rose Harsent was employed to clean the "Doctor's Chapel" at Peasenhall and that the accused had nothing to do with that particular community. No decision was arrived at then, but Gardiner was told to be careful in his relations with young girls. Gardiner admitted that he had been indiscreet, but promised to keep clear of Rose Harsent in the future.

Mr Wild's cross-examination here was fairly successful. Guy agreed with him that if there had been any truth in the story, the accused would have been speedily asked to resign — summarily ejected, in fact, from his offices at the church; but he denied the suggestion that he had on one occasion said that it was a trumped-up affair. The court then listened to Rouse telling of the familiarities he had noticed at the church. His story somehow did not ring very true, and it was easily shaken by the defence. Mr Wild skilfully showed the jury that the witness was one of those people who are continually bringing accusations against others.

Here, then, is all the evidence of Gardiner's alleged relations with the dead girl. This earlier history of the case may not *prima facie* seem to be connected with the actual circumstances of the murder itself; but it possesses a vital importance from the Crown standpoint because, if established, it constitutes a probable motive for the crime, the whole force of the argument culminating in the fact that Rose Harsent at the time of her death was six months advanced in pregnancy. The motive, shortly stated, was the removal of an imminent menace to the accused's respectability. The question now arises: Is there evidence enough to satisfy us that Rose Harsent was indeed Gardiner's mistress; or can we, with Mr Wild and the jury, dispose of it as nothing more than village tittle-tattle? If we discount the evidence of Mr Rouse, who we were told had a taste for squabbles, the testimony of Wright and Skinner still remains. They apparently had nothing to gain by Gardiner's disgrace, and if the story had originally been started as a prank, one would think that these two boys would have been brought to their senses by the man's wrath and his threat of legal proceedings. But, as we have seen, they told their story, and, in the transatlantic phrase, they stuck to it. Against this, there are the denials of Gardiner, supported by his wife's testimony — evidence weakened by self-interest, of course, the value of which could best be judged by those who saw and heard the Gardiners.

The next important matter relates to the letter in the buff envelope, which the girl received on the afternoon of 31 May. After Harry Harsent, a brother of the dead girl, had deposed that he had taken letters from the accused to his sister on several occasions, the postman spoke about the letter in the buff envelope, in which the Crown were specially interested. He had several times delivered letters to Rose which had been enclosed in similar envelopes. It appeared that envelopes of this kind were in use at the Drill Works, and the accused had access to them. Later in the trial a fierce battle of expert evidence raged round the handwriting in this document.

"There are liars," says the cynic, "damned liars, and expert witnesses," and a study of the expert evidence given here tends to make one believe that the expression is not too drastic. As a matter of fact, the administration of justice in our courts might be better served by the rigid exclusion of all such testimony except in cases where, owing to the technical nature of the subject matter, it is absolutely necessary in order to explain the points in dispute. The present practice in our courts goes far beyond this. Engineers of alleged eminence in their profession have spent hours in court explaining, and contradicting each other, about the ability of an open-ended spanner to slip off a nut. In medical cases, especially, there seems to be no limit to the latitude allowed, and much time is wasted. Of all the classes of expert evidence adduced for the so-called assistance of the court, that dealing with handwriting is among the most illusory. It depends in the main upon a number of similarities, the existence of which is strenuously affirmed and just as strongly denied. In no case does it afford any guidance beyond the point at which an ordinary man would arrive by a careful comparison of the documents.

In the case we are considering, it is perhaps enough to say that the discrimination of Thomas Gurrin, the handwriting expert for the Crown, and the best-known authority on the subject, was entirely discredited in the action of Charles Stewart Parnell in 1889 against the editor of *The Times* newspaper, where he was fully prepared to give his sworn opinion that the letters which the notorious Richard Piggott afterwards confessed he had forged were in the handwriting of Mr Parnell. There is, therefore, little to be gained from this evidence. In passing, however, we note a peculiarity common to the letter received by Rose Harsent and other letters admittedly in Gardiner's handwriting: in each case several words in the middle of sentences are commenced by a capital letter. As an item in a cumulative case, this resemblance is significant, but too much reliance should not be placed upon it.

It will be remembered that the writer of this letter instructed the dead girl to put a light in her window at ten o'clock for about ten minutes. Harry Burgess, a bricklayer, was called to say that he had spoken to Gardiner at about five minutes past ten on the evening of 31 May. Their conversation took place at Gardiner's front door, and Burgess remained there for a quarter of an hour. As he was going home, he noticed a light in the top window of Providence House. It would be wise not to pay much attention to this statement. Obviously, the imagination may enter into evidence of this kind, and, in addition, the fact that the storm was then raging is sufficient to discount it.

From the light in the window the Crown came to the matter of Gardiner's rubber-soled shoes. James Morriss, the gamekeeper, told of the footmarks he had traced between Providence House and Gardiner's cottage. When questioned by the police, Mrs Gardiner had readily produced the rubber-soled shoes. They did not appear to have been worn recently, and there were no traces of blood upon them, a point which the defence quickly turned to the advantage of their client. There were, in fact, no bloodstains of any kind upon any of Gardiner's clothing. The only trace of mammalian blood was a spot upon a clasp-knife which was found in the accused's possession. This knife had evidently been freshly cleaned and sharpened. It had been scraped inside the haft and the two blades bore signs of recent polishing. On examining the interior of the handle, Dr Stevenson, senior official analyst for the Home Office, had found a minute quantity of mammalian blood. The suggestion of the defence was that the presence of this blood was due to the fact that the accused had killed some rabbits shortly before and had used the knife to disembowel them. The absence of blood was a strong point in favour of the defence; but, against this, the Crown brought a neighbour to say that there was a fire in Gardiner's wash-house very early on the Sunday morning and that both the accused and his wife had been seen going there at an unusual hour. This was a rather dangerous piece of evidence, but Mr Wild's cross-examination was meant to show that the witness's imagination had played no little part in his recollections.

We have already dealt with that specious piece of evidence, the broken paraffin bottle with the tell-tale label, and have seen how the defence ridiculed the idea that Gardiner would leave such a glaring clue behind him. Later they strengthened their position by calling evidence to prove that the bottle had originally contained camphorated oil, which was prescribed by a local doctor for Mrs Gardiner's children, and that she had let Rose Harsent have some of the oil in the bottle for a sore throat. It was suggested that thereafter the bottle had been used by the girl for storing paraffin, that it had been placed upon a bracket behind the kitchen door — which was afterwards found broken — and that it had been knocked off on to the floor when the door was pushed open on the night of the crime. It was an exceedingly plausible supposition, and served to make the matter of the broken bottle with its label of little value to the Crown.

These were the principal points against the accused upon which the prosecution relied to secure a conviction. Their case ended with the close of the second day, but before that a young man named Davis spent an uncomfortable hour in the box. He was a young shop assistant who had written several questionable letters and verses to Rose Harsent. In respect of his more objectionable compositions, he was severely censured by the bench. But he was quite innocent of any connection with the murder, and this was admitted by the defence. At the same time, however, when Mr Wild addressed the jury he showed them how a case might have been built up against Davis. It was an excellent idea, his ingenious object being to demonstrate how easily a strong case might be constructed against a perfectly innocent man.

On the third day, Mrs Gardiner told her tale. She had never believed the scandal that linked her husband's name with that of Rose Harsent. On the afternoon of 31 May her husband had driven to Kelsale, and he had returned home at half-past nine. He stood at the door watching the storm for some time, after which they had supper, and then went to Mrs Dickenson's. She went first and her husband followed a few minutes afterwards. They left Mrs Dickenson's at half past one in the morning, when the storm was practically over. After they retired, her husband slept soundly, but she had to get up more than once during the night to see to one of her children who had been frightened by the storm. Thus she was positive that he had not been out of bed during the night. When she had given her evidence, Mrs Gardiner fainted and her cross-examination was delayed until next day. Mr Dickens did not shake her testimony, but as a defence the suggested alibi is obviously weak since no definite hour could be fixed for the murder and the accused was within a stone's throw of Providence House during the night and morning.

The behaviour of Mrs Gardiner is interesting. She was distressed and terrified in the box, and after her examination-in-chief she had a violent fit of hysterics. The next day, after cross-examination, she was obviously on the verge of another breakdown — so much so that her husband, sitting in the dock, burst into tears. These incidents could not fail to impress the jury, and they formed a basis for the last pathetic appeal by the defence. Mrs Gardiner's collapse in body and mind is strange when one remembers that all that was required of her was the truth about her husband's movements on the night of the murder. Certainly there had been much cruel suspense connected with the case, but a belief in her husband's innocence might have been expected to inspire her with greater fortitude, unless, of course, she was in weak health or abnormally temperamental.

When William Gardiner went into the box, he was taken through all the incriminating points that the Crown had raised. He denied that he had had immoral relations with Rose Harsent, stating that when he went into the "Doctor's Chapel" it was merely to help her to shut a heavy door which was stuck. The evidence of Wright and Skinner was entirely false. It was at his own request that the inquiry had been held at Sibton Chapel, and he had continued in his offices after the investigation. He never used buff envelopes for his correspondence, and the letter sent to Rose Harsent shortly before her death was not written by him. He had once received a letter from the girl about a church matter, but he had never written to her. Concerning the shoes, he was evidently contemptuous — in view of the storm — of Morriss's story of the footmarks. He denied any knowledge of the light in Rose Harsent's bedroom window, and declared he was unaware at that time that such a light could be seen from the roadway before his house. His wife, he now admitted, had gone to Mrs Dickenson's first on the night of the 31st; he had followed a few minutes later, after seeing to the children. They went to bed about two o'clock, and he was in his room until eight o'clock next morning. Mr Dickens cross-examined skilfully, but the witness emerged from the duel with credit. It was, in fact, an excellent appearance in the box, which must have assisted materially towards his acquittal.

That is a brief summary of the important evidence led at the second trial of William Gardiner. A fundamental axiom of English law is that a man must be presumed to be innocent until he is found guilty; and, therefore, Gardiner is entitled to the full benefit of the presumption since two exhaustive efforts by the Crown failed to lay the responsibility for the murder at his door. No one has the right to assert that a miscarriage of justice took place or to regard him otherwise than as an innocent man.

But the reader must naturally ask himself what opinion he would have formed had he been a member of the jury who listened to the evidence at Ipswich. In doing so, however, one must bear in mind what has so often been said by judges of the Court of Appeal, that to read a report of the evidence is far less informative than to see and hear the witnesses who gave it. Nevertheless, the report makes it clear that the case presented by the Crown was founded upon a number of incriminating circumstances, some of which pointed strongly and others with less force to Gardiner as the guilty person. Thus, in coming to a decision, one will have to ascertain whether these circumstances are merely a group of isolated coincidences or whether they form a chain of evidence that can only be explained by Gardiner's guilt. We imagine that even the accused himself could not deny that the cumulative case of the Crown looked very formidable; but the burden of proof was upon them, and if there is a reasonable doubt the accused is always entitled to the benefit of it. It may be that to the pure logician the reasonableness of a doubt does not depend on the result of a decision. But, fortunately for the conduct of everyday affairs, the pure logician is an extremely rare specimen. We may possess an easy feeling of certainty in deciding a trivial matter, yet, upon the same material, certainty may well be replaced by doubt if a man's life is threatened by our decision.

The Peasenhall Case

Perhaps the popular conclusion will be one of agreement with the majority of the jury at the second trial; or, at any rate, that the abortive conclusion of the Peasenhall Case was the best thing that could have happened in the circumstances.

The Murder of Mary Ashford

Anonymous
(From a Newgate Calendar)

THIS CASE is remarkable not only for the lamentable atrocity of the offence imputed to the unfortunate prisoner, but from the fact also of the brother of the deceased person having lodged an appeal, upon which the prisoner demanded "wager of battle".

Abraham Thornton was a well-made young man, the son of a respectable builder, and was by trade a bricklayer. He was indicted at the Warwick Assizes in August 1817 for the murder of Mary Ashford, a lovely and interesting girl of twenty years of age, whose character was perfectly unsullied up to the time at which she was most barbarously ravished and murdered by the prisoner.

From the evidence adduced, it appeared that the poor girl went to a dance at the Tyburn House inn, a few miles from Birmingham, on the evening of 26 May 1817, where she met the prisoner, who professed to admire her figure and general appearance, and who was heard to say, "I have been intimate, and I will have connection with her, though it cost me my life." He danced with her, and accompanied her from the room at about three o'clock in the morning. At four o'clock she called at a friend's at a place nearby called Erdington, and the offence alleged against the prisoner was committed immediately afterwards.

The circumstances proved in evidence were that the footsteps of a man and woman were traced from the path through a harrowed field near Erdington, through which her way lay home to Langley. The marks were at first regular, but afterwards exhibited proofs of running and struggling; and at length they led to a spot where a distinct impression of a human figure and a large quantity of coagulated blood were discovered, and on this spot the marks of a man's knees and toes were also distinguishable. From thence the man's footfalls only were seen, and, accompanying them, blood marks were distinctly traced for a considerable space towards a pit; and it appeared plainly as if a man had walked along the footway carrying a body, from which the blood dropped. At the edge of the pit, the shoes, bonnet, and bundle of the deceased were found; but only one footstep could be seen there, and that was a man's. It was deeply impressed, and seemed to be that of a man who thrust one foot forward to heave something into the pit. The body of the deceased was discovered lying at the bottom. There were marks of laceration upon the body; and both her arms had the marks of hands, as if they had pressed them with violence to the ground.

By his own admission Thornton was with her at four o'clock, and the marks of the man's shoes in the running corresponded exactly to his. By his own admission, also, he was intimate with her; this admission was made not before the magistrate, nor till the evident proofs were discovered on his clothes.

Her clothes, too, afforded most powerful evidence. At four in the morning, when she called at her friend's, Hannah Cox, she had changed from her dancing-dress. The clothes she had put on

The Tyburn House Inn

there, and which she had on at the time of her death, were all over blood and dirt.

The case, therefore, appeared to be that Thornton had paid attention to her during the night; shown, perhaps, those attentions which she might naturally have been pleased with; and afterwards waited for her on her return from Erdington, and after forcibly violating her, thrown her body into the pit.

The prisoner declined saying anything in his defence, stating that he would leave everything to his counsel, who called several witnesses to the fact of his having returned home at an hour which rendered it very improbable, if not impossible, that he could have committed the murder, and have traversed the distance from the fatal spot to the places in which he was seen, in the very short time that appeared to have elapsed: but it was acknowledged that there was considerable variation in the different village-clocks.

The case was involved in so much difficulty, from the nature of the defence, although the case for the prosecution appeared

Mary Ashford

unanswerable, that the judge's charge to the jury occupied no less than two hours. "It were better," he said in conclusion, "that the murderer, with all the weight of his crime upon his head, should escape punishment than that another person should suffer death without being guilty." This consideration weighed so powerfully with the jury that, to the surprise of all who had taken an interest in the case, they returned a verdict of Not Guilty, which the prisoner received with a smile of silent approbation, and an unsuccessful attempt at concealment of the violent apprehensions as to his fate by which he had been inwardly agitated.

He was then arraigned, *pro forma*, for the rape; but the counsel for the prosecution declined offering evidence on this indictment, and he was accordingly discharged.

Thus ended, for the present, the proceedings on this most brutal and ferocious violation and murder; but the public at large, and more particularly the inhabitants of the neighbourhood in which it had been committed, were far from considering Thornton innocent, and subscriptions to defray the expense of a new prosecution were entered into.

The circumstances of the case having been investigated by the Secretary of State, he granted his warrant to the sheriff of Warwick to take the defendant into custody on an appeal of murder, to be prosecuted by William Ashford, the seventeen-year-old brother and heir-at-law of the deceased. Thornton was in consequence lodged in Warwick jail, and from thence he was subsequently removed by a writ of *habeas corpus* to London, the proceedings on the appeal being in the court of King's Bench, in Westminster Hall. On 6 November, the appellant, attended by four counsel, appeared in court, when the proceedings were adjourned to the 17th, by the desire of the prisoner's counsel; and on that day the prisoner demanded trial by *wager of battle*.

The revival of this obsolete law gave rise to much argument on both sides; and it was not until 16 April 1818 that the decision of the court was given upon the question. The learned judges gave their opinions *seriatim*, and the substance of the judgement was that the law must be administered as it stood, and that therefore the prisoner was entitled to claim trial by battle; but the court added that the trial should be granted only "in case the appellant should show cause why the defendant should not depart without delay". On the 20th the arguments were resumed by the counsel for the slightly-built appellant (who, not unnaturally, was loath to engage in mortal combat with the defendant); but Thornton was ordered to "be discharged from the appeal, and to be allowed to go forth without bail".

Though the rigid application of the letter of the law thus, a second time, saved Thornton from punishment, nothing could remove the conviction of his guilt from the public mind. Shunned by all who knew him, his very name became an object of terror, and he soon afterwards attempted to proceed to America; but the sailors of the vessel in which he was about to embark refused to go to sea with a character on board who, according to their fancy, was likely to produce so much ill-luck to the voyage; and he was compelled to conceal himself until another opportunity was afforded him to make good his escape.

The *trial by battle*, which in this case was so remarkably claimed, may be thus described:

When the privilege of *trial by battle* was claimed by the appellee, the judges had to consider whether, under the circumstances, he was entitled to the exercise of such privilege. His claim thereto having been admitted, they fixed a day and place for the combat, which was conducted with the following solemnities:

A piece of ground was set out, of sixty feet square, enclosed with lists, and on one side was a court erected for the judges of the Court of Common Pleas, who attended there in their scarlet robes; and also a bar for the learned serjeants at law. When the court was assembled, proclamation was made for the parties, who were accordingly introduced in the area by the proper officers, each armed with a *baton*, or staff of an ell long, tipped with horn, and bearing a four-cornered leather target for defence. The combatants were bare-headed and bare-footed, the appellee with his head shaved, the appellant as usual, but both dressed alike. The appellee pleaded Not Guilty, and threw down his glove, and declared he would defend the same by his body; the appellant took up the glove, and replied that he was ready to make good the appeal, body for body. And thereupon the appellee, taking the Bible in his right hand, and in his left the right hand of his antagonist, swore to this effect:

"Hear this, O man, whom I hold by the hand, who callest thyself [John], by the name of baptism, that I, who call myself [Thomas], by the name of baptism, did not feloniously murder thy father [William], by name, nor am any way guilty of the said felony. So help me God, and the saints; and this I will defend against thee by my body, as this court shall award."

Abraham Thornton

To which the appellant replied, holding the Bible and his antagonist's hand, in the same manner as the other:

"Hear this, O man, whom I hold by the hand, who callest thyself [Thomas], by the name of baptism, that thou art perjured, because that thou feloniously didst murder my father [William], by name. So help me God, and the saints; and this I will prove against thee by my body, as this Court shall award."

Next, an oath against sorcery and enchantment was taken by both the combatants in this or a similar form: "Hear this, ye justices, that I have this day neither ate, drank, nor have upon me either bone, stone, or grass; nor any enchantment, sorcery, or witchcraft, whereby the law of God may be abased, or the law of the devil exalted. So help me God and his saints."

The battle was thus begun, and the combatants were bound to fight till the stars appeared in the evening.

If the appellee were so far vanquished that he could not or would not fight any longer, he was adjudged to be hanged immediately: and then, as well as if he were killed in battle, Providence was deemed to have determined in favour of the

truth, and his blood was declared attainted. But if he killed the
appellant, or could maintain the fight from sun-rising till the
stars appeared in the evening, he was acquitted. So also, if the
appellant became recreant, and pronounced the word *craven*,
he lost his *liberam legem*, and became infamous; and the
appellee recovered his damages and was for ever quit, not only
of the appeal, but of all indictments likewise of the same
offence. There were cases where the appellant might
counterplead, and oust the appellee from his trial by battle:
these were vehement presumption or sufficient proof that the
appeal was true: or where the appellant was under fourteen or
above sixty years of age, or was a woman or a priest, or a peer,
or, lastly, a citizen of London, because the peaceful habits of the
citizens were supposed to unfit them for battle.

It is almost needless to add that this remnant of barbarity has
now ceased to exist, an act of parliament, the introduction of
which was attributable to the above case, having removed it
from the pages of the lawbooks by which our courts are
governed.

Editor's Note
Adding to the abounding coincidences in the annals of murder,
early on the morning of Tuesday, 27 May 1974 (the anniversary,
almost to the hour, of the murder of Mary Ashford), a twenty-
year-old girl named Barbara Forrest was strangled to death in a
field at Erdington, within 400 yards of the site of the pit in which
Mary's body was found. Like Mary, Barbara Forrest had been
to a dance on the night before her death; had gone to a friend's
home to change her dress. The police arrested the superintendent of the children's home where Barbara Forrest had
worked. The alibi claimed by the man was soon proved to be
false; there were bloodstains on his clothing. He stood trial at
Birmingham Crown Court in March 1975; but at the end of the
prosecution case, the judge agreed with his counsel that there
was no case to answer, and directed the jury to bring in a verdict
of Not Guilty. The acquitted man's surname was Thornton.

The
Raising of the Guernsey Farmer

Richard Whittington-Egan

ITS MELLOW bricks and seasoned timbers baked in the summer suns and weathered by the winter snows of a hundred years, the old house called Nuthurst lay basking like a sleepy cat in the soft, warm sunshine of the August afternoon. Set against the picturesque background of the little Surrey village of Lower Knapphill, it looked like an American tourist's picture-postcard dream of an old English country house. I watched two children playing happily on its baize-green lawn, the echoes of their laughter drifting across the bright-banked beds of sweetly-smelling flowers.

It would be difficult to imagine a scene to which the description "sinister" could less aptly be applied. And yet . . . as I stood there remembering — another August . . . the laughter of other children tinkling in that same garden — that word "sinister" came scudding up like a black cloud into my mind, dimming and chilling the sunlight.

Knowing what I knew, it needed only a small effort of imagination to conjure up the sad spectre of a little old man with a thin, drooping moustache, whose especial pride and pleasure it had once been to care for that lawn, and who, one August half a century before, had met a cruel and unlovely fate amidst all this loveliness. To this day, the story of how death came to him remains a puzzle, which not even the sequel of yet another mysterious death has entirely solved.

Back in June 1926, a young couple named Lerwill — William and May — were the tenants of Nuthurst. They had rented the house, furnished, for six months, and moved in with their two children, a nanny, and an old family friend who lodged with them as a paying guest — a highly paying guest, as it proved. He was a seventy-seven-year-old, retired gentleman-farmer from the Channel Island of Guernsey, Hilary Rougier. A bachelor, deaf and solitary in his old age.

By all accounts, Mr Rougier was a kindly, amiable old man — if not exactly rich, certainly not short of money, and, so far as the Lerwills were concerned, most unusually generous. They, for their part, seemed to be devoted to him, and, as one of their servants put it, "looked after him as they would their own father".

It was shortly after their arrival at Nuthurst that the old gentleman's health, hitherto remarkably good except for occasional attacks of asthma, began to cause the Lerwills some mild anxiety.

On 23 July, the local GP, Dr A. H. Brewer, was called in to see him. Dr Brewer did not, however, view his patient's condition with any alarm. He diagnosed slight bronchial trouble, wrote out a prescription for a simple cough mixture, and took his departure. The doctor came again on 28 July, found Mr Rougier much as before, certainly no worse, and said he would call again in a fortnight. But, at about half-past eight on the morning of 14 August, Dr Brewer received an urgent summons from Mrs Lerwill. When he arrived at Nuthurst, he was taken to an upstairs bedroom, and there he saw Rougier, lying in bed, livid, deeply unconscious, and quite obviously dying.

Some hours later, Dr Brewer was not surprised to learn that Rougier had died, and he had no qualms about issuing a certificate to the effect that death was the result of a cerebral haemorrhage.

Nineteen months went by. The first tentative buds were beginning to haze with green the gnarled old trees in the beautiful parish churchyard of St John's, near Woking, when, on the morning of 16 March 1928, the men with the spades arrived.

Quietly they made their way to the unmarked, untended grave in which Hilary Rougier lay. Quietly they began to dig. A Home Office exhumation order in their pockets, they had come to raise the dead.

The coffin was removed to Woking Mortuary, and there Sir Bernard Spilsbury, the Home Office pathologist, carried out a post-mortem. He looked for evidence of cerebral haemorrhage. There was none. In fact, there were no signs of any kind to indicate a cause of death.

As Sir Bernard deftly removed the internal organs, preparatory to dispatching them to the forensic analyst, Dr Roche Lynch, Dr Brewer stood quietly at his side — to quote one of Spilsbury's biographers, Douglas G. Browne, "yet another busy general practitioner placed in the unenviable position of watching a faulty diagnosis being exposed".

The train of events which led to the raising of Hilary Rougier began with the discovery by Rougier's relatives — his sister, Mrs Ellen Cary Smith, and his niece, Mrs Ethel Hilliard — that he had left only £79. Whereas he should, they reckoned, have been worth at least £5,000 or £6,000 — a reckoning with which Mr Arthur Wilson Crosse, the solicitor who had drawn up Rougier's will for him in 1919, agreed. On the relatives' behalf, Mr Crosse made certain discreet inquiries, and secured evidence that the missing money had found its way into the pockets of the Lerwills. Various payments of sums ranging from £40 to £950 were traced to them, and a bearer-cheque for a massive £1,850 had been paid into Mrs Lerwill's bank account.

The authorities, presented with the sum of these findings, agreed that it amounted to reasonable grounds for suspicion and probatory action.

While Dr Roche Lynch was making his chemical tests and analyses, the Surrey County Constabulary, under the command of Detective Superintendent Ernest Boshier, were busy with investigations of their own.

At Nuthurst they found a locked cupboard in which was a bottle of laudanum. Miss Mary Hope, who had let the house to the Lerwills, said that her late father had been a doctor, and that this was his drug cupboard. She remembered the laudanum bottle's being there, but added that there had been more liquid in it when she last saw it, and that a piece of cork now floating in the liquid which remained was certainly not there previously. And Superintendent Boshier pointed out that, although the cupboard was locked, it was easy to open without a key because of a defective hinge.

By the beginning of May, Dr Roche Lunch had found morphine — a derivative of laudanum — in all the organs submitted to him, and, on 17 May, an inquest was opened at Woking in an atmosphere decidedly hostile to the Lerwills.

Dr Brewer gave evidence that never in the course of his visits to Hilary Rougier was he permitted to see his patient alone, and that Mrs Lerwill did all the talking, even answering for Mr Rougier when the doctor put questions to him. Richard

Hilliard, husband of Rougier's niece, said that when Mrs Lerwill telephoned the news of the old man's death, she suggested cremation. And Mrs Ellen Cary Smith, when shown a number of cheques alleged to have been signed by her brother, bluntly declared her opinion that some were forgeries.

William Knight Lerwill told the court that he was of no fixed occupation, and said that the money which Rougier gave him from time to time was to help him. It was given freely, gladly, and as an absolute gift. He was not, he went on to say, even in the house on the day that Rougier died, although he had looked in briefly during the Friday afternoon — because his wife had told him on the telephone that she was very worried about Rougier's condition.

Lerwill further said that he had, some time previously, bought laudanum for Rougier, who had wanted it to treat his spaniel's claws, when the dog was suffering from eczema. Despite a widespread search, the police were never able to trace any record of this alleged purchase.

Concluding his evidence, Lerwill stated that he had known Rougier since he (Lerwill) was a child of six or seven, and that their relationship had always been more than friendly.

Asked by Mr Crosse if he did not think it an extraordinary thing that Mr Rougier should die just at the time when he had got rid of all his money, Lerwill replied, "No, I do not."

Mrs May St Leger Lerwill was called next. She said that Rougier's health had been deteriorating for some time, and that she had thought that he rather overdid things. Dr Brewer's statement that when he came to examine Rougier she monopolized the conversation was untrue. She had merely answered for Rougier because he would not fully answer questions for himself. She knew nothing, she said, of financial matters. She had no money of her own. The bank account was opened in her name because an action was pending against her husband.

While Mrs Lerwill was giving her evidence, something occurred which many people said was "a sign" that her husband was guilty — the chair on which he was sitting suddenly collapsed, depositing him on the floor.

I can reveal that the cause of Mr Lerwill's literal downfall was something far less dramatic than divine intervention. The truth of the matter was told to me by Superintendent Boshier's son, Eric, when I went to see him at his house at Guildford. Back in 1928, Eric Boshier, following in his father's footsteps, had joined the Surrey Constabulary, and was serving at Woking. "One night some of us young constables were larking about, wrestling, in the section house," he said, "and one of us was thrown on to a chair, breaking it. A pot of glue was hastily found, and the chair stuck together and stowed away in an out-of-the-way place. Came the Rougier inquest, and every chair that could be found was commandeered. It was just sheer chance that Lerwill got the chair which we had broken and so inexpertly 'mended'."

Eric Boshier also told me: "I was in the coroner's court during the inquest and had the chance to have a very good look at Lerwill. I didn't take to him at all. He had a sort of secretive, furtive air about him. I know that my father was most anxious that there should be an arrest in the case, and he was absolutely convinced that Lerwill had done it."

On 30 May, the sixth day of the hearing, the inquest was concluded. After an absence of half an hour, the jury returned the curious verdict that "Hilary Rougier died from morphine poisoning, which was not self-administered". And there, on that question-begging note, the affair seemed to have ended.

Later that year, 1928, Mr and Mrs Lerwill brought actions for libel against the *News of the World,* and received what were for those days substantial settlements, rumoured to have totalled about £5,000. Taking with him the bulk of the money, William Knight Lerwill decamped to Canada, having abandoned his wife and children.

We next hear of him back in England in 1933, using his middle name, Knight, as his surname, living mainly in seedy boarding-houses in the Paddington and Cricklewood districts of London, and writing letters on the notepaper of exclusive West End clubs.

Then, in March 1934, he turned up unexpectedly at the house of a lifelong friend at Brighton. Haggard, poorly dressed, he said that he was starving and had only two shillings in the world. But he had great expectations. After mentioning that, as was true, he was an expert horseman, formerly known in Sussex riding circles as "Gentleman Jock" because of his immaculate appearance and stylish handling of horses, he told his friend that he had met a man in London who knew his reputation and had given him the job of buying him ten thousand pounds' worth of bloodstock and steeplechasers.

Whether or not the friend believed this story is a moot point, but he gave Lerwill a meal and lent him ten shillings to get to the North Devon village of Combe Martin, where Lerwill had relatives, including a brother named Thomas.

Lerwill arrived at the Pack of Cards Hotel, Combe Martin, on Sunday, 11 March.

One of his first actions was to call on a Miss Mary Kearney, who lived in a house in Buzzacot Road, which she rented from Lerwill's brother. Having introduced himself, Lerwill told her: "I am your landlord. I've had a motor-smash a little way down the road. I wonder if you'd be good enough to let me have three pounds, as I'm a trifle short of money." Although Miss Kearney had never met Lerwill before, she was happy to oblige with a cheque.

On Wednesday, 14 March, Lerwill was walking through the main street of Combe Martin when he saw the local policeman, PC Yelland, approaching.

In the polite way of villagers, Constable Yelland called a greeting to him — whereupon Lerwill pulled a small bottle from his pocket, swallowed its contents, and fell dead on the pavement. The bottle had contained prussic acid.

Why did he do it?

Did he fear arrest in connection with a recent accumulation of frauds? Or was there — had there been ever since an August day eight years before — another fear that rustled unceasingly in the dark corners of his brain?

Did he, in a moment of panic, imagine that the fear had suddenly been made flesh: that, by some chance-in-a-million trick of fate, a secret which had so long lain hidden had been dragged forth, like Rougier from his grave, to herald a retribution so terrible — arrest, trial, the condemned cell and the hangman's hands — that death in a swift moment of agony would be the better part of the bargain?

A Short Walk to Eternity

Jonathan Goodman

IN THE several plays and ballads inspired by the murder in the Red Barn at Polstead, Maria Marten is portrayed as the pure, simple daughter of a Suffolk mole-catcher. Actually, to para-phrase Wilde's view of truth, Maria was rarely simple and, from the age of sixteen, never determinedly pure.

She had been delivered of at least three illegitimate children. The father of the first child, which was born in the spring of 1820 and lived only a few weeks, was Thomas Corder, the eldest son of a well-to-do local farmer. A year later, when Maria was twenty-one, she gave birth to a son by Peter Matthews, the rakish brother of the lady of the manor of Polstead; this child, Thomas Henry, survived, and Matthews paid the Martens £5 a quarter towards its support. In 1826 Maria brought forth a child by twenty-three-year-old William Corder, the younger brother of Thomas; the child died — perhaps unnaturally — within two months and was secretly buried in a field at nearby Sudbury.

According to a contemporary description and appraisal of William Corder:

> He was five feet, four inches in height, and of slender make, and had a remarkable inclination to stoop forward in his walk, and held the lappel or breast of his coat in his left hand, when doing so. His complexion was fair, but not sickly; his face much freckled, and his eyes extremely weak, so much so that he was often obliged to put a book very near them, in order to read its contents. . . . This young man appears to have indulged an ungovernable propensity for for-ming intimate connexions with females, not withstanding which he was, in general, extremely cautious in his amours, in order to prevent discoveries. When the secret was disclosed, he used to boast of the favours with which he had been indulged, with a criminal flippancy.

After the death of the baby, Corder and Maria quarrelled frequently — chiefly, it seems, over Peter Matthews's most

175

recent quarterly payment, which Maria (with good reason) accused Corder of stealing. Her father, apparently feeling that an unhappy marriage was better than no marriage at all, repeatedly reminded Corder of his promise to make Maria his wife; but Corder always either evaded the issue or named a date for the wedding and then concocted a reason for postponing it.

On 18 May 1827, a Friday, Corder arrived at the Martens' cottage and announced that he was taking Maria to Ipswich — ten miles or so east of Polstead — for their marriage. "The reason I go to Ipswich," he said, "is because John Baalham, the constable, came to me in the stable this morning, and told me he had a letter from a Mr Whitmore in London, to proceed against Maria about her bastard children." He persuaded Maria to pack some of her clothes and disguise herself as a man, and they set off towards a barn at the southern edge of the village; the building, which was leased by the Corders from Peter Matthews's sister, was known as the Red Barn because of its imperfect mirroring of sunsets. There — so Corder had said — Maria was to change into her own clothes for the trip to Ipswich. She was never seen alive again.

William Corder and Maria Marten

The Red Barn

The following Sunday, Corder again called at the Martens'
cottage. He and Maria were not yet married, he said, because
the licence had had to be sent to London for signature; he told
Anne Marten, the step-mother, that Maria was staying at
Ipswich with the sister of a friend of his. The reason for his
"returning" to Polstead was that all his brothers were now dead
and his widowed mother needed his help in dealing with family
business. The weeks passed, and Corder told different stories to
different people to account for Maria's absence and to explain
why no letters were received from her.

Apart from her family, the person most anxious to obtain
news of her was Peter Matthews, who seems to have believed
that if she were married he would no longer need to subsidize
Thomas Henry. On 26 August Corder wrote to him:

Sir,
   In reply to your generous letter which reached me yesterday, I
beg to inform you that I was indeed innocent of Maria Marten's
residence at the time you requested me to forward [a] letter . . . and
will candidly confess that Maria had been with a distant female
relation of mine since the month of May. About five weeks ago they
both went into Norfolk to visit some of my friends. On Friday week I
received a letter from my kindred, who informed me that Maria was
somewhat indisposed, and that they were then in a village called
Herlingly, near Yarmouth.

I received an answer by the next post and enclosed your letter for Maria, which I found reached her perfectly safely, as I took the Yarmouth coach last Wednesday from Ipswich Lamb-Fair, and went to Herlingly, when I was sorry to learn that Maria's indisposition was occasioned by a sore gathering on the back of her hand, which caused her great pain, and which prevented her from writing to you, as her fingers are at present immovable.

Knowing you would be anxious to hear from her, I particularly wished her to write the first moment she found herself able, which she promised very faithfully to do. I gave her a particular account of our dialogue at Polstead Hall, not forgetting the remarkable kindness I received from you, which I shall ever most gratefully acknowledge. . . .

I remain, Sir,

Your most humble and obedient servant,

WILLIAM CORDER

Corder finally left Polstead for London on 18 September, exactly four months after Maria's disappearance. Confident, apparently, that he could continue his deception indefinitely, he made no attempt to hide his whereabouts, and a month later wrote to Maria's father with the news that the marriage had taken place:

> The Bull Inn,
> Leadenhall Street,
> London
> Thursday, 18th Oct.

Thomas Marten:

I am just arrived at London upon business respecting our family affairs, and am writing to you before I take any refreshment, because I should be in time for this night's post, as my stay in town will be very short — anxious to return again to her who is now my wife, and with whom I shall be one of the happiest of men.

I should have had her with me, but it was her wish to stay at our lodging at Newport, in the Isle of Wight, which she described to you in her letter, and we were astonished that you have not yet answered it, thinking illness must have been the cause. In that she gave you a full description of our marriage, and that Mr Rowland was "daddy", and Miss Rowland bridesmaid. Likewise told you that they came with us as far as London, where we continued together very comfortable for three days, when we parted with the greatest respect. Maria and myself went on to the Isle of Wight, and they both returned home.

I told Maria I should write to you directly I reached London, who is very anxious to hear from you, fearful lest some strange reason is the cause of your not writing. She requested that you would enclose Mr Peter's [Matthews] letters in one of your own, should he write to you, that we may know better how to act. She is now mine, and I should wish to study for her comfort, as well as my own. Maria desired me to give her love to Nancy [Maria's sister], and a kiss for her little boy, hoping that every care is taken of him; and tell your wife to let Nancy have any of Maria's clothes she thinks proper, for she says she has got so many they will only spoil, and make use of any she may like herself.

In her letter she said a great deal about little Henry, who she feels anxious to hear about, and will take him to herself as soon as we can get a farm whereby we can gain a livelihood, which I shall do the first I can meet with worth notice; for living without business is very expensive; still, provisions are very reasonable in the Isle of Wight, I think cheaper than any part of England.

Thank God we are both well, hoping it will find you all the same. We have been a good deal on the water, and have had some seasickness, which I consider to have been very useful to us both — my cough I have lost entirely, which is a great consolation; in real truth, I feel better than I ever did before in my life, only in this short time. Maria told you, in her letter, how ill I was for two days, at Portsmouth, which is seven miles over the sea to the Isle of Wight, making altogether one hundred and thirty-nine miles from Polstead.

I would say more, but time will not permit; therefore, Maria unites with me for your welfare, and may every blessing attend you. Mind you direct for W.M.C. at the Bull Inn, Leadenhall Street, London. Write tomorrow if you can; if not, write soon enough for Saturday's post, that I may get it on Sunday morning, when I shall return to Maria directly I receive it. Enclose Mr Peter's letters and let us know whether he has acknowledged little Henry. You must try and read my scribble, but I fear you will never make it out.

I remain your well-wisher,

W.C.

I think you had better burn all letters, after taking all directions, that nobody may form the least idea of our residence. Adieu.

Thomas Marten replied at once, and on Monday, 23 October, Corder wrote:

I received your letter this morning, which reached London yester-day, but letters are not delivered out here on a Sunday: I discovered on making inquiry yesterday. However, I could not get through my business before this afternoon, and I am going to Portsmouth by this night's coach. I have this day been to the General Post Office, making inquiries about the letter Maria wrote to you on the 30th of

September, which you say never came into your hands. The clerk of the Office traced the books back to the day it was wrote and he said a letter, directed as I told him to you, never came through their office, which I think is very strange. However, I am determined to find out how it was lost, if possible, but I must think of coming over the water to Portsmouth, which I will inquire about tomorrow, when I hope to find out the mystery.

It is, I think, very odd that letters should be lost in this strange way. Was it not for the discovery of our residence, I would certainly indict the Post Office, but I cannot do that without making our appearance at a court-martial, which would be very unpleasant for us both. You wish for us to come to Polstead, which we should be very happy to do, but you are not aware of the danger. You may depend, if ever we fall into Mr P——'s hands, the consequences would prove fatal; therefore, should he write to you, or should he come to Polstead, you must tell him you have not the least knowledge of us, but you think we are gone into some foreign part. I think, if you don't hear from him before long, you had better write and tell him you cannot support the child without some assistance for we are gone you know not where.

If you tell him you hear from us, he will force you to say where we was, therefore I think it best not to acknowledge anything at all. I enclose £1, and you shall hear from us again in a short time. This will not reach you before Wednesday morning, as I am too late for this night's post. You said your wife did not like to take any of Maria's clothes; she said in her last letter that her old clothes were at their service — I mean your wife and Nancy; but she shall write again as soon as possible. I must now bid you adieu. The coach will start in about ten minutes. I have been so much employed all this day that I could not write before. Believe me to be your well-wisher for your future welfare,

W.M.C.

The correspondence between Corder and Thomas Marten makes it clear that Matthews had decided to discontinue the payments towards the upkeep of Thomas Henry; the risk of his trying to trace Corder and Maria was no doubt magnified by Corder into an ideal excuse for staying away from Polstead and for not revealing the address on the Isle of Wight (a place which, as Corder took such pains to point out, was 139 miles from Polstead, just about as far south as it was possible to go without leaving the country; to Marten and his wife, neither of whom had ventured more than a few miles from their village, the island must have seemed as remote as the Indies).

Corder remained at the Bull for a further week, and would

probably have stayed longer had he not met a prostitute who knew of his connection with Polstead. Fearing that she might inform the Martens of the meeting, he hurried away to the small town of Seaford, on the coast of Sussex.

He returned to London in November. Having gone to extreme lengths to prevent one marriage, he now went out of his way to arrange another, inserting the following advertisement in the *Morning Herald* of 12 November and the *Sunday Times* of the 25th:

> MATRIMONY. A private gentleman, aged 24, entirely independent, whose disposition is not to be exceeded, has lately lost the chief of his family by the hand of Providence, which has occasioned discord among the remainder, under circumstances most disagreeable to relate. To any female of respectability who would study for domestic comfort, and willing to confide her future happiness in one every way qualified to render the marriage state desirable; as the advertiser is in affluence, the lady must have the power of some property, which may remain in her own possession. Many very happy marriages have taken place through means similar to this now resorted to, and it is hoped no one will answer this through impertinent curiosity; but should this meet the eye of any agreeable lady, who feels desirous of meeting with a sociable, tender, kind and sympathising companion, she will find this advertisement worthy of notice. Honour and secrecy may be relied on. As some security against idle applications, it is requested that letters may be addressed to A-Z, care of Mr Foster, stationer, No 68 Leadenhall Street, which will meet with the most respectful attention.

The advertisement attracted ninety-nine replies. The first forty-five were handed over to Corder as a batch, and he never bothered to collect the rest. Such a large response can probably be ascribed to the sheer length of the advertisement; this, as well as making the advertisement more eye-catching, indicated that "A-Z" was better off, or perhaps more open-handed, than most matrimonial advertisers, who condensed their conjugal desire into a couple of lines.

The Martens' cottage

Matrimonial advertisements were almost as much a feature of the newspapers of the 1820s as are used-car advertisements in the newspapers of today; even so, they were considered "not quite nice". It was a minor social sin for an unattached woman who did not work for a living to be seen glancing at the matrimonial columns, and the idea of actually replying to an advertisement was tinged with scarlet. Many of the women who replied to Corder's advertisement used up sheets of notepaper in explaining how they had "inadvertently", "accidentally", or "by the merest chance" happened to notice the word MATRIMONY; how, despite themselves, they had been forced to read on; and how, after considerable mental anguish, they had allowed their womanly feelings to overcome the guilt and embarrassment of communicating with "A-Z". Several replies claimed to be from go-betweens but were patently from excessively shy principals; there was no mistaking the true go-between letter, the most blatant of which came from a father offering his daughter's hand, sight of prospective husband unseen — "you can call here at any hour and take her away". Few of the letters were as brief, open, and to the point as the first in the following selection:

Sir,
     I have taken the earliest opportunity of addressing you with these

few lines. According to your advertisement, as you being the age that will suit me, twenty-four and I am eighteen, so I think Providence as ordained that you and I shood come together, for I am not very pleacntury situated myself, and it appears that you are not. I am of very cheerful disposition, and shood study everything for your comfort and happiness. If it will suit you, the most convenient time to see me will be at eleven o'clock in the morning, and three in the afternoon. If I do not see you in a day or two, I shall think that you are suited.

Till then, adieu.

Another letter, a small masterpiece of emphatic gentility, began:

When a female breaks through the rules of etiquette justly prescribed for her sex, as a boundary which she must not pass without sacrificing some portion of that delicacy which ought to be her chief characteristic, it must be for some very urgent reason, such as a *romantic* love, or a circumstance like the present; and in answering your advertisement, I feel that I am, in some degree, transgressing the law alluded to, and yet the novelty and sentiments of the advertisement itself, so entirely different from the language generally made use of (and which alone induced me to answer it), almost assure me that no improper advantage will be taken of the confidence I place in the honour of the writer: however, as you request that no person will write from motives of curiosity, I trust that no feeling of that nature actuated you in giving me this opportunity; but enough of preface.

Several timid pages later, the writer at last braced herself and came to the point:

From the tenor of your advertisement, I presume fortune is but a secondary consideration; a companion only is wanted who would sympathise in all your joys or griefs, one who would return kindness with kindness, love for love, and, as I perfectly know my own heart, as far as regards those qualities, I do not flatter myself when I say that such a companion would I prove; and where confidence was shown, the fullest would be returned. Pardon the warmth of my expressions, nor think me forward in offering them, as I am no giddy girl: nor am I a romantic old maid, but a warm-hearted affectionate girl, whose age qualifies her to pass between the two characters, being just turned twenty-one.

In contrast, another of the replies displayed a daunting confidence:

If you really are inclined to marry, and all is true which you state, I think I am the person. My age is twenty-two, and am happy to say possess a most amiable disposition; can play the piano-forte and sing tolerably well; also other accomplishments which I think not worthy of statement. I have always been brought up domesticated, and am quite able to manage, let my situation be what it may; my wish is to settle in life, provided I meet with one who I think deserves such a wife as I shall make. . . .

P.S. I have no fortune till the death of my mother.

Although a number of women admitted to having fallen on hard times, only one indicated the circumstances of her fall:

I have moved in society perhaps not inferior to the rank you hold; but, by a deviation from rectitude, which was occasioned by the too easily listening to the flattery of one whose vows I foolishly believed to be true, I am entirely deserted by my family, and banished from society; nevertheless, I flatter myself that I do not altogether merit such a fate, for I do assure you that no one could have acted more prudently than I have done since the unfortunate circumstance happened, which has very much destroyed my peace of mind; but I still hope to see better days.

I am two-and-twenty years of age, but have not the least pretension to beauty—quite the contrary. I have a sweet little girl, who is my greatest comfort; she is sixteen months old, and is beginning to prattle very prettily; I have no fortune whatever, but am supporting myself by needle-work at present, until I can meet with something more to my advantage. I mention these facts that you may not be led into any error; for I should be extremely sorry to act with any duplicity towards any one, and I leave you to consider how far your generosity will extend to appreciate my wrongs, and excuse my past misconduct.

Corder's motive in advertising for a wife is by no means clear. During the short stay at Seaford, he had met a shy, slightly deaf young woman called Mary Moore who was on holiday there; her home was in Gray's Inn Terrace, London, where she lived with her mother and brother, and ran what would nowadays be called a nursery school. Corder and Mary Moore did not exchange addresses and, so far as is known, made no arrangement to continue the friendship — yet a week or so later they met again in a pastrycook's shop in Fleet Street. Perhaps this first London meeting was a coincidence. But it can hardly have been a coincidence that Mary Moore answered the "A-Z" advertisement in the *Morning Herald*. Within a week of Corder's receiving her letter, they were married under special licence at St Andrew's Church, Holborn.

It seems, then, that Corder inserted the advertisement for no other reason than that Mary Moore should answer it — but why he, or she, considered it necessary to effect a further introduction, and by the rather illicit means of a matrimonial advertisement, is a complete mystery.

The newly-married couple settled down just outside London, at Grove House, Ealing Lane, Brentford, and Mary Corder started a girls' school. (The house was found for them by Thomas Griffiths Wainewright, who was an acquaintance of Corder's; an artist, and probably a murderer, Wainewright is the subject of Wilde's "Pen, Pencil & Poison". He thought of painting Mary Corder, but decided that her eyes "baffled" him: "they were like two lost stars that have strayed into a human face from the heavens".)

For the short time they were together, Corder and his wife were very happy. According to Wainewright, "Corder was inordinately fond of her and was for ever praising her virtues, squeezing her hand and whispering endearments to her. . . . I urged them to live on the continent." Corder was to regret not taking that advice.

During the early months of 1828, Anne Marten claimed that she was having a recurring dream in which she saw her stepdaughter being murdered and buried in the Red Barn. On Saturday, 19 April, more to put an end to his wife's pestering than because he believed in clairvoyance, Thomas Marten searched the barn; noticing loose earth around some large stones, he started to dig and before long came upon a sack containing a badly decomposed body that was later identified as that of Maria Marten.

A warrant for Corder's arrest was issued, and he was soon traced to Brentford. He was taken back to Polstead for the inquest; on the way there, he and his escort stayed the night in a back room of the George Inn at Colchester. Before going to bed, he was allowed to write a letter to his mother:

Dear Mother,
    I scarcely dare to presume to address you, having a full knowledge of the shame, disgrace and, I may truly add, for ever, a stain on my family, friends and late-formed connexions. I have but a few minutes to write; and being unfortunately labouring under this unfortunate charge, I have to solicit that you will receive Mr Moore [his wife's brother, a jeweller] on Friday morning, with whom, probably, may be my injured, lawful — and I must do her the justice to say — worthy and affectionate wife. I have always experienced

from every branch of their family the kindest treatment — hope and trust that the same will be returned from you the short time they continue in this part of the country, which, I am sorry to have to state, is to hear the event of this dreadful catastrophe. I am happy to hear you are tolerable, considering the present circumstances. I may, perhaps, be allowed an interview with you in a day or two, but that, I find, is very uncertain, I must beg to subscribe myself your unfortunate, *though unworthy* son,

W. CORDER

The words "though unworthy" were crossed out, but were still legible. Corder afterwards said that he wished to burn the letter, but the police refused to allow this, and it was handed over to the prosecution as evidence.

Following the inquest, at which the jury returned a verdict of wilful murder against him, Corder was taken to Bury St Edmunds Jail to await trial. On 28 April he wrote to Mary Corder:

My much injured and afflicted wife,

I arrived at this solitary prison on Friday, at ten o'clock at night, after a most dreadful day of misery. That night and the following day I was labouring under the most unimaginable affliction, alas! being confined by myself, without a single individual to ease me of my grief; on Saturday night I was quite worn out, and it pleased God to relieve me with sleep. The next morning (Sunday) I was summoned to attend chapel; but I must first tell you, the minister brought me a Bible and Prayer-Book on Saturday, and hearing of my awful situation, a sermon was preached on the occasion; the text was taken from 5th chap. 2nd Corinthians, 10th verse; the words particularly reminded me of the Day of Judgement, where we must all one day appear, and "receive according to the deeds done in the body whether good or bad". . . . I cannot but reflect upon the good advice which you have so often bestowed upon me, a poor lost sinner, unworthy of any one blessing. Yes, my dear wife, I feel persuaded my sins are more in number than the hairs of my head. Were it possible, how gladly would I fly to receive instructions from you, but alas! the time is now past.

I have made application for you to visit me an hour or two daily, thinking you might have taken lodgings at Bury; but that favour, I find, is not allowed; so that I am altogether deprived of my only earthly comfort, excepting through your pen, from which I hope to derive some consolation; and by searching the holy word of God, I hope to find forgiveness, through the merits of Jesus Christ, who came into the world to save sinners. Oh! that I may be one of the chosen people; yet how can I expect his brightness to shine upon me, knowing that I have always neglected to attend to his holy word. Our minister has kindly offered me any of his religious books, for on religion I must now build my hopes. My time is short — I must soon depart from this vale of misery, and true it is, man has but a short time to live, and even those who may now be in a good flow of spirits and health, if they look over a short space of time, they will be no more seen for ever. For my part, I could wish it were tomorrow, but God's will must be done. I cannot forget your severe affliction, and my dear mother's and sister's. Were it not, my dear wife, for the afflictions of those I have left behind, I should be better able to prepare myself for another world. . . .

With respect to this world, Mr and Miss Orridge [the prison governor and his daughter] have offered me every favour their regulations will admit of, and we are all allowed common necessaries, with which I have reason to hope your good brother will supply you, and I am anxious to hear how he was received at my mother's on Friday. When you feel disposed, come and see me, which I think had better not take place at present, as you will be allowed so few minutes with me, and that in the presence of a third person. Let me hear from you as soon as possible. I have not been able to write to mother, nor any of my friends. I shall be happy to receive a few lines from your brother, although I do not feel able to write to him. May God bless and protect you. I subscribe myself

Your unfortunate and almost broken-hearted husband,

WILLIAM CORDER

That letter, when published after Corder's death, caused offence to many people. One commentator referred to its "obscene juxtapositions", while another wrote:

What an incongruous animal is man — how unsuitable are Corder's expressions in comparison with his character. The letter contains the effusions of a captured murderer, writhing under the pangs of guilt (for he says, "I must soon depart from this vale of misery"). Upon what principle, therefore, can we reconcile his spiritual quotations, and his hope of becoming "one of God's chosen people"? The tongue even of Charity is mute.

Corder's anxiety to ensure financial security for his wife, who was several months pregnant, appeared in many of his letters to her. On 2 May he wrote:

My beloved wife,

As it is necessary to provide for the support of nature during the time we are in existence, I wish to know if you feel perfectly satisfied with respect to my property. . . . Remember, I have no one in this world but you to consult, and should it not be to your entire

satisfaction, I entreat you to inform me. I am at liberty to make an
alteration you think proper. I gave —— all the money I took wit
me, excepting three sovereigns, in consequence of the officer
threatening to take it from me, saying I should pay my ow
expenses. I have several times attempted to write to my mother bu
this disgraceful event prevents me. I cannot — I dare not addres
her.

 Yours, &c.,

WM. CORDER

Mary Corder, who had by now taken lodgings in Bury S
Edmunds, was allowed to visit her husband. After she had see
him on the morning of 3 May, he wrote her a long lette
expressing his anticipation of an after-life; parenthetically, h
begged her "not even to look at a newspaper, as there are s
many ready to represent me in the blackest colours". Sh
replied the same day:

> My dear husband,
> I know that there are a number of idle reports published; bu
> when we consider that it is by such reports those who write them ge
> their living, it is a little excusable. Although no one would like t
> have all their faults and every error painted in their blackest colour
> to the world — pray be of good cheer, as we are not to be judged by
> sinners like ourselves, but by one who will pardon us if we
> repent. . . .
> Write me a few lines every day, if ever so few — I am fearful you
> do not eat — I have left all to follow you — let me know what you
> want, and while I stay here, it shall only be to attend to your
> comforts.
> God bless you,
> Adieu,

M. CORDER

The apparent ease of Mary Corder's combining of practicality
with saintliness must have made missionaries who could not
infallibly resist envy envious. Shortly before returning to London for a brief while to attend to business relating to Corder's
property, she wrote to him:

> Do not let the affairs of this world trouble you; I think the sooner
> they are settled the better, as it will be a relief to you as well as
> myself. I do not feel so happy when I stay away from you, and I have
> endeavoured to conform to come once or twice a week, as I fear it is
> troublesome to Mr Orridge. I am a little more reconciled to my lot
> now, but cannot at present bear the idea of seeing you so seldom. I

188

will try at some future period. We have never been separated since we were married, only once, for a day or two, and then, you know, a few hours appeared years. . . .

I shall be so happy when my mother has let the house, as she purposes coming to me — I wrote her last night. Let me entreat you not to think so much about me — I have One to protect me. When I was last in London I could neither eat nor drink; it then cost very little to supply me with food. I now feel a great consolation at being so near you, and I wish our friends were also near us. I dare say some of them will come shortly. The time appears very long to us, but it will soon wear off. Adieu, God bless you.

Try and compose yourself — you would be surprised how I sleep; you have heard me say, if I have anything in the shape of trouble, I always sleep soundly — try and take pattern by me. You are very low-spirited today — but you know not what happiness awaits us both. Let me see tomorrow that you have profited by my advice — you will have a letter ready for me tomorrow.

Did you want the tea-spoon I sent you? — it is not borrowed — I bought or rather paid for it. . . . Adieu, God bless you once more.

Your ever affectionate wife,

M. CORDER

The trial began on Thursday, 8 August. The surgeons who had examined Maria Marten's remains had adumbrated so many possible causes of death that the Crown elected to indict Corder on several counts, each a different method of murder, and including shooting, strangling, suffocating, stabbing, and even burying alive. The jury retired at ten minutes past two on the second day of the trial; they returned thirty-five minutes later with a verdict of Guilty, and Lord Chief Baron Alexander set the execution for the following Monday.

On the eve of the execution, after seeing his wife for the last time, Corder was persuaded by Governor Orridge to make a confession:

> Bury Gaol, Aug. 10, 1828,
> Condemned Cell.
> Sunday Evening, half-past 11.

I acknowledge being guilty of the death of poor Maria Marten, by shooting her with a pistol. The particulars are as follows: — When we left her father's house we began quarrelling about the burial of the child, she apprehending that the place wherein it was deposited would be found out. The quarrel continued for about three-quarters of an hour, upon this and other subjects. A scuffle ensued, and during the scuffle, and at the time I think she had hold of me, I took

the pistol from the side-pocket of my velveteen jacket, and fired.
She fell, and died in an instant. I never saw even a struggle. I was
overwhelmed with agitation and dismay. The body fell near the
front doors on the floor of the barn. A vast quantity of blood issued
from the wound, and ran on to the floor and through the crevices.
Having determined to bury the body in the barn (about two hours
after she was dead) I went and borrowed the spade of Mrs Stow; but
before I went there, I dragged the body from the barn into the
chaff-house, and locked up the barn. I returned again to the barn,
and began to dig the hole; but the spade being a bad one, and the
earth firm and hard, I was obliged to go home for a pickaxe and a
better spade, with which I dug the hole, and then buried the body. I
think I dragged the body by the handkerchief that was tied round
her neck. It was dark when I finished covering up the body. I went
the next day and washed the blood from off the barn floor. I declare
to Almighty God I had no sharp instrument about me, and that no
other wound but the one made by the pistol was inflicted by me.

I have been guilty of great idleness, and at times led a dissolute
life, but I hope through the mercy of God to be forgiven.

W. CORDER

Witness to the signing by the said William Corder,

JOHN ORRIDGE

Sunday Evening, half-past 12 o'clock

While Corder was completing the not entirely credible confession, people were already arriving outside the prison to
witness his hanging. According to the anonymous author of *An
Authentic History of Maria Marten:*

By six [on Monday morning] vehicles of every description lined the
streets, until every stable and yard was full, as were the inns and
public-houses, so that adequate accommodation could not be afforded to man or beast, and hundreds who had not been provident
enough to bring food with them were obliged to go to the place of
execution hungry. The visitors consisted of every grade in society,
but there were more labouring men than any other class: for
although it was a fine harvest-day, the reapers, &c., for miles
around, "struck", and came in gangs to witness the end of the
murderer. Among the visitors were an extraordinary number from
Polstead, who started from their places of abode at midnight.

Long before the hour arrived, every foot of ground was occupied
in the pasture, and the buildings and trees which stood within view
of the scene of death had their occupants.

At half past eleven o'clock, Mr Orridge announced to the prisoner that the time had arrived when he must resign himself to the
officers of justice, and submit to the usual preparation for execu-

Corder on the morning of his execution

tion. Awful annunciation. Although Corder was well aware of the precise time fixed for his exit from this world (and he could see the minutes glide away by the prison dial which was within his view), he appeared to start when the announcement was made, but he soon recovered himself, and earnestly called upon God for mercy.

He then took the arm of one of his attendants, and descended to a room immediately under his cell, where his arms were pinioned and his wrists tied by Foxton, the executioner who officiates at the metropolitan prison of Newgate. (Such was the certainty which the local authorities entertained of a conviction, that they sent "a retaining fee" to the finisher of the law: and in order to ensure his important services, ordered him to proceed to Bury forthwith, and he actually started, with a double set of furniture [ropes], as Jack [Ketch] calls them, before the prisoner was put upon his trial, and arrived at the place of destination twenty hours before it terminated.)

The procession was then formed in the usual manner, in order to advance towards the scaffold. Corder was sometimes at the side and sometimes at the rear of the clergymen. His walk was not firm, neither could it be termed very unsteady, except when he once made a trip against a pebble. He was dressed exactly the same as on the days of the trial, with the exception of his having substituted a pair of speckled worsted stockings for the silk and cotton ones.

The executioner standing ready with the cap and rope in his hand, the prisoner was conducted to the fatal plank, whence he was to be launched into an eternal world.

The prospect from the place where the wretched criminal stood is of the most beautiful description. The foreground consists of softly-swelling or gently-rising hills, which are bounded in the distance by extensive plantations of evergreens, so that they form a sort of picturesque amphitheatre round the prison. But to his view, upon whom the eyes of thousands were fixed, this lovely scene of romantic beauty had no charms; and almost as soon as he glanced upon it, it was shut from his sight for ever.

When the prisoner first made his appearance on the scaffold, there was a momentary buzz in the crowd, and all the men took off their hats.

The apparatus for the execution was exceedingly simple, and much smaller than the ponderous machine used at Newgate. Instead of being straight, the cross-beam is a kind of slender curve with holes perforated in it for the insertion of the rope.

When the prisoner beheld the executioner ready to receive him, the sight of the rope did not seem to be appalling, for he readily turned towards the minister of justice, and appeared anxious for the close of the dreadful scene.

After the cap had been drawn over his face, Mr Orridge spoke to him, and immediately told the executioner to turn it up. Mr Orridge then said to Corder that if he had any declaration to make, that was the time. At this moment, the prisoner seemed unable to stand, and an officer supported him. The greatest silence prevailed; but the crowd manifested an anxiety to know what the malefactor had said. Mr Orridge then advanced to the front of the platform, and in a loud voice proclaimed — "The prisoner acknowledges his sentence to be just, and declares that he dies in peace with all mankind!" A number of persons then said, "Does he? — then may the Lord have mercy upon his soul!"

After the executioner had fixed the rope to the beam, and was busy in tying what he calls the "mysterious knot", it was suggested to him that he had left too much for what is technically called "the fall", in consequence of which he reluctantly took part of it up, and it was quite evident that the executioner did not relish this interference with his public functions.

Everything being completely adjusted, the executioner descended from the scaffold, and just before the Reverend Chaplain had commenced his last prayer, he severed with a knife the rope which supported the platform, and Corder was cut off from the land of the living. Immediately he was suspended, the executioner grasped the culprit round the waist, in order to finish his earthly sufferings, which were at an end in a very few minutes. In his last agonies, the prisoner raised his hands several times; but the muscles

The execution of Corder

soon relaxed, and they sank as low as the bandage round his arms would permit.

Immediately after the corpse had been taken into prison, there was a considerable scuffle among the spectators, numbers of whom wished to obtain a piece of the rope. That the cord made a considerable sum there can be no doubt, for when Foxton was questioned about his prequisites, he replied, "What I got, I got, and that's all I shall say, except that that there was a very good rope."

Corder's last letter was delivered to his wife soon after the execution:

My life's loved Companion,

I am now going to the scaffold, and I have a lively hope of obtaining mercy and pardon for my numerous offences. May Heaven bless and protect you throughout this transitory vale of misery, and when we meet again, may it be in the regions of bliss! Adieu, my love, for ever adieu! In less than an hour I hope to be in heaven. My last prayer is, that God will endue you with patience, fortitude, and resignation to his Divine will — rest assured that his wise providence will work all things together for your good.

The awful sentence which has been passed upon me, and which I am now summoned to answer, I confess is very just, and I die in peace with all mankind. I feel truly grateful for the kindnesses I have received from Mr Orridge, and for the religious instruction and consolation I have received from the Reverend Mr Stocking, who has promised to take my last words to you.

Adieu. — W.C.

THE ARTS THEATRE

MARIA MARTEN

(OR THE MURDER IN THE OLD RED BARN)

by The Hon. ————— (a Gentleman)

Mr. Mark Dignam as
WILLIAM CORDER

Revised and Reformed and the Company assembled and rehearsed by
MR. A. CLUNES

Programme Price Sixpence

*Cover of the programme for a production at the Arts Theatre, London,
in December 1952.*

The Poetry of Desiré Landru

William Bolitho

FOR THE space of a hundred miles' zone round the city of Paris are rich farming lands, split up into wedges of varying size by the radiation of the railway system. On these artificial routes runs, inwards, the current of food-stuffs to the central markets. Outwards to every segment of this agricultural circle there is a reflux of Parisians of all classes in the summer, to make the fortnight, month, or longer, stay, which is the institution of *villégiature*. In this region, southward, lies Gambais, where Henri Desiré Landru rented his villa.

Gambais differs in no other way from its sister-villages in the neighbourhood. The nice balance of their distance from the Colossus City has had uniformly two effects on their character. First, their ancient quiet has been outwardly intensified. They have no permanent cinemas, few cafés, rare and rudimentary shops. With Paris within an hour's railway-journey, who would want to shop or buy amusement for himself in Gambais? But all the noise of the world passes in the summer evenings through the main street, which sometimes is a roaring dust-flue containing a current of high-powered motor-cars that pass on their business.

Round this bed for the traffic stream, the village lies quite isolated; hundreds of concentric crooked streets, old and silent as the galleries of wood-beetles in a rafter. In the early morning, cocks call across from one high wall to another. At noon dogs slumber undisturbed on the door-sills; in the first cool of the evening a hay-wain creaking with its weight turns down the alleys to its home-arch. With this subtly decadent stillness, Paris has stamped these thousand villages with another mark. They are materially more rustic than any other villages in France. But there is no gossip. Collective curiosity, corporate censure, is as dead there as their streets. For better or worse, the villages of the zone are discreet extensions of the residential quarters of the

city, where there are no "neighbours". All round the mould-
ering nucleus of old houses in a Gambais where the peasant
landlords sleep, is a thick crust of gimcrack, walled villas, each
with its iron gate, its *cheval-de-frise* of broken glass, its hidden
garden, where live the Parisians in fully-paid-for enjoyment of
that capital city — luxury to which they are accustomed: privacy. The same unselective destiny as houses the Parisians in the
great tenements at home, distributes them in their *villégiatures*,
with no more discrimination or classification than a spade.
Asmodeus could show off as varied a sight under the roofs of the
villas of Gambais as in old Spain. An aged courtesan with a
corrupt boy may share a party wall with a domesticated banker;
a shy misanthrope who has survived a *cause célèbre* may walk in
his garden and faintly hear on one side of him, out of sight next
door, the laughs of a gay student and his grisette, on the other
the daily scoldings of a virtuous couple. Philosophers, artists
and devils, fools, misers, or drug-eaters — all may imaginatively
be found among the summer tenants of Gambais in any year. It
is probable (and the village gossips, having blunted their teeth
years ago in the research, have come to that opinion) that the
majority of their city tenants are, like the rest of humanity,
timid, rather dull people, to whom the problem of money is the
warp and woof of life. Among them, though, in the year 1918,
was Henri Desiré Landru.

As the roads and rails through this root-zone of Paris con-
verge, they seem physically to contract, and to concentrate the
look of the country. At a certain distance, the fields and pastures
are squeezed into the allotments of the market-gardeners,
which form a mosaic bowl of green round the outskirts of the
city, with ragged indentations into that first Circle of Power, the
industrial suburbs. This industrial circle is the outer structural
support of a myriad-meshed web of lives inside it: like the rim of
a wheel. Here the mechanical pressure on the green country is
completed. The gardens become narrow backyards, smutted by
the furnace-chimneys that drop heavy shadows over them. Like
grass under a stone, their produce has no chlorophyll; pallid,
swollen vegetables reared under glass like bacilli in a laboratory.
Here are the catacombs of mushroom-growers. From here
comes the livid asparagus of Argenteuil. The residue of the
forests that have ventured to this region is squeezed out of
orifices between the giant cells of these factories to make the
Paris Avenues, and sent on in parallel rays across shrieking

Landru's house at Gambais

tramlines, under groaning cranes, down dreary combs of drink and bicycle shops, through the abandoned pents of the old fortifications, centrewards. In this labyrinthine corridor Landru had his run and his home-earth.

From the points where they cut the circumference of Paris, the lanky lines of trees are ruled by straight-edge in a hundred radials to the hub, which is the Bourse and the banking quarter of ferro-concrete palaces. Here is the other structural element of the city, the roaring, vibrating money quarter, from the steps of whose Greek temple goes out at all the noon hours a clamour louder than an orchestra of steam-hammers: the axle of Paris, the buyers and sellers of shares.

Round this Bourse focus at various tangents, drawn by history of numerous centuries, are all the great lineaments of the city. Southwards, in a shaky line, the ruins of a land-owning feudality, the Boulevard St Germain, pious and old, doubled by the logical terrace of the ministries, the parliament, the Academy, beginning with the shrine of the army, the Invalides, and ending with the law courts and Notre-Dame. Northwards is the freehand vector of the industry of amusement, which starts in a dazzle of electricity on the boulevards, shades away quickly through the equivocal bars of Lorette, and the rendezvous parlours of St Lazare, blazes up again for a moment on the heights of Montmartre, a bonfire for the whole world, then, damped down every yard, along the straight strategical boulevards round the Gare de l'Est, it fades at last into the gloomy prostitution of the Outer Barrier, where the great shadows of the factory walls begin again. In every segment, chord, diameter of this living diagram where Landru had in his life-time business, its entire population followed his fate with passion and allied in his punishment. His hunt led him up the narrow back stairs that lie behind the palaces, his longings and sins knew both the staring lights of the theatre quarter, where he found Fernande Segret, and the clandestine perfumes of certain rooms near by, where he met Andrée Babelay, the palmist's assistant. When he was young and a choir-boy he loved Notre-Dame. When he was a man, his dossier and profile portrait was stacked handily in the file drawers of the Paris Préfecture. His hopes were at the Bourse-Centre, his garage at the Industrial-Rim, his trade at remote Gambais; academicians, duchesses, actresses fought to stare at him on trial with the miscellaneous riff-raff who live on holiday. The working people of Paris envied them. They would much rather have witnessed Landru marched down the Champs Élysées than the Allied Prime Ministers.

A whole city, a whole time, thus seems after a ghastly and mocking manner to be summed up in this individual, or at any rate to have a distorted reflection in him. No flat mirror, passive in itself, could have achieved this function; no nonentity. Landru was certainly a personality; if not a vehicle of power: a living allegory of large and obvious content, in which millions of nerve-racked, disillusioned men recognized a hideous likeness, and being momentarily without dignity, were forced to laugh at it, as if they had discovered an ape successfully masquerading as one of themselves.

The personality of Landru, and the extraordinary social phenomenon of his reaction on his times, are both to be studied together. Paris in 1919 was, more than all the other capitals of the world, a city of survivors. Every citizen counted his limbs and was amazed to be alive. Every one, when the cannons on the Seine fired their blanks for victory, started out of a hypnotic nightmare that had lasted four years, or like a Crusoe home at last threw himself with joy into that latest scandal of the village which assured him of his return. Returned soldiers, reading of Landru, heard for the first time since they entrained, of the old things, the old games, the old scenes which they were hungry to re-explore. They read of concierges, of palmists, of whores and cooks and Saturday nights; all the traditional puppets of civilian life, the libretto of a pantomime they had half forgotten. They heard the old jokes, now attributed to Landru. They followed with delighted recollection the street names in the accounts of Landru's crimes. This host back from killing, or suddenly relieved from the fear of being killed, with the taste of despair still under their tongues, learnt with a roar that a little funny man had all these years behind their backs been conducting a private war of his own, earnestly mimicking theirs, even to the casualties. Four years of intermittent abstinence had made all the men women-hungry, all the women starved for men: the very mention of their old sport of love raised their hysterical laughter to a shout. In the court, when the prosecutor in his charge came to the statement, "Landru had relations with 283 women," we heard that cry: admiration, regret, desire, which the fathomless law of human expression turns into "prolonged hilarity". It lasted until the judge, who had orders to extend his natural patience, prepared to clear the court. All these were reasons for the passionate interest of the Paris public in Landru. The case was the lay Te Deum for resurrection, the horseplay festival of peace, indecent as birth, stupid as war, unrulable and spontaneous as all the movements of the mob. On the whole it profited public order. It straightened the forehead of the surly combatant, ready to massacre the profiteers who had won where he lost, this immense joke on all the *embusqués*. It was also a good joke against themselves. They howled loudest of all when they noticed Landru had a trench-beard like themselves; in a twinkling this badge of their past sufferings and deceptions was shaved off every face: with it the *Poilu* surrendered the badge of his dangerous segregation from the rest of the nation.

The established forces of government, the press of information and the oligarchy of Clemenceau and Mandel seized willingly on the opportunity. The newspapers, bewildered at the sudden absence of a war communiqué, flung themselves eagerly on this first peace-news. The ironic despot Clemenceau, charmed with the discovery of a screen to push in front of the plans for a peace settlement he wished to elaborate undisturbed, gave murky instructions to the police and the magistrates to "cherish the Landru case". The mob in cry after their murderer did not notice, or were delighted to notice, the concomitant shortness of news about the Peace Conference. The raging protests of the liberals of all the opposition at the fantastic doings of the tyrant, in high politics, so found no echoes. Clemenceau carried to an end the French participation in the Treaty of Versailles — with the help of Landru — who thus unexceptionally enters into political history at its modern turning point.

The intersection of Landru's fate-line with public history lay in a china shop, the "Lions de Faience", in the Rue de Rivoli: more precisely, on the left hand of the cash-throne, at the end of an alley of pots and glasses, from which, as he spoke to the cashier, he could be seen by a person standing at the other end, though barred off by a crowd of shopping

Henri Desiré Landru

women. It was 12 April 1919, a Saturday. This shop (to attenuate the accident) is not an insignificant place, but one of the very numerous institutions around which the doings of Paris tend to collect; not *any* china shop, but the one place in the city where broken sets of out-of-issue pattern may be completed. At one of the restaurants in the Bois, a patient customer may confidently expect to meet sooner or later any particular moneyed pleasure-seeker in the world. At the shop in the Rue de Rivoli, if you wait long enough, you may count on re-meeting any woman of the lesser French bourgeoisie, once at least in her lifetime, and most of their husbands, all who have ever received a wedding present of a dinner-service and employed a servant who can crack a cup.

On Saturdays, the goods on display are retired half an inch from the edge of the shelves, to avoid breakages; Mademoiselle Lacoste was unable to cleave the crowd in the direction of the man she had recognized. But from a hundred tea-sets away, she identified his fawn-coloured beard, his polished scalp when he lifted his hat, his attitude, which was as unmistakable as his step if she could have heard it above the loud confusion of a great shop in full sale. As soon as she might, she veered under the cashier and asked and received from her the name of the polite customer. He was one Guillet, Lucien, engineer, 76 Rue de Rochechouart on the hither slope of Montmartre, who had bought a tea-service for his wife, to be sent immediately to his flat. Mademoiselle heard the name with grim unbelief, then, like a lean middle-aged Angel of Vengeance, stepped out to the nearest Commissariat of Police to announce that, unaided by all their efforts of the past months, she herself had at least found the address of Fremyet, engineer: abductor, seducer, sequestrator and, in her suspicion, slayer of her sister, Widow Buisson. Also in all probability of the so-called Dupont, suspected of the same offences on the sister of Madame Collomb, with which lady she was in relations since the coincidence of place, Gambais, from which both women had disappeared, had been revealed to her by the magistrate charged with investigation into her own case.

The Commissioner received the information with mediocre enthusiasm, but sent her on to the Central Bureau. Here they were more interested, mainly because of certain identities in the description of this Fremyet or Dupont or Guillet with a swindler named Landru for whom they had been long in search. The next morning two detectives went to the given address, above a jeweller's shop, a small neat flat, and there arrested Guillet, who made no trouble about admitting his real name was Henri Desiré Landru (Nandru, the first press reports have it), fugitive from a sentence of a criminal court for fraud in 1913. With him they took away his companion, a tall, ugly girl, very coquettish, named Fernande Segret, who wept all the short time of her detention. In the afternoon, the two were brought back in a cab to their flat, to be present at the impounding of their papers; when that long operation was finished, the man asked to be allowed to take his leave of Fernande, whom he understood was immediately to be released. He kissed her and, according to a strong legend, which she herself supports, said or hummed, with an operatic gesture and a "pale smile", the favourite little melody from *Manon Lescaut*: "Adieu, notre petite table".

With this verse the Landru case began. Whether or not the incident, at that place and time, was true, whether, after he had seen the brigadier turn over, at first curiously, then carefully, the leaves of the twopenny notebook covered with black waxed cloth that lay on top of the drawer, Landru could so have mastered his despair as to remember to be true to character, and even emblematical, it is now a matter of temperament to decide. It is certain, and as historic as anyone could wish, that the story that this hand-cuffed man under suspicion of two murders took leave from his mistress with the best-known sentimental phrase of the best-known sentimental opera in Paris, was handed to the reporters by the police the next day, and because of its "news-value" placed Landru for the first time on the front page of the press. The great public — and the whole of the unwritten art of newspaper production holds in this — always reserves its interest for the things it already knows. The incidence of a tune which every midinette had in her heart in an affair not obviously at this stage remarkable, explains the early precipitation of the press on the Landru story. Next day, when the "lost-dog" reporters called again for news and heard that the accused Landru was something of a wit, a fish that showed fight and would need playing, they knew that the first real peace news had arrived, and sorrowed to realize that the special correspondents would take its further course out of their hands.

To a chosen pack of these latter, Monsieur Dautel, commissioner in charge of the case, now showed the notebook itself. This dirty little thing, which the detectives had found on their second visit to the flat in the Rue Rochechouart, was one of the prime properties of the case, almost equally with the phrase from *Manon*. The one is a clue to the depths of Landru's mind; the other contained, as you shall see, the whole police case against him. It was ruled in money-columns in the customary pale blue ink. It was almost covered with a close writing in pencil, most of it the petty accounts of a methodical man; but near the beginning was this strange inscription jotted across the lines:

A. Cuchet. G. Cuchet. Brésil. Crozatier. Havre. C.t. Buisson. A. Colomb. Andrée Babelay. M. Louis Jaume. A. Pascal. M.Thr. Marcadier.

Dautel pointed out the significant occurrence in this abracadabra of the names Pascal and Collomb, or Colomb, as it was spelt: two missing women, whose sisters had already formally recognized in Landru the lacking Dupont and Fremyet. Further, the name Buisson corresponded with that of another woman, reported by her family as missing in September 1917. This woman's concierge had been put before Landru and had recognized him as a constant visitor to her vanished tenant.

The accounts were all on this pattern:

Expenses of 25 December.
2 Metro tickets, returns.
Invalides, 0,40.
One single 3,95.
One return 4,95.
One ticket (single Tacoi) 2,75.
Ticket (return) 4,40.

13 March.
2 tickets (return) 9,90.

27 April.
Meeting f. Pascal 4,90.
Biscuits, Malaga.

4 April.
Invalides, cab 3.
Tickets 3,10-4,95.
Post-chaise 2,40.
Houdan (St Lazare), 10 francs.

18 January.
Post-chaise (Diligence) 1,75.

From these entries the police was able to trace successively ten persons who had disappeared after relations with Landru. It is convenient at this point to give their names and some description of them, together with others not mentioned in the notebook.

WIDOW CUCHET claimed to be thirty when she met Landru in 1914. She was a domestic servant with a son of sixteen or seventeen, and several thousand francs of savings, of which Landru quickly defrauded her, but was pardoned months before her final disappearance. Widow Cuchet had no more colour or taste than water; from January 1915 to the day that the police seized the notebook it was as if she and her son had evaporated.

WIDOW GUILLIN, a respectable woman of fifty-one, with a fortune estimated by her family at 40,000 francs, lonely and discontented, disappeared two months later.

WIDOW BERTHE HEON, who came from Le Havre (and is apparently included in the list under that name), was fifty-four years old. She lived in a small shabby milieu of old women with incomes. She disappeared three months after Widow Guillin.

WIDOW COLLOMB was of higher social class. She was the "woman in a blue silk dressing-gown" in the case, that is, it was she who was seen by neighbours of the Gambais villa in the walled garden in that attire for a few mornings before she too vanished. In her life was one of those incidents which are only romantic because of the exotic names in them: she had had a child by a lover in Guatemala, who was being educated in a convent at San Remo.

ANDRÉE BABELAY, a servant girl of nineteen years old, who worked for a palmist in the St Lazare quarter. A big lumping hussy, whose case stands by itself, for she had no money.

WIDOW JAUME, from the quarter of small tradesmen and skilled workmen, Belleville. A stout, sentimental woman of forty-two, whom Landru wooed with flowers.

Then ANNETTE PASCAL, an Arlésienne, with large black eyes and false teeth. Landru's *denuciatrice*, Mademoiselle Lacoste, was her sister.

MARIE THÉRÈSE MARCHADIER, known in the brothels of various garrison towns as "La Belle Mythèse", still flamboyant at thirty-seven. She had wisely saved enough out of her military admirers to equip a small hotel in the interminable Rue St Jacques; it was in a negotiation for the sale of this business that she met Landru.

MME. CUCHET.

MME. LABORDE-LINE.

MME. GUILLIN.

MME. HÉON.

MME. COLLOMB.

MME. BUISSON.

MLLE. BABELAY.

MME. JAUME.

MME. PASCAL.

MME. MARCHADIER.

Landru's victims

The Poetry of Desiré Landru

There were others: MADAME LABORDE-LINE, who came from Buenos Aires (hence *Brésil* in the list!); WIDOW BENOIST, or BENOÎT, a buxom cashier at a *beuglant* — one of the lesser music-halls near the Rue de la Gaiété. Others again whose names filled for a day a column of sensation, then dropped out of the case, either because they had been traced or from inability of the police to find anything definite about them. Effaced, half-existent women, all of them, whose personality was not strong enough to leave even a distinct trace in the memories of their friends.

These identifications by the police were not at all simultaneous. Intervals of weeks, sometimes months, separated them. Each as it was announced had the air of a present to the public, a treat in reward for its patience over the interminable negotiations of the Peace Conference, which on such occasions became a secondary affair. Paris was thus fed irregularly with rich and indigestible repasts of blood and sex: perhaps the only food which its enervated palate could have stood. Often the announcement of the finding of a new "fiancée", the spiced details of her seduction by the strange creature in the cage at the Santé, exciting guesses at the way of her murder, would unaccidentally coincide with the bare announcement of the latest decision of the Big Four; so with red jam the nasty pill would pass down. There was a conjuration of chance in favour of the cranky despots who were making the treaty; the debasement of the currency, the badgering of Germany into life, the licence to all the hobbyists of Europe to create and kill nationalities at their fancy, the mass-betrayals and bribings, the huge spree with the profits of the deaths of twelve million men, which left not only Europe but Asia in more certain danger of war than it was in 1914: these were all safely smuggled, as far as the population in whose midst they were done were concerned, under the mackintosh-tails of our seedy little murderer. . . .

In the moment of destiny, the French had their heads buried in a *feuilleton* — a serial story.

At least, its central figure, this Landru, could rival in his life and character most of the personages in past *romans à succès*. With a little jogging from the journalists, the examining magistrate had fixed the main traits of his subject: Landru's deep and luminous eyes, his hypnotic charm, his inflexible assurance, his wit, his mystery; and Landru did his best to live up to this schedule. Even when he stood in full light before the reporters

207

at Versailles, they continued to write about his "black beard", though it was too obviously a tawny ginger, because the public expected a black beard in its satyr. His *"rouspetance"* was doctored by able wits, and when it failed into a grumpy silence or mere insolences, epigrams were attributed to him, some say from canonical anecdotes of Clemenceau himself. The mawkish was out of fashion; in those days Landru gave us what we wanted. As Clemenceau did, he faced his horrors as we wished we could, with a bright eye, a rasping tongue, a sang-froid which had a savour of desperate rebellion. "Prove it," he would answer contemptuously to the magistrate when a new abomination in his past was spread traitorously in front of him. "I'm a man of honour, and won't say," was all threats and wheedling could ever find out about the ends of these sinister idylls. When they shook his notebook, his damnation, in his face (the reports told us), they could get nothing from him but a laugh, a real laugh, and a waggish "I must have been a thrifty man."

By skins as an onion is peeled, the detectives opened up each of his impostures, towards the first facts of his boyhood and birth. He was born in Paris, in the 19th arrondissement, in 1869. His father was a stoker at the *Forges de Vulcain*, a self-bettering man; all identifiable trace of his mother has disappeared. Desiré Landru was "un petit garçon très doux, très timide et très caressant". In his embryo is indeed little of the finished grotesque that the whole of 1919 is jabbering about. Perhaps only this, that he was too shy to play with other boys. He had a sweet voice, and the clergy, who esteem this type of boy, soon found him and gave him a place in the choir of St Louis-en-l'Île, where he sang alto to Sunday nave-fulls of Bonapartist tradesmen. His voice cracked late, when he was fifteen years old. The curé, to keep him, allowed him to serve the mass, and wear a dalmatic at the festivals, whence the tradition that he was actually received to the order of sub-deacons. When he was sixteen, he passed the entrance examination to the École des Arts-et-Métiers which prepares for the profession of mechanical engineering: here again there is a vague echo of his later life, for his favourite imposture was to take the part of an engineer; and he was always ready with impressive technical words. He was conscripted before he had qualified. He was sent to the garrison town of St Quentin, where his punctuality and submission, qualities prized by officers as well as priests, soon gained him sergeant's stripes. With the idea of shortening his time with the colours, after four ears he married, and soon after was released to civilian life. Meanwhile his father had yielded to lifelong ambition and joined the collared classes. He had abandoned the factory, and found precarious work as a publisher's canvasser; and Desiré, on his return, was obliged to follow him upwards. Besides, there was now no more money to support him for the final year at the school; young Landru was placed as book-keeper and general clerk. So for years the family added chapters that matched each other.

But in 1900, the year of the Paris Exhibition, the father being feverishly occupied with the thousand new chances it had the air of bringing to his career, Desiré Landru went into a metamorphosis which changed him from the sentimental, softish fellow hitherto into an impudent swindler. This change, instead of having no explanation, as many have said, has too many. They range from the magical hypothesis of the alienists: that Landru must have fallen off a ladder, or in another way received a blow on the head, which blow or accident there was a great bother to find.

The undoubted antecedence of the theory to the evidence makes the latter, and its explanatory worth, very suspect. In the history not only of remarkable persons such cracks are common. Before accepting them as sufficient causes for the strange and sudden changes that make mass-murderers out of mild book-keepers, or (as it has been done) saints out of wastrels, and poets out of pig-keepers, other less alarming possibilities must be explored. Much of modern criminological theory, like the earlier nonsense of Lombroso that they have, under pressure of ridicule, discarded, certainly comes from the baseless and unconscious pride of honest men who refuse to see in a felon a like animal to themselves, of like instincts, feelings, methods, a lost straggler from the army, not an alien tribesman. If anyone wishes to cure himself of this error, let him, in the privacy of the night, set himself the little exercise of reckoning, in his own life, the exact number of years' imprisonment he himself would have accomplished had he unfortunately been caught in every lawless act, even the most insignificant, and had had the misfortune of being sentenced on such occasions to the maximum penalty of the law. It is not necessary to add to this the probably unsound evangelic reckoning of all crimes of intention, though the total from this latter method will assist powerfully in seeing the resemblance. "There, quite conceivably, go I," the majority of

honest men, with awe if not piety, may say to most petty swind
lers and thieves as they stumble down from dock to prison. And
from swindlers to the lowest hell which we are visiting there is
as we have found, a quite practicable path down. So, in this case
of Desiré Landru we will not believe that he is a hand-watch tha
one bang on the case deranged, but that he came under a law o
metabolism that works, though in infinitely varying degrees and
periods, in the lives of all human beings. At the age of thirty
years, quite an ordinary period for a man to reflect on his life
measure his situation, and if he finds it displeasing reform it, this
Landru reviewed, we may legitimately suppose, his past and
present, and then firmly decided to try another road to the
future.

The slow accumulation of his experience had come to persuade him that submission did not pay. The sight of the unusual
luxury and heightened life that the Exhibition brought to the
city sharpened his desires, and by natural maturity, his
adoration of ecclesiastical scents and sounds and sights had
developed into other desires which promised less vague and
more realizable satisfactions. He knew he needed more money,
more freedom, more solitude from men and more of the company and pleasures of women. So he set himself to his first small
fraud, which prospering, another, and so on until, with a terrible
shock, no doubt, he found himself at his first conviction, in 1900,
in Paris.

It was still confidently hoped that two years' hard labour was
the right medicine for a case like this; once more it failed. It
failed, not only because a prison condemnation makes the
future exercise of any honest trade or occupation difficult,
except that of the common labourer, but still more because of
the mental obstacle of the convicted man's intimate way of
thinking. It Landru considered that he was guilty, the terrible
suffering of two prison years might frighten him from his ways,
in spite of the after-difficulties of an honest life; but it is wrong to
suppose that a swindler, a man who is rather more than less
egotist than the normal, denies himself in the solitude of his cell
from the almost universal pleasure of believing oneself in the
right. The pupal Landru, like the fully-developed mass-
murderer that he grew into later, not only found excuses for
himself, in the personal causes of the action that had brought
him there, and in the practical morality of the times around him,
but he definitely considered that he had been unjustly injured

or a piece of sharp business in no way out of the ordinary. So the mill of the law has failed with him. It turned him out still harder than he went into its maw. He is caught again in 1904 for the same offence, and given another two years' hard labour; then in 1906, thirteen months; then in 1909, three years; then at Lille, in the same year while serving the sentence, another three years; finally, on 20 July 1914, he was sentenced, by default, for fraud to four years' imprisonment and *relégation*, that is, lifelong obligation to reside in New Caledonia. It was to inflict on him the performance of this sentence that the police were looking for him throughout the war period. The manner of his frauds showed a nice gradation in the art of the confidence trick, with a noticeable tendency to choose victims among women, and these of a certain age and sort. It may be laid down that in Landru's pre-war career the women always grew older and uglier, and that his means of meeting them narrowed more and more to the columns of the newspaper. In his last bloodless case, the fixed type is reached: he advertised for second-hand furniture, met an elderly widow and bilked her of payment for the sale of her goods.

Here, openly, is a resemblance between Landru and English Smith[1]: both second-hand dealers, both preying on women. They were, in fact, in the same branch of trade, which will make their dissimilarities the more interesting. His last condemnation had made Landru a desperate, hunted man; only the war, and the general disorganization of the police service that followed its outbreak, saved him from a living death in Cayenne. For he was like all his class, an animal that had his habits; the hunters were perfectly aware of his appearance as well as his methods and forms, even of the stereotyped formulae of his advertisement. August 1914, though it saved his skin, almost ended him by hunger. All business in these first months ceased. There was no one to sell or buy, and Landru, slinking about the outer labyrinth of Paris, was hard put to it to get a meal a day. Even a day may hold many resolutions to a destitute man; it was on 14 August 1914 that he appears to be in the midst of his first murder. . . .

Sooner or later, on the way he was going, he was bound to

---

1. *Editor's Note.* George Joseph Smith, the "brides-in-the-bath" murderer; an account of his exploits appears in *The Seaside Murders*, Allison & Busby, London 1985.

stump his nose against the barrier that separates crime into two parts, when in the course of a deception he was certain to notice and ponder that the logical conclusion of a fraud was to kill the victim, and so take, not a pittance, but the whole. In the days of mobilization, with starvation at his heels, Landru does not even check at it, but bursts through as if it were made of smoke. In a few days he met the Widow Cuchet and her son André, deceived them, trapped them, robbed them, and abolished them. On 14 August he is selling a tobacco-pipe belonging to the boy; in January 1915 mother and son are vanished from the earth, from the stepping-stone of a villa which Landru hired in Vernouillet, a village in the *villégiature* zone of the city. By July of the same year the last possessions of the unfortunate couple were sold, and in the following month he is in the midst of the murder of the Widow Guillin. . . .

In two characteristics Landru leaves that impression of hocus-pocus which was behind the name one of his victim's friends gave him of "Mr Mystery". There was the conjuring away of his bodies, which I will discuss; and then there was his fascination of women. First we must clear away the charlatanry, his own and that which hurried journalists wrapped round him. Landru's magnetic eyes were a fable; they were only queer eyes, two shining black spots at the bottom of depressions, fixed unchanging objects that appeared artificial as if he had been fitted with two glass eyes, of a fanciful make, rather than the eyes of a dominator or seducer. These eyes gave no confidence, but rather the effect of an infirmity. Unless women are to be fascinated by curiosity alone, they had no part in his success. Landru's whole look, in fact, does not explain even the humblest of his conquests. He was a shabby, bowed little man, fitted for peddling or any form of selling in which pity besides business has to matter. As to his manner, that is different. His speech was highly persuasive to a certain class of women and young persons, for he had a great deal of calm, always based himself on the most assimilable form of reason, Law, and ornamented every statement with technical words which gave them an appearance of great dignity. When in argument, he would not allow the contradictor to state his own case, but he would do it for him quickly and fairly, then demolish it, gravely and sometimes with an expression of sympathetic regret. In his walk and when standing, he contrived by slowness and deliberation to expunge the last trace of anything ridiculous in his seediness, by which it appeared to many merely another mark of distinction, as if he was a millionaire too preoccupied to trouble about clothes. His poor physique often prepossessed women among whom a certain thinness is instinctively believed to be a sign of a sort of worldly innocence that disarms mistrust and calls for protection. Many of Landru's women felt he needed protection.

On the whole, then, Landru gave the impression in his world of a distinguished gentleman, poor, perhaps, but learned and serious, as it were an unofficial professor, whose crankiness was very respectable. Even in the court of Versailles many of the witnesses, and — supreme tribute — among them concierges, could not bring themselves to speak of the poor devil standing between gendarmes in the dock on their right otherwise than as "Monsieur" and "Ce monsieur". This effect indeed was not universal: certain families, among them the Lacostes and the Collombs, people of a higher social rank than the rest, disliked him from the start, and may even, as they declared in court, have taken him to be "a very fishy person" when they met him in the company of their enthralled sisters. But it was true for the majority of those humbler women with whom he had contact; it would partly explain how these "sou-gripping" charwomen could have so tamely lost their heads to his frauds.

But there was much more in Landru, much that cannot be explained, either by his quackery, or still less by any erotic superstition about him. This second charm can be put: that he knew what he was after in life. To women (I am not sure of men) this is doubtless the strongest lure in the world. However it is looked at: that Landru had will, or direction, or a theory, or a belief, it means in practice that he was positive to the same degree that they were negative and so they followed him, as by an electromagnetic law, or as one man walking firmly and straight through a crowd of saunterers will draw them infallibly after him. All the women whom he destroyed were completely lacking in this purpose: the young Babelay unconsciously, her elders with the sting of knowing that they had few more years in which to discover the secret without which they were mere flotsam. This man who had overawed them with his supposed culture drew them pantingly after him with the hope that he possessed the plan they had missed; he promised to let them share it with him in marriage. Again it must be observed that the bait was not simply, or even chiefly, one of the senses; most of them were widows, none virgins, and even at fifty a woman who desires sexual intercourse in Paris need not go to the point of making an advertisement-marriage to enjoy it without publicity. The marriage offer that Landru set out was perfectly understood by both parties to include much wider benefits than "love": to the woman it meant the whole of that vast range of benefits that the institution everywhere endows her; lifelong financial support, as the least though solidest, and still more (for they were all self-supporting) whatever deep needs of human kind are expressed by "company" — which in the case of this man meant a full share in the secret and meaning of life which everything, from his absent eyes to his confident walk, advertised that he possessed. They fell on Landru, as lost trippers in an artificial labyrinth will cling to a passer who says and shows that he knows the way to the centre. Past the menopause, all of them, they knew — counting back from the unreality to which they had come, a life entirely meaningless and useless, in which they were not even happy — that every single act since they were born, their sleep, their work, their sufferings, were equally unreal. They had not even that last means of illusion in the life of a woman, that last substitute for a purpose, a man to themselves. In ordinary times, this bitter consciousness would have been unobtrusive, lulled by the comfortable materialism around them of millions who left the Sphinx's riddle alone. But a war to a spinster is like a ball in the house next door, a wild and fascinating carousal of sound and adventure to which she has not been invited. Let no one, pacifist or patriot, imagine that the masses read the war-communiqués. But in huge Paris there were drums in the air, which made it a frenzy to be alone. Age, sex and time were in complicity with Landru. He was the male, the master of the secret.

They knew he had it, because of his air, because of his eyes (that did not move like their own), because he told them so, and because he believed it himself. To this pedlar, these peaked seekers were clients come to offer a bad bargain: their wrinkled cheeks and dyed hair, their sticks of furniture and savings, together with the make-weight of their intimacy, against the fabulous value of his possession, himself and his secret. He had no more doubts than sun and moon, otherwise the spell had never been.

But what it was he believed, the nature of the charm in his possession that would have made the life of a washerwoman and a superannuated whore at last worth living, is more obscure.

That these uneducated women never could discover it, and had to content themselves until the brutal end with mere hints, need not discourage all investigation; nor that the drama-drunk audiences at Versailles, and the hasty mob of reporters, and even the judges and pleaders intent on their own ambitions, never guessed it, and felt that Mr Mystery was well named. For these were all burning the Guy of Paris in the bonfire of their return, in clothes which they had themselves dressed him. An effigy of their old bogy, the Satyr of the Bois de Boulogne: their mood was not for research, but a hilarious hunting. He was the resuscitation of the national joke against sexual impotence, this man who had "had relations with two hundred and eighty-four women", which lies as deep in the French subconsciousness as its brother, the fear of being a cuckold, in England. Covered with traditional rags, daubed with the traditional paints, the mysterious little fellow on his carnival throne was as safe from observation as he had been at Gambais. Even now, when the revellers have gone, it is a daring thing to pick about among his embers for his great secret, for it was deeply embedded in that ultimate cubby-hole of any human man, his personality. If it were not that he had himself half-betrayed it to one woman, and that woman, Fernande Segret, worked by a mixed motive of her poverty and her notoriety, had not given it to us in a curious little pamphlet of her *Memoirs*, we might turn in despair from the search. We have this document. In it like an insect in a thick glass bottle we can vaguely see this queerest of mass-murderers moving to and fro and study him at ease.

At first, in these *Memoirs*, it is only the minor interest of his ways and wiles that catches our attention: his manner of approach, the system of his lies, how he behaved when seized by an angry and respectable mother, or how he looked after a return from a Saturday to Monday, which we know from an easy comparison of dates must have been filled with one of his black idylls at Gambais. Such passages as this satisfy our lesser curiosities:

> Arrived at our destination, scarcely had we gone a few yards on the pavement when a man accosted us, saluted us very respectfully, and addressing himself to me, with a voice whose charm and softness surprised me, asked if we would allow him to accompany us for a few minutes. It was the unknown of the tramcar [who had stared at Fernande Segret and her friend fixedly a short time before]. We refused the invitation with a smile, and quickened our pace to get

away from him. But our follower would not be shaken off. Rather
cheekily he suggested that young girls in Paris go out all too often
alone, with the risk of being accosted by bad characters, and all sorts
of annoyances from men. Such a statement made us laugh loudly;
our follower took advantage of it to stay. As we were certain we
would soon give him the slip, we exchanged some commonplaces
with him. He talked on, abundantly, with a most lively wit, and
every subject he touched on he seemed to be at home in.

On a later occasion, Fernande again meets the man, Landru, who
"confided to me that he was a manufacturer, owner of an automo
bile and of a garage near Paris, and of a sweet little villa at Gambais
where he liked to do a rest cure from time to time. 'My father,' he
said, 'was a very rigid and austere man, and always kept my mother
ignorant of his business. I suffered much, for I had a boundless
affection for her. . . .' His eyes shone as he spoke of his mother, and
he gave the impression of much emotion."

Fernande Segret, who "*subissait les apprehensions d'une épo
que où la guerre laissait aux jeunes filles peu d'espoir sur leur
avenir*", allowed him to call on her family, whom he charmed
with gifts of flowers and genteel, grave ways. He claimed to be a
refugee from the war region, by which he explained the lack of
identity papers, necessary before there could be a marriage.
Here is a party at the Segrets', which is as curious in its way as
the grasshopper's method of laying its eggs.

The following Wednesday, we were all seated with him at a family
dinner. Grandfather was with us, and I noticed at once by his happy
smile how much he appreciated the lively conversation of Lucien
[Lucien Guillet, Landru's pseudonym in the incident] and how
much he liked the many attentions which his neighbour at the table
showed on him. That evening Lucien was dazzling in his "go" and
comicalities. Without ever forgetting that he was in the presence of
ladies, he poured out jokes, witty retorts, and even juggled for us
with the napkin rings in a clever way, all the time garnishing his talk
with the most wonderful puns. At dessert, as we were on the subject
of music-halls, he recalled the triumphs of stars of the past, whom he
had known, and sang for us some lines of a once famous song, "Le
Bal à l'Hôtel de Ville". So he attracted the liking of all, and no one
had eyes all the evening for anyone but Monsieur Lucien.

This impression, so obviously authentic in its reporting,
Landru added to by many another device. "We were at the
critical moment of food restrictions. Neither *petits fours* nor
pastry were any way to be had, but nevertheless he managed

always to bring us all these prohibited delicacies, and when we showed our delighted surprise, he would answer that if one really wanted anything, one could always get it."

At the house-warming of his flat in the Rue Rochechouart:

> There an unforgettable spectacle shone on our eyes. It was not a mere flat on which the door opened, it was a real greenhouse. The dining-room was nothing but an immense basket of flowers. I have never seen such a display, in size or variety. He had with careful taste mixed humble violets with the rarest gardenias, and everything was so well arranged with such harmonies of colours, such taste in the bouquets, that mother and I looked at it as if we were paralysed. "You must have robbed the Nice flower train," I said at last. . . .

Finally, the difficulties of the identity papers having been recognized as insuperable, Fernande avows that she went to live with him, in the flat at the Rue Rochechouart, with the tacit permission of her mother. After some time, "Lucien" asked her to visit his little property in Gambais. They went down by train, and hired bicycles at the station of Gambais.

> At last we passed the cemetery, and then, before we entered the village, Landru waved to a little house, buried in the trees, still far off, and murmured to me happily: "There is my little paradise."
> We jumped off our bicycles and entered the grounds. The garden seemed to me very large, but it was completely neglected. A few half-wild roses, some geraniums run to seed in a jungle of weeds and bushes.

At this point Fernande, after having inspected the house, which was practically without furniture, and where "none of the rooms seemed to be used for what it was intended", makes the characteristic remark: "Wouldn't it be possible to let my family come and live here?" It was the high season for the Gotha raids. But Landru evasively refused.

These and fifty other such passages show the value of this little document, saved from banality by the happy simplicity both of the narrator and the editor. It allows us to see the greatest murderer of our times with limpidity, as he went about his business. For though it is certain that this girl was in no immediate danger during this period, yet it is equally sure, both *a priori* and from fragmentary revelations in the evidence at the trial, that the manner, the technique, employed by him in the snaring of his victims was the same. But this is only the husk of Landru, and having followed with delight the curious detail of his ways, we must return to our deeper research of what he meant to the long muster of these unhappy women, and why.

For granted that Landru was in love with this girl who has given us his secrets, with her airs and simpers, as he assuredly never was with the elderly row of victims, with whose spoils she was thus elegantly seduced, she certainly was not in love with him, and the attentions over which she rolls such a greedy little tongue replaced with her accordingly the overwhelming, obscure passion which was the cord that held the others to Landru, whose roots we have set ourselves audaciously to explore. Again we have to thank the news-editor for light; without prompting from a skilled publicist trained in the tradition of *documents*, Fernande, the scatterbrain, would doubtless never have thought of giving us Landru's letters, which have the clue; nor perhaps of recalling that queer simulation of suicide which rushes to our help when we were almost turned back in despair. Here, first, is the letter which is reproduced in facsimile in the *Memoirs*:

Thursday evening.

I am, my pretty little friend, in a sorry state which draws me near your caressing heart to find consolation and forgetfulness of my pain. I must tell you that first of all, mustn't I? Don't be alarmed, it is nothing you have done, you would never do me harm; I myself am the cause, but I cannot yet quite explain it. Yesterday I saw your beautiful eyes, so deep, so stirring, clouded with a little worry. I cannot ignore that I must have been the cause since there was no one near except ourselves. But what can it be? Can I have said a word or a phrase that shocked you? Or anything else of the many things that I have been trying to think of, in vain? That is how I look at it, and it leads me to examine many matters which in my happiness at having you by my side I did not think of, in the sheer joy of my heart at being filled with you. Unfortunately, implacable reason when one dissects it shows a thousand things, perhaps mistaken, but perhaps, ah me, nearer truth. From this number, I have excluded the idea that you were hurt because I cannot bring you a quite new love. Certainly your beautiful soul deserves it, and I long to be able to do so. But we have promised to be frank with each other, and I will tell you everything about myself which you would like to know, or which it is good for you to know. But please, please don't press me too soon. I am by nature, by life, by reason of my real loneliness, spiritual and material, a hermit, and utterly reserved. Perhaps you will find many new things in me, more than you could suppose. It is for you who have so much good sense to see that you don't ask too much from me at a time, and I will see to it, in compensation for all that hard experience has taught me, that no troubles you have and are good enough to confide in me can touch you. Another of those hard truths which I have to recognize, and which, perhaps, is one of the reasons, or a part of one of the reasons, for your sadness, is the fact that I am no longer of the same charming and hopeful age as yourself. The years have been hard to me in all the painful acceptation of the term; if I have kept a body which is still supple and healthy, I owe it only to a strict hygiene and to the avoidance of all excesses. Certainly I am still vigorous, more so perhaps than many a young man of our city, but the years have marked their imprint on me and I would take it as a stupidity to try to hide it. But for you, little friend, whose very walk is pretty, whose fresh smile and eyes have a right to happiness, to dream, can I have the right to consider myself even as a chance pal without presumption? Don't protest out of politeness. I know myself pretty well. If I have some qualities, I have also great faults; the balance is against me if I weigh them up. Only, if that could explain it all, a very great friendship, and, I fear, a feeling much deeper than affection draws me to you and grows daily as I find in you those precious treasures of the heart and head which I fear are so little appreciated in these times. Where am I going, little friend most dear, under your darling leading? and where are you pulling me? What will I be to you? What do you want to be to me? All these thoughts, all these reflections and a thousand others, as I have said above, make me try to find the reason for your little sadness. Tell me, beloved friend, and let your heart open a little. You will find, perhaps, a cure, certainly a friend who is indulgent, affectionate and attentive, whom you need never fear to come to whatever it may be. We don't know each other very well yet, but I have a presentiment that we will both learn to appreciate each other better in frank confidence. Would you like that? and isn't it too much to ask you? There are still other reasons that I have thought about, but those are more delicate and need to be discussed by word of mouth. They will not be mentioned by me unless I cannot find the reason for that cloud over your eyes, and when circumstances give me my chance.

Excuse my rambling prose, but the very thought of seeing you sad torments me. You alone can with one word calm me and give me back the so great happiness of seeing those deeply dreamy eyes, whose memory haunts me day and night, clear and sparkling once more. Goodbye, don't make me wait too long; whatever your answer, it will be welcome as coming from you and I will take it without a murmur. You will have, all the same, the respect, the good will, and if you wish — on your darling little hands, the best kisses of your

LUCIEN GUILLET

Then, here is the mock suicide:

When he had gone, I shut the door quickly, almost sure that he
would come back five minutes afterwards. I gave my visitor his
leave, but hour after hour passed and there was no Lucien. On
reflection, I imagined him so upset that suddenly I felt extremely
miserable. I knew how bizarre he was, how complicated, and that
day he had seemed so troubled that I asked myself whether perhaps
he would not do something rash in his despair. That idea would not
leave me; at last I began to think that he must have committed
suicide. To reassure myself I decided to put on my hat and pay him a
visit. It was about six o'clock in the evening. I found his door open
and, timidly feeling my way in the darkened flat, I entered. I called.
No answer. Terrified, I hurried through the rooms one by one.
Then, on his desk, placed so that they could not fail to catch the eye,
I saw several leaves of paper with his writing on them — pieces of
poetry, all expressing sadness and despair. Here is one of them
which I remember:

> Dieu, soutiens mon courage et chasse comme une ombre
> Des biens que j'ai perdu le souvenir si doux.

On another page I then read these lines (from the libretto of Gou-
nod's *Faust*):

> *Vains, echos de la joie humaine,*
> *Passez . . . passez votre chemin. . . .*

Slowly and hesitating, I then entered his room. On the sill I stopped.
A really macabre scene had been prepared. In its usual place I found
my photograph, bordered with crêpe, and in front of it a chair
placed like a *prie-Dieu* as if he must have been meditating there as
one does before an idol or a holy picture. The floor was strewn with
faded rose-petals. I was sorry now that I had not understood him. I
bitterly regretted the harsh words I might have said to him, and I felt
capable of anything to recall them, if there was still time. . . .

At this propitious point Lucien, who had been hiding in a
cupboard, reappeared . . . and the chief chapter in their idyll
commenced. Without the letter, I would still believe in the
rose-petals on the floor, for it is only the finest of a thousand
other incidents which, though decimated by criticism, can still
rally enough survivors to prove that *this* was the Landru that
sold shrewd housewives' possessions under their nose, and
whom retired prostitutes — wariest of womenkind — followed
to their death like hypnotized lambs. The elementary stages of
his attraction can be arranged thus: (1) Landru — any man, who

brought "company" to solitary women marooned in exciting times, the petty swindler whose exemption from the trenches gave him, like thousands of others, an exceptional chance with the sex. (2) Landru — lodestone, the man with a purpose, in which these disoriented women longed to share. Here is his magnetism. But it is the honest magnetism of the compass, which has no truck with the supernatural.

Up to this point he shares with Smith, who used both these baits. Smith, too, presented himself to lonely women, and magnetized them with the positive goal they felt he possessed. It was not one in which they could possibly share — can indeed any mortal ever share the path another has found, or partake of his reality? The utter belief of both men in themselves, and confidence in their aim, sucked in, dragged towards themselves and swirled in a rush the unsettled, groping wills of their victims. In Smith, as in Troppmann, as embryonically in Burke,[1] no doubt, this goal was simple: to make a secure fortune for the self which he adored and pitied. But Landru has a more complicated heaven to which he no less remorselessly steers, and in return his net is of steel to their hempen ropes. Smith's women clung to him always when he was there; they wavered, as the story of Bessie Mundy showed, when he was away. The Kincks came to Troppmann's rendezvous, though they doubted and feared. But the satellites of Landru were as inexorably fixed to his personality as the outer and inner stars to their orbit and their sun. He was almost the founder of a religion; he was the equal in mastery with Rasputin, and Brigham Young, and the Old Man of the Mountains, the first assassin. This power of Landru, which went as far as death, was above that of his rivals in proportion to the height of his obsession over theirs, and its vastly wider content. This is the third spell of Landru, by which he traffics in immortal things, in the mysteries of life itself, and reveals himself to his bedazzled initiates as Landru — the poet.

I am ashamed to ask you to notice the abominable commonplaces of his letter and his *mise-en-scène*, and only because in translation some of them may have disguised themselves. His

---

1. *Editor's Note.* Jean Baptiste Troppmann, French mass-murderer, executed in 1870. William Burke, of the Edinburgh firm of Burke & Hare, suppliers of fresh "specimens" to Dr Robert Knox's school of anatomy; executed in 1829. An account of the Burke & Hare case appears in *The Pleasures of Murder*, Allison & Busby, London 1983.

"eyes clouded with a passing pain", his "charming and hopeful age", his "precious treasures of heart and head", his "lonely soul", and especially his years that are "hard in all the painful acceptation of the word", need no labels. His phrases are of the same atrocious banality as the mechanism of his suicide, from the enshrined photograph of that poor slut, to the used lines from the hackneyed opera. However, not only are they, I suspect, much above the common level of middle-class love-letters, but in the milieu in which Landru lived, to which he belonged, most commonplaces are rejuvenated by their novelty and may be used and felt as expressions of real feeling. Doubt not that they were so used, or that Landru himself could smile at the old-fashioned details of his love-game that conquered the sentimental Fernande. To the poor widows of his intimacy, to himself, this man was a poet, an artist. In his intercourse they felt the divine glows of idealized emotion, which only Shake-speare and Beethoven can give to the sophisticated: Landru's contact brought perfumes unknown to them before from the very bouquet of life. His presence had vague harmonies for them of things they had heard faintly in their youth; his talk was full of sweet words: loneliness, love, regret. This he could do, because his own mind was full of them. No one who has pored over the whole body of evidence in the Landru trial and case can doubt that we are here in the presence of a self-deceiver, a being who has fabricated out of his nature and his reading a dream, or fiction of things, in which he is the hero, and in which he has fortified himself against reality by an ingenious rampart of lies.

The only other view possible, that he was a perfectly awake murderer, that all his romanticism was hypocrisy, easy as it would make the infliction of his punishment, only leaves his nature a mystery unparalleled in the animal world, wherein reasonable beings may not rest unless all explanations have been proved vain. Or it slides into a statement that he was mad, of which even his acute defender Maître Moro-Giafferi could find no evidence. The inner life of Landru was a daydream, different only in furniture from that which Troppmann and Smith possessed, in that it was more poetic, more literary, than theirs. That it was inferior, trite poetry, and feuilletonesque literature, does not allow of question. But even in their degra-dation, the arts do not entirely lose their character: there is a music of the roundabout, and the street-song, and the prole-tariat of great sad modern cities have their folk-culture as well as

the ancestral peasants, which though as degraded and adul-
terated as their food-stuffs,.yet contrives in a way that should
excite our wonder and pity to flavour and express that strange
life. Landru brought to his women the sadness of a street-organ,
the romance of a sentimental ballad, an assimilable mystery of
the arts. For that ultimate reason they followed him as the
animals followed the god-like piper of Thrace who afterwards
too went down to hell. They were not drawn so far by anything
altogether base. And this must have been his ultimate secret.
Nor to Landru was it base; he never meant that they should
share in it. He was deluded by his own illusion. A sentimental
love, going to music from *Manon Lescaut*, was his own goal, his
sincere religion.

Which like a mystical tradesman he worked for by day to
enjoy by night. He had the protective faculty of strictly separ-
ating business which had to be done from the life for whose
accomplishment he carried it on. As with Smith, his stingy
neatness is not a sign of an insensitive man, but rather of the
opposite: a man who cannot kill or steal without hypnotizing
himself with all the apparatus of business. It is for this that we so
often find, to his ruin, a diary and petty accounts in the desk of a
multi-murderer. It was so with William Palmer, it was so with
Landru. And all of them were sustained in the anguish of the
dock by believing themselves back into pettifogging business
men and county court lawyers.

For at last the trial arrived, and we may turn our attention to
Landru's great antagonist — society. The daily badgering of the
monster in his cage by the examining magistrate had lasted from
13 April 1919 to November 1921. His use of the government had
ended, for the dictatorship had fallen long ago, the people were
restive for their final treat. But all this racking had not drawn out
of the man a secret, the only one the examiners hoped for, how
he had disposed of his corpses. The villa in Gambais had been
excavated and sacked from rafters to cellar, without any result
but a handful of charred bones which only cranks in the anatomy
school could swear were not rabbits' bones. The kitchen stove,
on which the spiritual eyes of thirty million people were fixed
ever since Salmon the reporter had playfully hinted that Landru
might have used it as a private incinerator, had been dismounted
and brought as a trophy; on Landru's own suggestion, the
discomfited experts had scraped the soot out of the chimney for
analysis, with no better result. Landru, like Smith, would have

to be condemned only on coincidence.

This failure of the investigators undoubtedly worried the responsible minister, that is a certain Monsieur Ignace, the chief tool of the dictatorship. Landru had been extremely useful, but it would never do to allow him to be acquitted, ridiculously, as was likely to happen in Paris, where criminal juries are always dramatic. As a terribly sure safeguard from this possibility, Ignace sent the trial to Versailles. The Versailles juries seldom erred in mercy; they were drawn from a population of small farmers, rentiers, and master-workmen who believed in the law. From the moment of that decision Landru was as doomed as if infected with a cancer of the throat.

The selection of the law officers was as delicate as the partition of roles in an amateur theatrical society. Every judge on the list had influence; every one demanded the right of presiding over the most famous case in French criminal history. The judging in such an affair was not empty celebrity; during its course the judge was the most esteemed figure in society, for he had the allotment of the court-tickets, one of which every great lady in the city *must* secure. At last the claims, political, social, of Mr Counsellor Gilbert prevailed for the post of principal judge: a very social eminence, a man of the world and fashion, whose tact and appearance — his magnificent and well-groomed beard, his manicured gestures — hold some reminiscence of the great magistrates of Balzac. The less but still pretty office of Advocate-General, or prosecutor, was awarded to Maître Godefroy, a bearish determined fellow who was evidently making great progress in the "career"' For Landru's defence the prize had long been taken: Maître Moro-Giafferi, a risen Corsican, with the largest and most profitable practice in France, as well as the assured commencement of a remarkable political career on one side or the other, had, in the first month of Landru's success, seized it for himself, and was, long before the trial, in enjoyment of its luscious fruits of publicity.

So much preliminary drumming on the likelihood of enormous crowds at the opening of the case had the contrary effect: on the first day and until the truth was incautiously published by the reporters, the court was only moderately full. It was a hall the size of a meeting-house, distempered in a grim shade of green, whose only ornament was a huge gas-chandelier, gummy and long unused. The weather was cold, the light hard. In front of the judge's bench was a table covered with "material evidence", the heavier parts of which were stacked far into the body of the court, so that the witnesses on their way to the stand had to pick their way among the burst mattresses, the dismounted iron bedsteads, past a rusty stove, and look at the silky Gilbert across a square rod of false hair, cardboard boxes of bones, jewellery that all looked sham, books and iron bric-à-brac, the lesser spoils of Landru's victims. The front of the court thus had the sordid and depressing air of a house-removal. At the other end, there was a dock, strongly barred off, where throughout the trial the ticketless public stood in a slab: pale-faced rogues, gamboge-tressed women without hats, truant workmen, and inquisitive middle-class women from Paris, all day obsessed with the wish to gain a place nearer the front. In front of them were twenty rows of school benches, where the reporters of the world press scribbled and quarrelled.

On the third day the court changed: the whole of leisured Paris came to fight for places: a special train was run from the Gare d'Orsay in time for the opening. Both the cavernous corridors and the wet street outside were thick all day with a crowd that pushed like a panic in a theatre to get in. Gilbert's careful plans to admit only the flower of his friends were wrecked by force of numbers. The sovereign people itself had come to enjoy the function of judging. A place inside, instead of being the present of a magistrate, was only to be won, like all the other privileges of a democracy, by competition, and became a trophy of ferocity in a woman, or cunning strength in a man. The successful part of the nation once inside, consolidated positions, squeezed up beside the judge on his bench, forced its way beside the jurymen, and occupied every window-ledge. The principle of representation was abandoned; society moved itself to share in the condemnation and punishment of the offender. From this confined rabble at every significant point of the trial rose various sounds, ignoble roars of laughter, infamous grumblings, and yells of delight and excitement. It was never quiet. The ordinary machinery of justice clogged, only with the greatest hardship managed to enter into action at all. The jurymen took two hours and the assistance of a platoon of police to get to their box. The judge, though he had a private entrance, was often late. The reporters, unofficial delegates of our world civilization, abandoned their earlier composure in the crush and, fearing to be excluded from the function by which they earned their living, scuffled with the mob and fought their colleagues each for his own hand with no less determination.

The French dock is a long bench, raised to the same level as the judge's desk. In this, above the fleshy figure of his counsel, Moro-Giafferi, was the profile of Landru, russet and bleached bone. The horrible patina of the gaol was on his naked cranium, which seemed to shine in the wintry light from a window behind. His coat, which he never removed, was a mackintosh of the military cut fashionable when he was arrested: a shade lighter than his beard, which was trimmed in the shape of a fan. In the street he might have passed as one of those innumerable petty speculators that dealt in army stores. But on his dais, framed by the broad blue gendarmes, with the aura of his iniquity, he seemed unlike any human seen before, as Napoleon might have appeared on the day of his anointing. His skull was certainly strange, with its dead colour and incandescence. His nose was the greatest rarity, as thin and transparent at the bridge as a sheet of greased paper. When he sat and listened to the long requisitories, he could be taken for an actor in his carefully attentive pose, but so thin and delicate that one could notice the outline of the small, sharp elbow through his sleeve. We saw his full-face but rarely: when he entered, stumbling and blinking through the side-door that ended the stone stairs from the prisoner-yard every morning; and sometimes when he turned to the roaring arena to protest. Then we caught a glimpse of his cavernous eyes, which never lost their abstraction even when he was shouting. Usually his manner was chosen and finicky, but after a few minutes in this style he would drop back into the Paris twang. When Fernande Segret was giving her evidence, he closed his eyes; once when the rough Attorney-General, coming to the matter of Thérèse Marchadier's pet dogs which were found strangled with a waxed thread under an oleander clump at Gambais, rushed at him the question: "Is that how you killed all your victims, Landru?" — he seemed scared, and shook. Once, at eighth repetition of the question, "What became of this woman, Landru?" he lost his temper and stood up, shaking his long, large hands with rage. He had many poses. He seemed sometimes like a fox, with his snout finding danger in the air; sometimes he seemed false, sometimes he seemed like a wood-insect, with undefined antennæ that felt their way along the board in front of him. Sometimes he would pause and slowly take out, wipe and don a pair of gilt spectacles before an answer;

then he seemed simply a prematurely old man. Usually he was obviously immersed in a private dream; but he took great pleasure in the whirling combats between the hairy prosecutor and his sleek Corsican defender. He had a weakness for minor details, on which he extended himself, until he suddenly remembered some warning he had had of the danger of these tactics and sat down. The judge, after a few days' brow-beating, treated him with consideration. Both of them were interested in the crowd: the judge stroking his beard with his soft white hand, the accused sideways, without completely turning his head, as if he were eavesdropping.

As in all multiple-murder trials, the evidence was largely a repetition; each new victim had been met in the same way, traced in the same way, perhaps killed in the same way, it may be by this abominable new weapon of a waxed thread round the neck while asleep, which no agonizing effort could disengage. Probably, too, Landru disposed of their bodies in the same way; like Pel and Soleillant dissecting them minutely, then burning the pieces to ashes in a red-hot stove, then no doubt by the aid of his motor-car strewing their few pounds of relics in the hedges of distant lanes. The witnesses stepped after each other monotonously: concierges in Sunday clothes, little old women with dingy reticules, dry-eyed sisters, moustached detectives with long and precise records of their failures. The crowd, subtly changing every day, ceased to pay any attention to these. It fed its thousand eyes on the figure in the dock, which grew lighter and more transparent every day, like a discarded carapace. Landru fell into somnolences that lasted hours, during which the heaps of papers in front of him had obviously no part in the reverie. The classic attitude of the mass-murderer towards his punishment.

Maître Moro-Giaffери, who at first had difficulty in inducing his client to resign the first role to him, composed dramatic tantrums, revolved his black professional sleeves at the more honestly bad-tempered red advocate opposite, then, having had his effect, subsided, and put on pince-nez. The judge, badly handled by indignant reporters in the press every morning, let an elegant melancholy creep over him, and little by little abandoned any effort to cow the crowd, which every day grew wilder and more primitive as the great moment of condemnation approached — and as the stage-element in its composition gradually gained the majority. Caricaturists, who, in the first days had timidly made their sketches using their knees as easels, now boldly advanced among the undergrowth of *pièces de conviction*, blocking the defence's view of the witness-rail, and drew Landru to the life at three feet from his eyes. This seemed to please him and amuse him; at a sign from one of the artists he would turn his head at the angle they wanted. And a more encumbering breed, the press photographers, doggedly impudent, lugged their ungainly apparatus into similar good positions and took time-exposures of the court. To no avail — for the ration of winter light, already insufficient for their purpose, was now always barred off by the backs of those who had climbed into the window-ledges. Most photographers having failed, the cameramen took to the expedient of hanging incandescent lamps of great power over the prisoner's bench, when the court was not sitting, so that at any rate the great moment and most interesting expression would not escape them and the millions for whom they deputized.

So the time arrived: the jury after all these days had nothing before them but coincidence; but it was enough. Ten women (the prosecution fixed on this number somewhat arbitrarily) who had known, loved and followed Landru had vanished. In his possession were their papers, their birth certificates, their marriage papers, all the paraphernalia with which the human ant-hill tries to fix separate personality, without which there could be no emigration from France. Against this, Moro-Giafferi could only weakly hint that possibly Landru had shipped them to the brothels of South America, where common superstition had it there came no newspapers. The man himself, in his extremity, had never dared to make such a defence. He relied on the weary romanticism of "an honourable man will never tell a woman's secret", which, carefully weighed by the stony jurymen, came to much the same thing. But to this the terrible quietus of the prosecution struck mortally: What? Women of over fifty? Women whose false hair, false teeth, false bosoms, as well as identity papers, you, Landru, have kept, and we captured? The jury retired.

In these moments, while prisoner and judges were withdrawn, the court crowd, this assembly of a modern people which had just sacrificed 1,500,500 of its young men to preserve its institutions and its culture, was extraordinary. It had been waiting from an early hour to keep its place, and in its joy at success gave itself over to a debauch. These thousand compressed bodies were the elect of all Paris, all France, arrived by their abilities to the most coveted spectacle of the century: the sight of Landru's condemnation. They could not move, but within the inches of every one's power, they rioted with abandon. The shrill cries of women at the daring contacts of their neighbours, the screams, the high giggles of chorus girls, the shouts of rage or pleasure of the men, combined in a chorus. It filled the street outside, and filtered no doubt to the ears ofthe man waiting in the cold cell somewhere beneath, wrapping himself close in the warm quilt of his sentimental daydreams. It was not the cold formula of a delegated justice, but the voice of outraged society itself, doing its own justice. A thousand incidents kept the crowd alive while the tedious jury kept it in waiting. Girls pulled by the legs tumbled from their perch in the windows, strong men forced themselves from three places distant upon each other and revenged their dignity on some enemy with blows, which, falling generously on the people between, were returned, or saluted with bellows of pain. At last the jury, ill at ease and silent, filed back and the door opened for Landru. Immediately there was a frenzy. As the man stood half bowed forward to catch his fate and his sentence, at precisely the right moment the photographers fired their illumination. There was a great glare of light over him. From every part of the massed hall arms protruded upward with black boxes, cameras which aimed at him. And as though in the throes of an eruption, figures shot themselves out of the crowd-level with hands waving and their faces distorted with the effort of their struggle. One man (according to some, it was the dean of the Comédie Française) actually succeeded in leaping to one of the advocate's benches, and stood there, hilarious, with opera-glasses to his eyes, greedily scanning the lost criminal's expression.

When the court was empty, the servants found the floor strewn like a holiday beach with bitten sandwiches, papers, bottles, and other unmentionable, unmistakable traces of their presence which human beings, alas, must leave on a spot where they have been long hours kept immobile without privacy.

This immission of the sovereign people into judgment and punishment, or rather the disrespectful publicity given to it by the exasperated reporters, troubled the government. They determined therefore that the final act, the execution of Landru, should be guarded, and only enjoyed by appointed proxies. Before dusk, troops took up their stations, and as soon as the trams stopped running, pickets enclosed the space of road out-side the prison of Versailles, which is next door to the court. All the cafés and houses within this area were searched. Those numerous strangers who, having shared or missed the condemnation, wished to witness the execution and had hidden themselves, sometimes in the most humble compartments of these places, were rigorously expelled beyond the barrier. Only the reporters were allowed to remain; these spent the night in billiards and dozing. Before dawn the guillotine was reared on the side-walk, before the principal door. At the appointed hour, before it was light, that door opened, and with tied feet, his chest bared by the executioner's shears, and ghastly rags of shirt hanging over his bound arms, Landru was jostled to the towering machine that in a flash ended him and all his secrets.

At that moment, by some error of the guards, a tram filled with workmen on their way to the yards was allowed to pass, and their curious crowded faces received the last sight of the living head of Desiré Landru.

Acknowledgements and Sources

IN ADDITION to those given in the text: "The Killing at Road Hill House", the example of murder for revenge in *Murder and Its Motives* (Harrap, London 1952), is published by permission of Joanna Colenbrander, for the Harwood Will Trust; "Death on the Via Davana", which first appeared in the *Leicester Graphic*, is published by permission of the author; "The Puzzle of Rumsey House" is composed of extracts from *The Life of Sir Edward Marshall Hall* (Gollancz, London 1930); "Herbert Armstrong, Poisoner", originally published in a paperback, appeared in this amended form in *Crime & Detection* No. 1, June 1966; "The Origin of the 'Gigman'" is from *Murders and Murder Trials, 1812–1912* (Constable, London 1932); "The Frozen Footprints" is published by permission of the author; "The Tragedy of Amy Robsart" is from the second volume of *Great Stories of Real Life*, edited by Max Pemberton (Newnes, London 1929); "A Ritual Murder", extracts from *The Sex War and Others* (Peter Owen, London 1973), is published by permission of Margaret Heppenstall; "The Peasenhall Case", extracts from the introduction to *Trial of William Gardiner* (Hodge, Edinburgh 1934), is published by courtesy of the late James Hodge; "The Raising of the Guernsey Farmer" is published by permission of the author; "A Short Walk to Eternity", from *Posts-Mortem: The Correspondence of Murder* (David & Charles, Newton Abbot 1971), is published by permission of the author; "The Poetry of Desiré Landru" is composed of extracts from *Murder for Profit* (Jonathan Cape, London 1926).